TEACHER PREP

MERRILL
PRENTICE HALL

Teacher Preparation Classroom

See a demo at
www.prenhall.com/teacherprep/demo

Your Class. Their Careers. Our Future. Will your students be prepared?

We invite you to explore our new, innovative and engaging website and all that it has to offer you, your course, and tomorrow's educators! Preview this site today at www.prenhall.com/teacherprep/demo. Just click on "go" on the login page to begin your exploration.

Organized around the major courses pre-service teachers take, the Teacher Preparation site provides media, student/teacher artifacts, strategies, research articles, and other resources to equip your students with the quality tools needed to excel in their courses and prepare them for their first classroom.

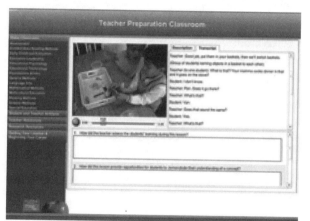

This ultimate online education resource will provide you and your students access to:

Online Video Library. More than 250 video clips—each tied to a course topic and framed by learning goals and Praxis-type questions—capture real teachers and students working in real classrooms.

Student and Teacher Artifacts. More than 200 student and teacher classroom artifacts—each tied to a course topic and framed by learning goals and application questions—provide a wealth of materials and experiences to help your students observe children's developmental learning.

Lesson Plan Builder. Step-by-step guidelines and lesson plan examples support students as they learn to build high-quality lesson plans.

Articles and Readings. Over 500 articles from ASCD's renowned journal *Educational Leadership* are available. The site also includes Research Navigator, a searchable database of additional educational journals.

Strategies and Lessons. Over 500 research-supported instructional strategies appropriate for a wide range of grade levels and content areas.

Licensure and Career Tools. Resources devoted to helping your students pass their licensure exam; learn standards, law, and public policies; plan a teaching portfolio; and succeed in their first year of teaching.

How to ORDER *Teacher Prep* for you and your students:

For students to receive a *Teacher Prep* Access Code with this text, instructors must provide a special value pack ISBN number on their textbook order form. To receive this special ISBN, please email **Merrill marketing@pearsoned.com** and provide the following information:

- Name and Affiliation
- Author/Title/Edition of Merrill text

Upon ordering *Teacher Prep* for their students, instructors will be given a lifetime *Teacher Prep* Access Code.

COLLABORATIVE
INDIVIDUALIZED
EDUCATION PROCESS

RSVP to IDEA

EVIE K. GLECKEL
Keene State College

ELLEN S. KORETZ
Assumption College

PEARSON

Merrill
Prentice Hall

Upper Saddle River, New Jersey
Columbus, Ohio

Library of Congress Cataloging-in-Publication Data

Gleckel, Evie K.
  Collaborative individualized education process : RSVP to IDEA / Evie K. Gleckel, Ellen Koretz.
    p. cm.
  Includes bibliographical references and index.
  ISBN-13: 978-0-13-112593-3 (pbk.)
  ISBN-10: 0-13-112593-1 (pbk.)
  1. Children with disabilities—Education—United States. 2. Individualized education programs—
United States. 3. Special education—United States. I. Koretz, Ellen. II. Title.
LC4031.G545 2008
371.9'043—dc22
                                     2007034970

Vice President and Executive Publisher:
  Jeffery W. Johnston
Executive Editor: Ann Castel Davis
Editorial Assistant: Penny Burleson
Production Editor: Sheryl Glicker Langner
Production Coordination: Thistle Hill
  Publishing Services, LLC

Design Coordinator: Diane C. Lorenzo
Cover Design: Craig Mangum
Cover Image: Fotosearch
Production Manager: Laura Messerly
Director of Marketing: David Gesell
Marketing Coordinator: Brian Mounts

This book was set in Meridien Roman by Integra Software Services. It was printed and bound by
R. R. Donnelley & Sons Company. The cover was printed by R. R. Donnelley & Sons Company.

Pearson Education Ltd.
Pearson Education Singapore Pte. Ltd.
Pearson Education Canada, Ltd.
Pearson Education–Japan

Pearson Education Australia Pty. Limited
Pearson Education North Asia Ltd.
Pearson Educación de Mexico, S.A. de C.V.
Pearson Education Malaysia Pte. Ltd.

10 9 8 7 6 5 4 3 2 1
ISBN-13: 978-0-13-112593-3
ISBN-10:   0-13-112593-1

Preface

RSVP to IDEA captures our shared vision about the special education process, one that incorporates the *spirit* and requirements of the Individual with Disabilities Education Act (IDEA) and its reauthorizations. The content has evolved from our work in the field as practitioners in schools, educational consultants, workshop and project facilitators, and field supervisors and professors in undergraduate and graduate education and special education programs. Based on our experiences and informed by IDEIA 2004, our purpose for writing this book is to give the complex demands of the legislation form, function, and meaning so teams move through the special education process cooperatively, understanding what they are doing and why.

Through the lens of the RSVP Model, comprised of **r**esponsive **s**tages, **v**oices, and **p**ractices, the book provides a collaborative problem-solving and decision-making approach that follows a progression of linked stages through the special education process. The structure guides teams in working proactively and systematically to individualize tiered assessment, planning, instruction, and interventions to address identified area(s) of concern. The framework provides purposeful ways for evaluating student needs, building comprehensive pictures of learners, and designing corresponding instructional education plans and programs (IEP) that enhance growth and support teacher implementation.

In the RSVP model, the IEP document is treated as a valuable blueprint for working with identified students while providing evidence of compliance with legal mandates. We contend that the education plan is only as relevant and useful as the information it contains. The document is only as effective as the description of the learner it conveys. The narrative is only as relevant as the assessment data collected to understand the student as a reader, writer, mathematician, and/or member/participant in the classroom community. The student profile is only as pertinent as the details it provides for informing the instructional plan and educational program. The IEP is only as valuable as the road map it presents to individualize instruction and meet student needs in or out of general education. The design and implementation of the individualized education plan, program, and document is only as effective as the collaborative and collective team efforts used to build them.

We have developed this book to capture the cooperative nature of the special education process. We believe the implementation of IDEA is strengthened when there is schoolwide commitment to adopt its goals, ways of thinking, and practices where everyone sees their responsibilities as opportunities to contribute to positive outcomes for students and to develop individualized programs. Through shared ownership, teams work to claim the _I (individual) and E_ (education) in IDEA and the IEP, making the thinking, strategies, and actions explicit to demystify the process, give value to IEP paperwork, open lines of communication, clarify roles, examine and concretize practices, and advocate for systematic activity from prereferral to program implementation and evaluation.

Text Features

The text is organized according to the stages of the RSVP model to provide a systematic and comprehensive approach to implementing special education legislation meaningfully. Following the introduction in the first chapter, each subsequent one describes a stage of the RSVP model and includes:

- *Think-abouts* at the beginning of the chapter to serve as advanced organizers that preview the content covered and highlight key points
- *Figures* to illustrate concepts presented
- *Toolboxes* to prompt thinking and practice through guideline questions, checklists, and examples of assessment and instructional approaches, applied to reader, writer, mathematician, and participant member of the classroom community
- *Case study* to present Paul as an example of how to move through the stages of the RSVP model, culminating in excerpts from his IEP
- *Chapter Review: Focus and Decisions* to recap the stage presented in the chapter, highlighting key questions and decision points
- *Apply and Learn* to pose reflective questions at the end of the chapter to develop competence and thinking of presented concepts related to the stage

Chapter Summaries

Chapter 1, "RSVP to IDEA: A Model for Shaping the Special Education Process," challenges schools to rethink responses to IDEA 2004 to capture its spirit and comply with its regulations. The RSVP model (Responsive Stages, Voices, and Practices) is introduced as a framework for moving through tiers of problem solving to arrive at data-based educational decisions in response to the challenges that students experience. RSVP guides a team approach to the thinking and practices involved in proceeding from the prereferral stage through assessment and planning to develop IEPs as blueprints for student outcomes and as a guide for program implementation and progress monitoring. Chapter 1 sets the tone for the remaining chapters.

Chapter 2, "Stage I: Explore Prereferral Concerns and Options," examines a systematic, tiered approach to acknowledge student challenges, gain an understanding of what impacts his or her performance, participation, and progress, design modifications and/or interventions to support growth, and monitor their effectiveness. This chapter highlights the pivotal role of the general educator in being proactive during the prereferral stage. He or she works with parent/caregivers and other professionals to understand student needs, brainstorm and develop in-class solutions, and implement and document the outcomes of attempted modifications and interventions. As a result of prereferral efforts, the decision to submit a referral for special education evaluation is weighed collaboratively. Guidelines are outlined for submitting formal referrals to ensure that teacher and/or parent/caregiver voices and concerns are heard and direction for assessment planning is provided.

Chapter 3, "Stage II: Design the Collaborative Individualized Assessment Plan," underscores the importance of being deliberate and selective in approaching assessment decisions about the student in need. This stage establishes the direction for how the team comes to know the student. The chapter presents guidelines for bringing the multidisciplinary team together to develop a systematic assessment plan. The purpose is to engage team members in collaboratively discerning the "problem(s)," drawing from prereferral/referral information to make decisions about how to evaluate the student, what data to collect, and which tools to use. Together, they construct a logical assessment plan, thinking through what is known about the student, what they want to find out, and how to get the information.

Chapter 4, "Stage III: Collect, Chart, and Analyze Assessment Data," focuses on the team's initiative to gather information through authentic tasks to enhance understanding of student status (competence and challenges) with regard to the area(s) of concern. These tools can be formal or informal assessment instruments. Analysis of student performance is key to this cooperative venture. This chapter proposes procedures for collecting and charting data: selecting, developing, conducting assessments, and constructing common lenses for analysis. These steps require the collective efforts of the team to learn more about the student in a variety of settings, using different types of evaluation tools to learn as much as possible. Members evaluate assessments individually and across tasks to draw hypotheses and conclusions. They prepare to share their results with other team members.

Chapter 5, "Stage IV: Engage in the Individualized Education Program Meeting," focuses on ways in which the team collates assessment results to build a comprehensive picture of the student and use that description to design a cohesive instructional program for him or her. The emphasis is on the content and cooperative efforts of team members meeting to integrate assessment data and build an outline for the IEP. Each member shares results and viewpoints using consistent evaluation criteria established by the team.

Findings are interwoven to create a complete picture of the student in the area(s) of concern. This integrated picture is the reference point for constructing instructional plans and a blueprint for service delivery that leads to accessing general education with or without modifications and/or establishing specially designed instruction in or out of the classroom.

Chapter 6, "Stage V: Write the Individualized Education Program," focuses on how the writer composes the document to include the team's descriptions for each IEP component. This chapter suggests formats for collating and presenting the collaborative decisions the team made. Information and ideas generated during team discussions are articulated and written in the appropriate sections of the IEP document. Attention is paid to required/universal IEP components and ways to put words to ideas, communicate plans clearly, and meet standards for effective documents that establish individualized programs for students. The focus is on writing a comprehensive, well-organized, coherent, internally consistent document through which plans are clearly communicated.

Chapter 7, "Stage VI: Implement the Individualized Education Program and Monitor Progress," guides practitioners to prepare, deliver, and monitor the ways the education program is implemented. This stage highlights the importance of communication among the implementers to coordinate efforts and provide the student with a cohesive program. Some ideas are offered to support coordinated implementation efforts among special educators, classroom teachers, and paraprofessionals to implement plans and document student progress.

Chapter 8, "Moving Forward," emphasizes the need for a schoolwide commitment to the intent of IDEA, creating a cooperative special education process and programming to address the range of student needs and challenges. This brief chapter encourages schools to participate in dialogue to interface general and special education with fidelity, clarifying and adopting the tasks, roles, and responsibilities that foster team building. The ease and effectiveness with which a school or district implements the special education process requires frank discussions about defining the functions and benefits of special education, the roles of professionals, parents/caregivers, paraprofessionals, paperwork, and activity surrounding implementation of the law.

Acknowledgments

As we enter the phase of putting final touches on this manuscript, it is a time to reflect on the contributions of those of you in our lives that offered continued support through our long and sometimes arduous, yet rewarding, professional journey. We can only begin to express our gratitude for all you provided. It was the words of encouragement, patience with this never-ending story, the space you gave us to write, and the ideas and feedback you shared that helped us reach our goal to RSVP to IDEA in ways that promote a collaborative individualized education process.

We want to acknowledge public and private school students, classroom teachers, special educators, related service providers, parents/caregivers, and administrators with whom we had the privilege to work in a variety of roles over the years. What we share in this book comes from being with you side by side to teach from the heart and reach all students, striving to support positive learning, environments, and outcomes.

We want to recognize our students at Keene State College, Assumption College, Framingham State College, and Lesley University. Your desire and commitment to be effective educators through the quality of your work, poignant questions, and insightful discussions have informed our thinking, teaching, and writing. Ideally, you learned as much from us as we learned from you.

We acknowledge our colleagues, mentors, and families, with special appreciation.

To Faye Doolin (sister) for knowledgeable reminders about the individualized education process and its challenges, and colleagues Glenna Mize, Ginny Trumbull, Ann Beaudry-Torrey, and Katie Ahern for inspiring, encouraging, and giving feedback for moving this project forward. To Linda Brion-Meisels at Lesley University and Howard Muscott, Eric Mann, Linda Potter, and colleagues at the NH CEBIS: New Hampshire Center for Effective Behavior Intervention and Support, who prompted us to focus on proactive and intervention approaches to challenging behaviors.

To Bill Harp, Jay Simmons, and Judy Davidson at the University of Massachusetts, Lowell and the Keene State College Writing Task Force for their guidance in teaching how to write with conviction and purpose.

Margie Berenson, it is through our long walks, deep talks, special friendship, and your expertise in literacy that we continue the conversation around the reading and writing process and implications for practice.

We want to thank the people at Merrill/Prentice Hall for believing in our project. To Ann Davis, we are grateful for your understanding the messages of the manuscript, honoring its intent, and providing us with the insights and perspectives to convey ideas and organize the materials clearly. To Penny Burleson, we appreciate your ongoing patience as you answered our many questions and provided us with the needed structure for what to do when. We further want to express our gratitude to Allyson Sharp, who, with the support of Kathy Burke, Christina Robb, and Ed Weisman, believed in our project, promoted the concept, and provided substantive direction and feedback in its development stages. Thank you, Angela Urquhart and the staff at Thistle Hill Publishing Services, for your gentle and thorough approach to the production process.

To those colleagues who have served as readers of different drafts, your constructive criticism gave us the basis to rethink, revise, and rework. We appreciate your time, efforts, and honesty. Thank you for helping to shape this book: John Brewer, University of Northern Colorado; Gail Peterson Craig, University of Wisconsin, Superior; Mary G. Curtis, University of Texas, Brownsville; Dan Fennerty, Central Washington University; Barbara Fulk, Illinois State University; Gay Goodman, University of Houston; Jack Hourcade, Boise State University;

Joan Leatherman, Indiana-Purdue University, Fort Wayne; Courtney Moffatt, Edgewood College; Beverly N. Parke, Indiana-Purdue University, Fort Wayne; Windy Schweder, University of South Carolina, Aiken; Cathy Warmack, Murray State University; Nikki N. Washington, California State University, San Bernadino; Bettie J. Willingham, Barton College; and Nancy Yost, Indiana University of Pennsylvania.

We are indebted to our families. To our parents, Anna Katz and, in spirit, Maury Katz, Seena and Lou Rosenberg, and Lachie Koretz, your deep and unwavering love and faith in us have contributed to our strong sense of self and perseverance to stand by our convictions and accomplish our goal.

With much love, we give a most special thank you to our husbands, Garry and Mark, and our children, Missy and Jessie, and Eric, Pamela, and Andrew for their rainbows of patience, beliefs in our journey, love, understanding, push, reassurances, and reality checks. To our *kids*, we thank you for your gifts of listening, confidence in us, encouraging words, and unconditional love. Over the years, each of you inspired us to stay focused on this project through the ways in which you explore your own views, values, and dreams while pursuing how to make a difference in this world.

To our "Hons" and our very best friends, there is no greater love. Your understanding of our passion, belief in us as educators, willingness for this project to take precedence over many parts of our lives, and sacrifice of "together time" define the kinds of supports we needed to accomplish this professional milestone. Thank you. We cherish being in partnerships in which we are *free to be you and me!*

There is no greater test of a friendship than literally to write a book together. In retrospect, we have the luxury of knowing each other so well that we can claim this text is truly a collaborative effort, one in which we shared, relied on, listened, questioned, critiqued, debated, and learned from each other to convey what we understand about the special education process and how to meet the needs of learners, families, and professionals working together in today's schools.

To those we acknowledged and to those others who were also there for us along this journey at our respective colleges and in other parts of our lives, we share this achievement with you. We are grateful that we have such wonderful students, mentors, colleagues, editors, family, and friends.

Discover the Merrill Resources for Special Education Website

Technology is a constantly growing and changing aspect of our field that is creating a need for new content and resources. To address this emerging need, Merrill Education has developed an online learning environment for students, teachers, and professors alike to complement our products—the *Merrill Resources for Special Education* Website. This content-rich website provides additional resources specific to this book's topic and will help you—professors, classroom teachers, and students—augment your teaching, learning, and professional development.

Our goal is to build on and enhance what our products already offer. For this reason, the content for our user-friendly website is organized by topic and provides teachers, professors, and students with a variety of meaningful resources all in one location. With this website, we bring together the best of what Merrill has to offer: text resources, video clips, web links, tutorials, and a wide variety of information on topics of interest to general and special educators alike. Rich content, applications, and competencies further enhance the learning process.

The *Merrill Resources for Special Education* Website includes:

- Video clips specific to each topic, with questions to help you evaluate the content and make crucial theory-to-practice connections.
- Thought-provoking critical analysis questions that students can answer and turn in for evaluation or that can serve as basis for class discussions and lectures.
- Access to a wide variety of resources related to classroom strategies and methods, including lesson planning and classroom management.
- Information on all the most current relevant topics related to special and general education, including CEC and Praxis™ standards, IEPs, portfolios, and professional development.

- Extensive web resources and overviews on each topic addressed on the website.
- A search feature to help access specific information quickly.

To take advantage of these and other resources, please visit the *Merrill Resources for Special Education* Website at **http://www.prenhall.com/gleckel**

Brief Contents

Chapter 1   RSVP to IDEA: A Model for Shaping the Special Education Process   1

Chapter 2   Stage I: Explore Prereferral Concerns and Options   16

Chapter 3   Stage II: Design the Collaborative Individualized Assessment Plan   41

Chapter 4   Stage III: Collect, Chart, and Analyze Assessment Data   105

Chapter 5   Stage IV: Engage in the Individualized Education Program Meeting   146

Chapter 6   Stage V: Write the Individualized Education Program   191

Chapter 7   Stage VI: Implement the Individualized Education Program and Monitor Progress   244

Chapter 8   Moving Forward   265

References   273

Name Index   285

Subject Index   288

Contents

Chapter 1 RSVP to IDEA: A Model for Shaping the Special Education Process   1

The Special Education Process   2

The Challenge   2

An Introduction to RSVP   4

An Overview of RSVP Stages   5

Conclusion   13

Apply and Learn   15

Chapter 2 Stage I: Explore Prereferral Concerns and Options   16

Overview of Stage I   17

Step 1: Identify the Concern(s) and Initial Modifications   19

Write Objective and Informative Descriptions   20

Maintain Records of Behaviors and Performance   21

Access Student Perspective   21

Make In-Class Adjustments   22

Step 2: Involve Parent(s)/Caregiver(s)   22

Share Information Between Teachers and Parents/Caregivers   23

Set Up the First Conference During the Prereferral Stage   24

Step 3: Access Supports Through Formal or Informal Prereferral Options   26

Emphasis on Collaboration   27

Step 4: Initiate the Special Education Process   30

Chapter Review: Focus and Decisions   33

Stage I: Apply and Learn   35

Toolbox: Parent/Caregiver Contact, 37

Chapter 3 Stage II: Design the Collaborative Individualized Assessment Plan   41

Overview of Stage II   42
The _Know-Want-How_ Structure for Assessment Planning   43
Step 1: Start with What the Team _Know_s—Analyze Concern(s)   43
    Filling in the _Know_ Column in the _Know_-Want-How Chart   44
Step 2: Determine What the Team _Want_s to Learn—Raise Questions   45
    Filling in the _Want_ Column in the Know-_Want_-How Chart   45
Step 3: Propose _How_ the Team Finds Out—Select Assessment Tools   47
    Filling in the _How_ Column in the Know-Want-_How_ Chart   48
Step 4: Distribute Assessment Responsibilities and Map Out the Plan of Action—Schedule   56
The Collaborative Perspective: Planning Assessment as a Team   57
    Identify the Assessment Planning Agenda   58
    Understand the Roles of the Team Members   60
    Organize Through Note Taking   60
Chapter Review: Focus and Decisions   62
Stage II: Apply and Learn   62

Toolbox: Guidelines for Describing the Student: Reader, 65 • Writer, 70 • Mathematician, 75 • Participant in the Learning Environment/Member of the Classroom Community, 79
Toolbox: Collecting Assessment Data: Reader, 86 • Writer, 90 • Mathematician, 94 • Participant in the Learning Environment/Member of the Classroom Community, 98
Toolbox: Assessment Plan Form, 104

Chapter 4 Stage III: Collect, Chart, and Analyze Assessment Data   105

Overview of Stage III   106
Step 1: Access and/or Develop Assessment Tasks, Tools, and Activities   107
Step 2: Prepare to Conduct Assessments   109
    Developing Forms for Data Collection   112
    Task Records   112
    Evaluator's Copies   113
Step 3: Conduct Assessments   113

Step 4: Chart and Analyze Student Performance and Products   116
    Charting Data and Analysis   117
    Cross-Referencing Data   118
Chapter Review: Focus and Decisions   123
Stage III: Apply and Learn   124

Toolbox: Construction of Assessment Tools: Reader, 125 • Writer, 127 • Mathematician, 130 • Participant in the Learning Environment/Member of the Classroom Community, 132
Toolbox: Sample Analysis Charts: Reader, 134 • Writer, 137 • Mathematician, 141 • Participant in the Learning Environment/Member of the Classroom Community, 143
Toolbox: The Interaction Formula for Analyzing Individual Tools and/or Cross-Referencing Assessments, 144

Chapter 5 Stage IV: Engage in the Individualized Education Program Meeting   146

Overview of Stage IV   147
Step 1: Build a Composite Picture of the Learner Collaboratively   148
Step 2: Summarize, Draw Conclusions, and Hypothesize   150
    Preliminary Eligibility Decisions   152
Step 3: Develop Content of the Individualized Education Program   153
    Design Individualized Curriculum   154
    Plan Instruction   155
    Determine Eligibility   157
    Participate in Performance Assessments   158
    Engage in Transition Planning   158
    Identify Program Components   159
    Note Taking   159
    Agenda for IEP Development   160
Chapter Review: Focus and Decisions   165
Stage IV: Apply and Learn   166

Toolbox: Checklists to Guide Descriptions: Reader, 167 • Writer, 175 • Mathematician, 181 • Participant in the Learning Environment/Member of the Classroom Community, 184

Chapter 6 Stage V: Write the Individualized Education Program   191

Overview of Stage V   193
    Authoring the IEP   194

Step 1: Develop Profile and Present Levels of Academic Achievement and Functional Performance to Present a Comprehensive Picture of the Student   196

Profile/Learning Style/Impact of Disability   *198*
Present Levels of Academic Achievement and Functional Performance (PLOP)   *201*

Step 2: Record the Design of the Individualized Curriculum   203

Goals and Objectives   *203*
Write Observable, Relevant, and Assessable Goals   *204*
Write Observable, Relevant, and Assessable Objectives   *207*
Documentation of Progress: Identify Monitoring and Evaluation Strategies   *211*

Step 3: Write the Plan for Instruction   215

Explicit/Direct Instruction   *215*
Access to the General Education Curriculum   *216*
Special Education Services/Specially Designed Instruction In and Out of the General Education Classroom   *221*

Step 4: Identify Service Delivery Plan/Program Components   221
Chapter Review: Focus and Decisions   224
Stage V: Apply and Learn   225

Toolbox: Excerpt from an IEP: Paul as a Writer, 226
Toolbox: Criteria for Writing Effective IEPs, 233
Toolbox: Think-Abouts for Writing Educational Plans: Reader, 236 • Writer, 238 • Mathematician, 240 • Participant in the Learning Environment/Member of the Classroom Community, 242

Chapter 7 Stage VI: Implement the Individualized Education Program and Monitor Progress   244
Overview of Stage VI   245
Step 1: Prepare for Implementation   247

Plan Collaboratively   *249*

Step 2: Deliver the Individualized Education Program   250

Develop Co-Teaching Models and Paraprofessional Responsibilities   *251*

Step 3: Monitor Student Progress and Program Effectiveness   253

Monitor Student Progress   *254*
Monitor Program Effectiveness   *255*

Chapter Review: Focus and Decisions   256
Stage VI: Apply and Learn   257

Toolbox: IEP Implementer To-Do List, 258
Toolbox: Interaction Formula Co-Planning, 260

Chapter 8 Moving Forward 265

Building Capacity 266

Build Infrastructure 267

Build Collaborative Relationships and Professional Confidence and Competence 267

Toolbox: Action Planning, 269

References 273

Name Index 285

Subject Index 288

C h a p t e r **1**

RSVP to IDEA

A Model for Shaping the Special Education Process

As you read through this chapter, *think about how:*

- The reauthorization of the Individuals with Disabilities Education Improvement Act (IDEIA, referred to as IDEA 2004) challenges schools to rethink the special education process beyond the *letter of the law* requirements

- The model Responsive Stages, Voices, and Practices (RSVP) addresses the *spirit* of IDEA 2004 by supporting schoolwide adoption of its intentions while complying with its regulations

- RSVP represents the special education process as a *responsive* structure, which emphasizes *stages* of tiered problem solving, *voices* of collaborative teaming, and *practices* that inform data-based decisions from prereferral through individualized education plan (IEP) development, implementation, and evaluation

- Implementation of the RSVP stages leads to meaningful IEPs, programs, and documents that capture student needs and serve as blueprints for outcomes and service delivery

The Special Education Process

We're in the special education process together—classroom teachers, special educators, parents/caregivers, students, administrators, and related service providers. What is the process and ideology to which we are committed by law? How do we create a supportive system and collective ownership of the law and the process it proposes? How do we work together in meaningful ways to serve individual students? How do we translate the requirements of the law into constructive practices for educational professionals? How do we make sure that each tier of intervention and/or individualized education plan (IEP), program, and document is viable and valuable to support students, teachers, and parents/caregivers?

The Challenge

The reauthorization of the Individuals with Disabilities Education Improvement Act of 2004 (IDEA 2004) and its alignment with No Child Left Behind 2001 (NCLB) creates an opportunity for schools to reexamine and accommodate the demands of the legislation. It reaffirms a commitment to understand student challenges and provide appropriate educational opportunities. The law reframes how the diverse needs of students, families, and professionals are identified, understood, and served using general education classrooms, curriculum benchmarks, and programs as reference points. This necessitates developing working alliances and deliberate links between general and special education to establish teams, evaluation approaches, services, and programming that are *responsive* to learner and school needs. It proposes tiers of assessment, instruction, and intervention that draw from evidence-based practices, connect with general education standards, and commit to constructive outcomes for students, enhancing the proactive directions the special education process takes (Gartin, Murdick, & Nikki, 2005; Lewis, 2001; Mainzer, Deshler, & Coleman, 2003; Marston, 2005; Samuels, 2005; Smith, 2005).

The revisions to IDEA 2004 present the opportunity for professionals to institute productive ways to work together to explore and satisfy its requirements and intentions. The law sets the standards and course of action for the special education process, yet it requires an in-depth understanding and schoolwide interpretation and application of the regulations to ensure adoption of substantive practices and effective implementation. To advance the law's intended messages, schools must build *capacity* by creating a culture of cooperative commitment to merge general and special education services and to adopt and implement authentic assessment and data-based differentiated instruction, interventions, and progress monitoring. This requires agreeing to and engaging in a system of support that responds to student concerns with clearly defined procedures, articulated responsibilities, shared resources, and opportunities for professional development (Chamberlain, 2006; Horner & Sugai, 2000; Hyatt, 2007; Lewis, 2001; Marston, Muyskens, Lau, & Canter, 2003; Sarason, 1990, 1998; Sugai & Horner, 1999). The changes in IDEA 2004 create the challenge for schools and districts to involve professionals in collectively addressing the following questions:

- How do professionals understand the goals and purposes of IDEA 2004 and view them as shared responsibilities in today's schools?
- What is the succession of steps, tasks, and key decisions for moving through the special education process responsively?
- How do professionals draw from the law to engage in tiered problem solving as vehicles for adopting proactive preventive strategies for at-risk students, identifying their needs, and planning appropriate learning opportunities?
- How do professionals proceed to and through the IEP process when initial levels of interventions yield limited progress?
- What practices connect assessing and understanding learners with designing and implementing corresponding instruction, interventions, and environments?
- How do professionals develop and articulate useful IEPs, programs, and documents as comprehensive and realistic blueprints that address student needs and lead to learning outcomes?
- How is the special education process structured to engage team members in participation, collaboration, and accountability?

Even though the current legislation retains the 13 categories of disabilities, there is a shift away from using the definitions as central to validating student needs. Reliance on discrepancy models and test scores no longer hold the status for determining eligibility for special education services. Instead, the focus of eligibility determination calls for a series of deliberate decisions around evaluating student struggles in the context of and with reference to general education standards, expectations, and settings with recognition of cultural factors. This shift necessitates collecting instructionally relevant data, making classroom adjustments, and documenting student progress systematically to evaluate if, when, and how general education, with and without supports, benefits the student and/or whether alternative plans are required (Fuchs & Fuchs, 2006; Fuchs, Mock, Morgan, & Young, 2003; Obiakor, 2007; Reschly, Hosp, & Schmied, 2003; Vaughn, Linan-Thomson, & Hickman-Davis, 2003; Vellutino, Scanlon, & Lyon, 2000; Ysseldyke, 2001).

The prominent role of data collection gives more credibility to the use of authentic curriculum-based assessment for making student-centered decisions (Choate, 1992; Daly & Martens, 1997; Fuchs & Fuchs, 2006; Obiakor, 2007; Simmons, 2000; Wilson, Martens, & Arya, 2005). This change in focus requires refining the stages of the special education process to incorporate approaches for understanding individual student needs, which ultimately leads to developing practical and comprehensive education plans, programs, and documents. Making adjustments in the special education process according to revisions of the IDEA 2004 regulations is somewhat open ended, leaving specific interpretations to the discretion of each state.

An Introduction to RSVP

The model Responsive Stages, Voices, and Practices (RSVP) proposed in this book meets the challenge of translating IDEA 2004 into practice. It is shaped by the goals, tasks, and demands of IDEA to capture the spirit and letter of the law. It presents an integrated model for implementing the mandates, one that embraces ideology and intentions, addresses requirements, articulates the outcomes, explains the special education process, describes and organizes tasks, integrates corresponding practices and tools, and fosters the investment of practitioners (Sarason, 1982).

As the acronym suggests, RSVP treats IDEA 2004 as an invitation to work with others to reach students struggling in schools. The model regards the special education process as a *responsive* structure, which infuses linked *stages* of tiered problem solving, *voices* of collaborative teaming, and *practices* that inform data-based decisions from prereferral through IEP development, implementation, and evaluation. RSVP brings together the team of general education teachers, parents/caregivers, special educators, administrators, and related service professionals to fulfill responsibilities systematically throughout the special education process and commit to the spirit in which the law was written (Ysseldyke, 2001; Ysseldyke, Thurlow, Graden, Wesson, Algozzine, & Deno, 1983).

The six stages of RSVP give structure and direction to the activities associated with prereferral efforts, referral for special education evaluation, collection and analysis of assessment data, development and implementation of the IEP, and ongoing monitoring of student progress and services. The stages are interdependent and cumulative. Each stage of RSVP contributes to the accumulation of assessment data, a growing understanding of student challenges and strengths, ideas for instructional planning and actions, strategies to document and monitor responsiveness to interventions and behavior supports, and the development of learning experiences and educational plans to meet student needs while referencing general education (Fuchs & Fuchs, 2006; Marston, 2005; Muscott & Mann, 2006; National Joint Committee on Learning Disabilities, 2005; Prasse, 2006). Moving through the model rests on teaming and culminates in constructing IEPs that are relevant and usable documents, ones that inform the work of program implementers and expectations of parents/caregivers.

In Figure 1.1 the stages of RSVP are represented as a pyramid to address student challenges through a progression of successive efforts. The shape captures the intent to accommodate most at-risk students through tiered assessments and interventions tied to general education. The illustration further depicts subsequent and more intensive evaluation and planning toward IEPs when student concerns persist (Batsche et al., 2006; Horner & Sugai, 2001; Marston, 2005; Muscott, Mann, Benjamin, Gately, & Bell, 2004). The following narrative describes how the RSVP process interprets and represents the mandates of IDEA 2004 through an overview of six stages.

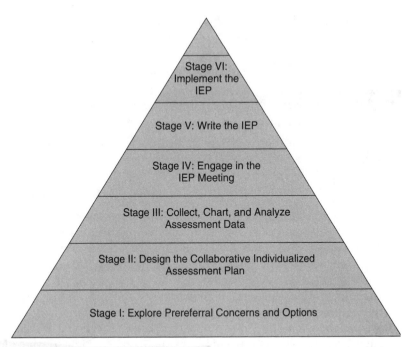

FIGURE 1.1 The RSVP Pyramid

An Overview of RSVP Stages

Stage I: Explore Prereferral Concerns and Options

Stage I highlights the roles, tasks, and thinking of general education teachers during the prereferral period as they explore concerns and corresponding modifications to address the challenges the student experiences. It provides guidelines for collecting informal data to understand student struggles, experimenting with a range of leveled interventions, contacting parents/caregivers, accessing supports and input from others, and documenting the effectiveness of efforts made on behalf of the learner. Depending on student responsiveness to interventions, the need for formal referral for special education evaluation is considered. Criteria for writing informative referrals are provided, if the decision is made to refer.

Stage II: Design the Collaborative Individualized Assessment Plan

Assessment planning draws from prereferral efforts and referral information to design a comprehensive approach for gaining a deeper understanding of student concerns, progress, and participation. This stage guides the team to make decisions about what data to collect, which assessment tools to use, and how to evaluate student performance. Team members construct a logical individualized assessment plan, thinking through what is *known* about the student, raising questions to determine what they *want* to find out, and matching assessment approaches for *how* to get the desired information.

Stage III: Collect, Chart, and Analyze Assessment Data

In Stage III, the team derives direction from the assessment plan to collect, chart, and evaluate the data, gathering detailed evidence of student competence and struggles in the area(s) of concern. Team members assess, analyze, and cross-reference student performance on a variety of assessment tasks and situations, synthesizing results, drawing insights, and making explanations about challenges and successes.

Stage IV: Engage in the Individualized Education Program Planning Meeting

Developing the IEP charges the team to integrate assessment results and draw conclusions to construct a comprehensive picture of the learner and discern appropriate starting points for instruction. This is the period in which members determine whether the student meets eligibility criteria, figuring out what interferes with progress in the general education classroom, whether adjustments to curriculum and instructional experiences are suitable, and/or whether his or her needs require specially designed instruction, interventions, and/or environments. Based on the team's integration of data, related educational decisions are made to design a responsive, cohesive program and plan according to student needs.

Stage V: Write the Individualized Education Plan/Program

Writing an effective IEP involves collating and reporting the information and ideas the team generates to create a blueprint for program implementers and a resource for parents/caregivers. Attention is paid to articulating the plan clearly to meet RSVP standards for comprehensive documents. As a result, readers understand student needs, proposals for instructional experiences, and ways to coordinate programming and services.

Stage VI: Implement the Individualized Education Plan/Program and Monitor Student Progress

Team members collaborate to transform IEPs into action, assign implementation responsibilities, coordinate instruction, and maintain ongoing communication in ways that ensure a cohesive program. When the IEP is informative, implementers have the basis to prepare, deliver, and document how the educational program is executed and how the student progresses. Ongoing data collection informs decisions around keeping to and/or modifying the IEP.

The stages of RSVP are connected to create a dynamic and proactive special education process based on understanding and valuing the IEP (see Figure 1.2). It involves:

- Proceeding through *tiered problem solving*
- Attending to *key decisions*

STAGE I: EXPLORE PREREFERRAL CONCERNS AND OPTIONS
Engage in prereferral efforts

    Step 1: Identify the concern(s) and initial modifications.
    Step 2: Involve parent(s)/caregiver(s).
    Step 3: Access supports through informal or formal prereferral options.
    Step 4: Initiate the special education process (submit referral for evaluation).

STAGE II: DESIGN THE COLLABORATIVE INDIVIDUALIZED ASSESSMENT PLAN
Conduct the Know-Want-How Assessment Plan Meeting

    Step 1: Start with what the team knows (about the student is as a reader, writer, speaker, listener, mathematician, and/or participant in the learning community). Analyze concern(s).
    Step 2: Determine what the team wants to learn. Raise questions.
    Step 3: Propose how the team will find out. Select assessment tools.
    Step 4: Distribute assessment responsibilities and map out the plan of action. Schedule.

STAGE III: COLLECT, CHART, AND ANALYZE ASSESSMENT DATA
Translate the Know-Want-How Assessment Plan into Action

    Step 1: Access and/or develop assessment tasks, tools, and activities.
    Step 2: Prepare to conduct assessments.
    Step 3: Conduct assessments.
    Step 4: Chart and analyze student performance and products.

STAGE IV: ENGAGE IN THE IEP MEETING
Synthesize Assessment Data, Determine Eligibility and Plan Instruction (IEP)

    Step 1: Build a comprehensive picture of the learner (in the area(s) of concern) collaboratively.
    Step 2: Summarize, draw conclusions, and hypothesize *what contributes to student competence and challenges*.
    Step 3: Develop content of the IEP:

        • Design individualized curriculum. (Establish next steps [goals, objectives, tools for documenting progress].)
        • Plan instruction. (Determine eligibility; identify teaching approaches, instructional materials, and modifications for access to general education and/ or specially designed instruction; figure out participation in performance assessment and transition plans.)
        • Identify program components. (Decide on service delivery.)

STAGE V: WRITE THE IEP
Compose the document

    Step 1: Develop profile and present levels of performance to present a comprehensive picture of the student.
    Step 2: Record the design of the individualized curriculum (goals, objectives, tools for documenting progress).

(continued)

FIGURE 1.2 The RSVP Stages and Steps

Step 3: Write the plan for instruction.
Step 4: Identify service delivery plans/program components.

STAGE VI: IMPLEMENT THE IEP AND MONITOR PROGRESS
<u>**Provide agreed on learning experiences**</u>
Step 1: Prepare for implementation.
Step 2: Deliver the individualized educational program.
Step 3: Monitor student progress and program effectiveness.
Step 4: Revisit IEP and make revisions as needed

FIGURE 1.2 *Continued*

- Adopting *practices* for assessment and educational planning
- Engaging *voices for collaboration*
- Treating the *IEP as a blueprint for student outcomes*, the culmination of the special education process

Tiered Problem Solving

Problem solving across the six stages of RSVP provides ways for teams to move systematically through the tiers of assessment, instruction, and intervention from prereferral to the IEP to placement to monitoring student progress and services. The use of such an approach keeps the focus on the intentions of the law to build an understanding of the challenges the student faces, address in-class solutions as the first priority, design constructive IEPs, and implement and reevaluate coordinated programs that impact the student. Team members cycle through efforts cooperatively to define the problem(s), prioritize concerns, analyze what is happening and why, brainstorm strategies and interventions, determine and implement action plans, and evaluate and reevaluate how the interventions do or do not result in student progress.

RSVP problem solving begins by examining and describing academic and behavior challenges and successes in the classroom, taking into account the demands that the general education curriculum, instruction, and setting place on the student. The description leads to different levels of modifications and interventions to accommodate and support the learner. The general education teacher starts by adjusting whole-class instruction, materials, structures, and arrangements that also benefits others in the setting. If issues persist, a more detailed problem analysis of needs is pursued to further determine distinctions among student performance, classroom expectations, and curriculum standards. As a result, supplementary small group and individual options are attempted to reach and teach the struggling learner.

When student progress is limited and it is deemed necessary to move to referral for special education evaluation, the problem-solving process then focuses on collecting more individualized assessment information to capture learner needs and specify more tailored teaching strategies and recommendations in the area(s) of concern. The team pursues more in-depth study of the student through more targeted assessment. The resulting data lead to further understanding of student struggles as a reader, writer, mathematician, and/or participant/member of the classroom, and defining his or her "present levels of academic achievement and functional performance." The comprehensive description of the student guides the articulation of an individualized education plan, which centers on relevant goals and objectives. The plan includes a set of solutions for accessing general education through adjustments and modifications and/or the selection of specially designed instruction and interventions. Through ongoing monitoring, student progress and program effectiveness are examined to determine necessary revisions (Fuchs et al., 2003; Marston, 2005; Marston et al., 2003; Prasse, 2006). Engaging in the problem-solving process rests on teams' wrestling with the succession of key decisions identified in the RSVP model.

Key Decisions

To respond to IDEA 2004 constructively, RSVP reminds team members to be vigilant about the key decisions they face as they move through the stages of the model to address the special education process. This requires them to examine what needs to be accomplished, who to involve, what questions to pose, what data to collect, what actions to take, and what potential outcomes are possible. When the decisions rest on referencing general education standards, collecting and using instructionally relevant data, and working collaboratively, teams have the wherewithal to substantiate and justify their positions and proposals as they make these determinations:

- Figure out the extent to which student challenges warrant concern
- Determine when and how to involve parents/caregivers
- Judge whether modifications to the general education and/or targeted interventions are sufficient and effective or whether more needs to be done
- Weigh the potential values of referral for special education evaluation
- Determine how to present collected prereferral data as part of a referral package
- Decide what evaluation questions respond to referral concerns and which assessment tools reveal needed information
- Evaluate whether completed assessments provide ample data to make instructional decisions
- Conclude whether the student meets eligibility criteria based on evidence collected and needs identified
- Figure out what constitutes a suitable educational plan to address individual challenges and promote student progress
- Decide how to apply IEP blueprints to daily practice
- Determine whether the program implemented is working and addressing the area(s) of concern, and make changes as necessary

The six consecutive stages of RSVP guide teams in making these key decisions explicit. Careful attention is paid to what and how assessment data are collected and used, how interventions are selected, how student responsiveness is appraised, how referrals are treated, what determines eligibility, and what informs IEP development. Emphasizing informed collaborative data-based decision making further affects how useful the IEP is in supporting program implementers and how invested they are in following and reevaluating the plans (Harber, 1981; Hosp & Reschly, 2003; Ysseldyke, 2001; Ysseldyke et al., 1983).

Practices: Tools for Organization, Assessment, and Planning

Essential questions provide direction for the tiered problem solving and key decisions inherent in the RSVP model. They underscore the importance of keeping the special education process practical and grounded in general education, *linking an understanding of curriculum demands, with how the student is viewed, with proposed ways to work with him or her.* Asking overarching questions helps organize the thinking and guide assessment and planning practices throughout the RSVP model to retain a student-centered focus, instructional relevance, and connections to general education contexts. The following questions steer teams on a proactive course of action to understand struggles of learners, make use of constructive assessment approaches, adopt instructional practices, and promote positive student outcomes in the area(s) of concern:

- What contributes to being proficient readers, writers, mathematicians, and participants/members of the classroom community?
- Who is the student as a reader, writer, mathematician, and participant/member of the classroom community?
- What types of instruction, interventions, and environments will promote student competence, participation, and investment as an effective reader, writer, mathematician, and participant/member of the classroom community?

The first question requires teams to understand academic and social competence with reference to grade-level standards, general education curriculum, and classroom expectations. The middle question frames what data teams collect to examine and comprehend individual student challenges and strengths in the area(s) of concern. The final question directs teams to connect assessment evidence to educational planning by coordinating what the student needs with what is to be done.

The essential questions are further defined in RSVP through the Interaction Formula as an organizational tool to build a comprehensive picture of the student and figure out individualized instruction or behavior plans. Use of the formula guides the team to sort out who the student is as a learner in area(s) of concern and what variables impact learning and teaching and instructional experiences and environments (Affleck, Lowenbraun, & Archer, 1980; Gleckel & Koretz, 1993, 1996; Price & Nelson, 2007; Wilson et al., 2005; Zigmond, Vallecorsa, & Silverman, 1983). Using the formula across the stages of RSVP provides a lens to systematically complete evaluations to capture student competence and challenges, establish curriculum and behavior expectations, select instructional materials and strategies, develop intervention plans, create learning environments, access general education, determine eligibility, and design programs and services that support student growth. Team members work together to apply the Interaction Formula (*What to Teach* + *How to Teach* + *How to Approach* + *Under What Conditions* + *Why Teach*) to:

- Know what to teach, determine the student skill competencies, and teach what is needed (What to Teach)
- Know how to teach, describe how the student responds to tasks and activities, and create suitable options for instruction and intervention (How to Teach)
- Know how to infuse problem solving into teaching, determine the thinking strategies the student uses, and develop strategy instruction to support learning and performance (How to Approach)
- Know what conditions promote participation, determine how the student engages, and arrange environments to support active involvement (Under What Conditions)
- Know why and how to motivate, determine when and how the student invests, and establish paths for commitment (Why Teach)

The Interaction Formula plays a key role in the ways team members grow to understand the student, figure out how to meet his or her needs, and design approaches to instruction and intervention as they proceed through the stages of the special education process. Using this formula facilitates the team moving from general to specific descriptions of the learner to designing increasingly individualized strategies and interventions. With detailed information, the team determines the significance of student need, eligibility, and related educational plans. It is adopting this thinking and corresponding practices that render the special education process as evolving, practical, comprehensive, and relevant.

Voices for Collaboration: Teaming

The RSVP model supports building the multidisciplinary team throughout the special education process, using the stages to bring the group of professionals, parents/caregivers, and the student (when appropriate) to work collaboratively. It guides them to develop a common understanding of the goals, to talk the same language, to complement each other's input and findings, and to share in decision making and problem solving, empowering all to be contributing members (Friend & Cook, 2000; Pugach & Johnson, 2002; Reeve & Hallahan, 1994; Walther-Thomas, Korinek, & McLaughlin, 1999). Team members engage in cooperative efforts as they attend meetings, assess students, design instructional plans, generate ideas for modifications and adaptations, implement instruction, and work with the student who is experiencing learning and behavior challenges.

The effectiveness of the multidisciplinary team depends on establishing working relationships to merge the richness of perspectives and expertise constructively. Throughout the six stages, members learn to give decisions and solutions a collective voice and make a shared commitment to accountability. It is through the structure and prompts of the model that members are coached to listen, raise concerns, ask questions, respond, give input, and share opinions. Setting ground rules for how to work together as a team consists of explicit agreements to come to meetings prepared, hear all voices, process differences, take on roles to facilitate exchanges and accomplish tasks, and monitor personal communication. Meeting agendas, which appear in subsequent chapters, help structure discussions so they are focused and productive, setting the expected outcomes, topics to be discussed, decisions to be made, and problem-solving process to follow. It is this team approach that contributes to the comprehensive understanding of student challenges and constructive plans for addressing them.

Individualized Education Plans/Programs as Blueprints for Student Outcomes

RSVP treats the IEP as a natural outgrowth of the special education process. It is the product of the team's collective problem-solving efforts, discussions, insights, brainstorming, and decision making. In the RSVP model, the education plan serves as the record of the team's work to respond to initial concerns regarding student performance and progress, collate assessment data to understand needs, and propose blueprints for individualized instructional plans and programs (Bateman, 1995; Drasgow, Yell, & Bradley, 1999; Drasgow, Yell, & Robinson, 2001; Huefner, 2000). RSVP guides the team to construct IEPs that are valuable tools for action planning and reflect the logic of the team's thinking and practices to support student gains.

The IEP serves as a reference tool from which to work and is evidence of meeting IDEA 2004 mandates. It is the product of systematic inquiry into what contributes to the challenges the student faces as he or she engages in school experiences. The quality and value of what is included in the IEP is judged by the extent to which it informs readers about student strengths and struggles and provides workable and relevant solutions, ones that transform into daily lessons, intervention strategies, and methods for documenting progress. It is critical for the IEP to set clear and realistic expectations for the student and implementers by articulating plans and programs that promise to be productive and worthwhile. A quality usable IEP reflects IDEA 2004 to address the student in the area(s) of concern. The document serves these functions:

- Reports challenges and performance
- Proposes focuses for instruction
- Sets criteria for student outcomes
- Designs techniques to monitor student progress and program effectiveness
- Outlines learning experiences to adjust the general education curriculum and/or offers specialized instruction
- Develops alternative testing plans, including statewide testing
- Creates plans for transition when age appropriate

The IEP presents guidelines for delivering services that identify when, where, how often, and with whom the student receives instruction. It takes into account the needs of the student and feasibility of implementation. More specific information on how to proceed through IEP development meetings, what formats IEP documents may take, and how to write IEPs is described in detail in Chapters 5 and 6.

Conclusion

The shift in the reauthorization of IDEA 2004 requires facing existing issues. This involves confronting traditionally held views about student challenges, the dichotomy of special and general education resulting in compartmentalized responsibilities of classroom teachers and special educators, and rote treatment of required special education steps marked by excessive paperwork and with limited attention to underlying critical decisions (Ysseldyke, 2005). It necessitates shedding the discrepancy model (IDEA 2004) and justifies the use of classroom- and curriculum-based measures for examining student needs.

The search is no longer focused on pathology but rather on adopting thinking and practices that support prevention and proactive approaches. This entails incorporating a problem-solving process for uncovering factors impacting student performance and behavior, addressing the range of individual needs, and designing corresponding programs and systems of delivery that support students and professionals. It requires being intentional about the types of data collected to inform each decision made throughout the special education process. These shifts involve developing an infrastructure in schools that supports merging ways for professionals, programs, and services to work collaboratively and sharing ownership of IDEA mandates and their implementation (Bryan & Bryan, 1988; Cook & Schirmer, 2003; Goodman & Bond, 1993; Lilly, 1987; Mainzer et al., 2003; Merrell & Shinn, 1990; Sapon-Shevin, 1988; Stainback & Stainback, 1984, 1985; Thurlow & Ysseldyke, 1982; Wang, Reynolds, & Walberg, 1986; Wiederholt, 1988; Wiest & Kreil, 1995; Will, 1986; Ysseldyke et al., 1983).

The emphasis of the RSVP model is to recognize and address existing issues by applying collaborative tiered problem solving, decision making, relevant practices, and IEP action planning, all of which are inherent in IDEA and throughout the special education process. This cumulative approach keeps the team focused on the educational life of the student. Developing constructive descriptions of learners and proposing educational plans that translate readily to daily instruction and learning environments make the goals and outcomes of the regulations practical. The RSVP Graphic Organizer in Figure 1.3 represents key aspects of the model. The remaining chapters of the book expand on the stages to support teams by providing specific steps, guidelines, and approaches for implementing IDEA 2004 meaningfully.

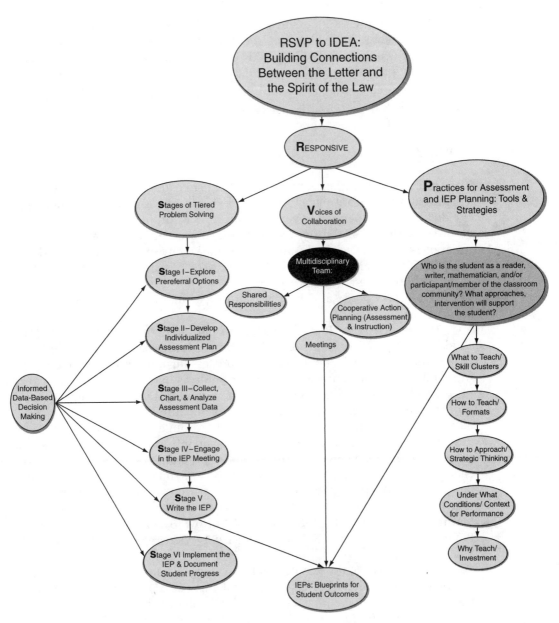

FIGURE 1.3 The RSVP Graphic Organizer

Apply and Learn

1. Think about a decision you have made in life. It may be big or small. Cut out strips of colored paper. Place each step of your decision on individual strips. Consider what influenced your decision. Write each influence on separate strips of white paper. Now arrange the decision steps and influence strips to represent the process you went through to make your decision, showing order and connections. What does it look like? What does the representation suggest to you? Compare your work with that of a peer.
   - How similarly or differently did you approach the decision-making process?
   - What about the decisions are sequential, confusing, messy, and/or neverending?
   - What were the roles of gathering information, internal dialogues, or external influences on your decision making?

2. Interview a special educator and/or classroom teacher about his or her perspectives as an advocate of special education legislation.
   - What aspects of the special education process does he or she discuss?
   - What are the purposes and benefits he or she sees in how the special education process operates in the school?
   - How are IEPs developed and used?
   - What are the drawbacks he or she sees with regard to how the special education process operates and IEPs are developed?
   - Summarize the responses you gathered. In what ways does this professional think about and/or address the *spirit of the law* and the *letter of the law*? What do you think is missing?

3. Examine the responses you gathered from the interviews with the teacher. Compare what the educator shared with regard to the RSVP stages and corresponding themes. What did you discover?

Chapter **2**

Stage I

Explore Prereferral Concerns and Options

As you read through this chapter, *think about*:

- The steps and related decisions during the prereferral stage; using tiered interventions to respond to described concerns and collaborative problem solving to access support

- The role of the general education teacher in responding to initial concerns regarding student challenges

- How to involve parents/caregivers in cooperative efforts to explore concerns and support in-class solutions

- The types of supports general education teachers seek to problem-solve with colleagues around student progress, participation, and performance

- How teachers and parents/caregivers make decisions about whether or not to refer students for special education evaluation

- What is helpful for teachers and parents/caregivers to include on a referral for special education evaluation

Overview of Stage I

Stage I of RSVP provides direction for systematically exploring student concerns and in-class solution options. The sequence of tasks described in this chapter provides a tiered structure for thinking about how to collect and make use of prereferral data to define student successes and needs to adapt and modify learning experiences and adjust environments. This stage guides data-based decision making that may avert or lead to referral for special education evaluation and presents what to include in a formal referral package.

Prereferral is the span of time when concerns are raised about how a student is responding to established curriculum standards and schoolwide behavior expectations. Attention is paid to how he or she participates in classroom activity, produces work, makes progress in academic and social areas, engages in the learning environment, and/or interacts with peers and adults. This period of time is marked by an emerging awareness of student challenges and an evolving approach to modification and intervention strategies to address struggles. IDEA 2004 sets the expectation for classroom teachers to assume responsibility for responding to student challenges in the general education context rather than moving directly to the special education process.

Prereferral is a proactive period of inquiry and exploration (Black, 2007; Buck, Polloway, Smith-Thomas, & Cook, 2003; Drasgow & Yell, 2002; Eidle, Truscott, & Meyers, 1998; Lewis & Sugai, 1999). The focus of this time is to understand student needs better and to support general education teacher attempts to create and implement adjustments and interventions while documenting the results. Informal steps move from raising concerns to pinpointing student struggles so graduated levels of adaptations and alternatives are developed as in-class solutions for the identified areas (Chalfant & Pysch, 1981; Chalfant, Pysh, & Moultrie, 1979; Fuchs, 1987; Fuchs & Fuchs, 1989; Graden, Casey, & Bonstrom, 1986; Graden, Casey, & Christenson, 1985; Lane, Pierson, Robertson, & Little, 2004; Pugach & Johnson, 1988). During this stage these actions are taken:

- Problems are initially identified and defined with reference to the demands of the general educational setting
- Informal data are collected to document and examine the concerns
- Communications with parents/caregivers are initiated or intensified and directed toward proactive and collaborative efforts to learn more about and address student in-class issues
- Conferences are set up with the student to invite his or her perspective
- Interventions are developed, instructional strategies are modified, environments are adapted, and materials are adjusted while the range of efforts and student responsiveness are documented
- Support of colleagues is accessed and recommendations for classroom modifications, interventions, and/or supplemental programs are pursued, implemented, and evaluated

• Options regarding referral for special education evaluation are weighed, and decisions are made in light of evidence collected around prereferral efforts

Growing apprehension on the parts of the general education teacher and/or parents/caregivers regarding student performance, participation, and progress give rise to activity during the prereferral stage. General education teachers pull back to acknowledge issues the student experiences, assess related situation(s), and consider what contributes to the challenges. They determine how evidence defines the concern in order to figure out options to support progress and in-class efforts. Parents/caregivers are invited to work with the teacher to share their input regarding student struggles and be involved in finding solutions. There is a commitment to implement modifications that adjust whole-group instruction to enhance student experiences in the general education curriculum and classroom. Efforts may progress to altering instructional approaches, materials, and environments and designing interventions to accommodate individual needs within small groups or provide differentiated instruction if warranted. These efforts are documented to evaluate student performance. How the student responds to the series of adjustments to learning experiences and environments helps determine whether attempted in-class strategies are sufficient, whether access to building-based supports and supplemental programs promises positive results, and/or whether formal referral for special education evaluation is justified (Batsche et al., 2005; Black, 2007; Gersten & Dimino, 2001; Horner & Sugai, 2000; Marston, 2005; Mastriopieri & Scruggs, 2000; Reschly, 2005).

Gaining an understanding of concerns comes from collecting informal data regarding how the student engages, performs, and produces in the context of the classroom structure, instruction, and curriculum. The intention of collecting these data is to discern a clearer appreciation of the student in the classroom setting as a reader, writer, mathematician, and participant in the learning environment and the classroom community. Observations, work sample analyses, and reviews of student records are the sources. The collection of data generated from these classroom activities allows for examination of matches or mismatches among student learning and/or behaving, teaching, and settings. Drawing conclusions from the information gathered helps account for what supports and impedes student progress and effectiveness, which leads to the development of levels of *explicit, intensive,* and *supportive* solutions (Bahr et al., 2006; Fuchs, 2003; Marston et al., 2003; Torgesen, 2002) designed to impact student achievement positively in the classroom.

When student needs and concerns persist, and before considering formal referral to special education evaluation, the general education teacher continues problem solving through the support and assistance of grade-level colleagues, a team designated to engage in prereferral efforts, or a peer assigned to facilitate addressing the issues the student presents (Bergan & Kratochwill, 1990; Chalfant & Pysch, 1981; Clark, 1999; Corrigan & Bishop, 1997; Graden et al., 1986; Harrington & Gibson, 1986; Lloyd, Crowley, Kohler, & Strain, 1988; Pugach & Johnson, 1988).

Cooperative efforts often yield a more insightful articulation of what happens when the student experiences difficulty, a clearer grasp of which tasks and activities are most challenging, and a richer pool of ideas to address concerns. Based on a collective understanding of student struggles, the variety of modifications to the general education curriculum, instruction, environments, and/or supplemental services is enriched when cooperatively brainstormed, implemented, documented, evaluated, and revised as needed (Buck et al., 2003; Chalfant et al., 1979; Pugach & Johnson, 1989).

If the prereferral strategies prove to address student needs, intervention approaches are continued and monitored, and no additional support is sought. If questions surrounding student status persist, the option to refer for special education evaluation is considered. Referral is an opportunity to gather more extensive information to deepen understanding of who the student is in the area(s) of concern and intensify the focus of interventions and modifications.

Formal referral is prompted, justified, and informed by the activities at the prereferral stage. It is critical that the corresponding referral documentation captures data collected and reports what is known about the student, interventions attempted, the resulting impact of efforts, and the remaining questions. This information, in turn, serves as the reference point to focus the special education evaluation team on developing an assessment plan that leads to generating usable data to understand student challenges.

The set of steps that follows explains connections among the thinking, practices, and decisions infused in stage I. With each step, the problem solving evolves, and approaches to intervention and progress monitoring intensify. With each step, the network of collaborative relationships grows to support the student, classroom teacher, and parent(s)/caregiver(s).

Step 1: Identify the Concern(s) and Initial Modifications

Beginning to explore student challenges is the first step in the search for in-class solutions. The general educator recognizes and describes emerging concerns, raises questions, and collects, reviews, and organizes information to capture a preliminary picture of student struggles in the classroom context. At the outset, the classroom teacher must clarify what those challenges are and what contributes to them. It is time to sort out and respond to initial reactions—those feelings of frustration, consternation, doubt; being caught up in what the student is not doing; uncertainty as to why progress is not made and/or questioning what to do. It is the time to describe the student as a reader, writer, mathematician, and/or participant/member in the classroom community.

Excerpts from a Case Study: Teacher's Initial Concern(s)

When Paul hands in writing assignments, they do not say much. They do not flow and give little voice to his thinking. This student is in sixth grade. What is going on?

Write Objective and Informative Descriptions

The goal is for general education teachers to develop their understanding of the initial concern(s) and build a practical definition of the problem(s). For general educators, this requires gathering evidence of student responses and performance relative to classroom demands: curriculum standards/benchmarks, behavior expectations, and instructional approaches, materials, tasks, and settings. This also involves reflecting on their own teaching related to the area(s) of concern and interactions with the student. The classroom teachers' role is to pull information together informally, contemplate the evidence, analyze what exists, and draft a preliminary description of the learner.

To develop the initial description of concern, general educators include objective, relevant performance data, drawing from observations, work samples, and conversations with the student. To get a handle on what is happening in the classroom, teachers define student behaviors, identify expectations for performance and behavior, and describe related circumstances or situations. To depict the concern objectively and constructively:

- ***Describe what the student is doing and saying, using observable vocabulary.*** Teachers record what they see or hear versus what they think is going on with the student. To prevent misinterpretation, use action words and behaviors that explain what the student is doing, be it *skipping unknown words* when reading aloud from a grade-level trade book, *counting on fingers* to calculate single-digit addition examples on a worksheet, or *pounding the desk* with a fist when her hand is raised and a peer is called on during large group discussion.
- ***Avoid using abstract, subjective descriptors.*** Nonspecific terms tend to devalue what the student is doing (e.g., *only* started his work, *barely* spoke), generalize what the student is *not* doing (e.g., *not* getting work done, *always* inattentive, *never* gets it right), make biased interpretations of behavior or performance (e.g., *manipulating, careless, uncooperative, stubborn*), or surmise what the student is feeling (e.g., *unhappy, distracted*). These descriptors tend to infer rather than report on the behaviors that comprise student performance or social/emotional responses.
- ***Identify curricular and teacher expectations for student performance and behavior.*** Explain what the teacher asks the student to do. These include the demands of the tasks (requisite academic and social skills and expected standards) and what the teacher asks of the student in response to directions, instructional approaches, and materials.
- ***Describe the academic and social learning environments and related situations.*** Outline the instructional and physical settings; grouping strategies, time on and pace of tasks, teacher responses, classroom arrangements, and setting structures (rules, procedures, transitions, etc.). Be sure to include what occurs prior to, during, and following the behaviors and performance.

Maintain Records of Behaviors and Performance

Descriptions of students are only as valuable as the information they contain. General education teachers use the classroom experience to gather objective data systematically. They conduct direct observations, write anecdotal records, and collect work samples to capture student concerns in the general education classroom. Maintaining records of student behavior and performance as they emerge requires teachers to adopt a system that is compatible with the way they work in the classroom. Here are some possibilities:

- Use *clipboard cruising*, making notes about student behaviors and responses to in-class tasks and activities as they occur. Arrange color-coded sticky notes, index cards, and/or stick-on name labels on a clipboard to jot down observations about students.
- Create checklists or rubrics relevant to academic and/or behavioral expectations and standards being observed (refer to grade-level curriculum standards).
- Organize a notebook and file folder system with sections for each student to collect information documented, individual student work samples, and corresponding rubrics.
- Record information anecdotally, noting behaviors and performance shortly after they happen or during a break.

Access Student Perspective

It is also helpful to gain students' own perspective as early on in the process as possible. Getting their views about performance and behavior in the area(s) of concern reveals more about qualities of work samples and anecdotal records. Take time to acknowledge the challenge(s) they experience, giving them a voice in sorting through the possible factors contributing to their struggles to shed light on what makes school hard and what would make it more constructive. It is valuable for students to hear that their efforts are recognized, in spite of work with limited accuracy or behaviors that feel *in trouble*. Listening conveys an awareness of the challenges students experience, communicates care and concern, and opens the doors to future discussion.

To learn more about student thinking, general education teachers intentionally engage students in conversation as they do work or during a private conference time. During independent work sessions, teachers ask students to talk through what they are doing, tell what they are thinking, explain what seems confusing, show what they can and cannot do, or describe their views of a situation. Teachers ask students to elaborate on a difficult situation through an in-class behavior contract or journal entry. Hearing what goes on for students adds dimension to tallying or analyzing the errors they make, invites students into evaluating their own learning and behavior, and provides insights into what does and does not work. Teachers capture the students' perspective by writing side notes on copies of work samples, journals, or behavior contracts.

Make In-Class Adjustments

Teachers review the information gathered to summarize findings and formulate an initial description of the student in the area(s) of concern. The focus is on describing academic and social struggles and successes, what the student does and what impacts his or her progress and effectiveness in the classroom setting. Teachers reference the following questions, derived from the Interaction Formula presented in Chapter 1, to help develop the description of who the student is in the area(s) of concern as a reader, writer, mathematician, and/or participant/member of the classroom community:

- What are the skills per cluster targeted by instruction that the student does and does not use? (What to Teach)
- How does the student respond to different instructional approaches, activities, materials, and tasks? (How to Teach)
- What thinking strategies and problem solving does the student use? (How to Approach)
- In what way(s) does the student respond to instructional arrangements and physical structures of the setting? (Under What Conditions)
- How does the student invest in learning? (Why Teach)

As teachers consider their understanding of the student, they come to grips with the need to do something different. General education teachers work to alter classroom expectations, adjust curriculum, redesign assignments, access alternative materials, and/or rearrange the physical and instructional environment to address student needs and competence. Keeping track of student responses to the modifications and interventions provides evidence of their impact on participation, progress, and performance and helps determine next steps.

Excerpts from a Case Study: Teacher's Initial Problem Description

When Paul hands in writing assignments, they are short with simple sentences and spelling errors. Paragraphs stay on topic but are not developed. When he completes written assignments, such as reader response logs, he tends to use simple bare-bone sentences strung together to convey a broad main idea. He uses manuscript that is hard to read. During morning meetings, classroom discussions, and literature circles, Paul shares his ideas and views in complex sentences. Supporting evidence: folder with samples of reader response logs and student journals.

Step 2: Involve Parent(s)/Caregiver(s)

As general education teachers work to unravel and address the challenges the student experiences, they reach out to parents/caregivers to inform them of the concerns, elicit their perspectives and support, describe student responsiveness to initial modifications and interventions, consider additional options for addressing student needs, and develop a cooperative plan of action. Involving parents/caregivers during this stage is an opportunity to gather more information about the student and establish a working alliance.

Approaching parents/caregivers to share concerns is facilitated when they are informed and involved in the life of the classroom. It is helpful when a foundation of school–home communications is established as a matter of practice, exposing parents/caregivers to classroom and school activity through open houses, conferences, class or school newsletters, volunteer programs, class presentations, and/or observation days. Access to the teacher through an exchange of notes, homework notebooks, e-mail, or call-in times helps families understand expectations and activity in the classroom as well as extends the level of comfort for all involved.

Developing positive working relationships with parents/caregivers and establishing avenues of mutual respect evolve from thoughtful interactions and attending to who they are. When teachers understand their own assumptions and beliefs, they build partnerships with the parents/caregivers through a two-way communication process called *cultural reciprocity* (Banks, 2001; Salas, 2004). Conversations communicating that cultural values and beliefs are recognized, appreciated, and respected take into account family structures, ethnicity, gender, religion, customs, language, socioeconomic challenges and work schedules, and views about education and special education. Becoming attuned to how cultural similarities and differences influence discussions around academic and social success and challenges, homework, and involvement in school leads to a collaborative understanding of student concerns, establishing priorities, and making recommendations (Obiakor, 2007). Using language that is readily understood and listening actively to parents/caregivers creates the context for sharing information, connecting to acknowledge cultural considerations and personal experiences, eliciting input, and promoting asking questions, thus establishing a comfortable situation for ongoing communication.

Share Information Between Teachers and Parents/Caregivers

It is the teacher's message of working together and sharing ideas that sets the stage for a productive relationship, and it is his or her style of delivery that enhances the quality of conversations about student challenges. It is important to balance concerns with positive anecdotes, giving parents/caregivers reassurance that time is taken to get to know the whole student. Offering information, asking questions, and making suggestions in a nonthreatening manner requires objective descriptions of student work and behavior, using examples to illustrate what is being discussed. The general education teacher creates a collaborative tone by facilitating a forum to discuss student status. Such a forum is an opportunity for the parents/caregivers as well as the teacher to share their insights and questions about the student's performance in the context of grade-level curricular and classroom expectations and with reference to the ways the environment and instruction are arranged.

Being mindful of the content of messages and the style in which they are delivered is crucial to working together, recognizing potential issues that may undermine the quality of such interactions (Clark, 1999; Lamorey, 2002). The atmosphere of such a meeting may initially be impacted by some of the views parents/caregivers bring to the conference. Their own past experiences as a student or with others in the school setting or their cultural beliefs may affect their participation in the meeting. Without recognizing these possibilities, parents/caregivers may appear confident, reserved, demanding, confused, or unrealistic about their child. These factors may be reflected in parent/caregiver conversation, tone of voice, body language, and may filter what and how they hear the teacher or impact how they feel they are treated. Attention to understanding where they are coming from by using positive communication skills may help avoid the parents/caregivers leaving the conference feeling blamed, defensive, guilty, dismissed, patronized, shut out, or judged. Being acknowledged, respected, and heard may lead to parents/caregivers feeling grateful, comfortable, pleased, or encouraged to participate. Dissipating potential issues by listening reflectively and balancing the content of conversation supports the development of this key partnership.

During discussion, pauses and open-ended questions promote conversation and invite sharing. Yes or no questions tend to limit what is said and possibly stifle the focus of conversation. The intent of working with the family in this way is to seek information and perspectives, engage in joint decision making, and enlist involvement in whatever ways feel comfortable and feasible. This give-and-take of listening, asking, and discussing communicates a mutual respect, acknowledges how well the parents/caregivers know their child, and recognizes teacher efforts to present documentation of how the student functions as a learner in the classroom and what he or she is attempting to do to accommodate the student. When conversations convey the message that *we're in this together*, teacher and parents/caregivers make concerted efforts to increase their collective understanding of the student, cooperatively explore possible interventions, and retain an ongoing dialogue to monitor progress and/or evaluate possible options and decisions.

Set Up the First Conference During the Prereferral Stage

Make the Initial Phone Call to Parents/Caregivers

When the teacher makes initial contact with parents/caregivers during the prereferral stage, it is important to explain concerns, convey a positive message, and limit alarming them. A phone conversation serves as the icebreaker to set up a meeting time and invite parents/caregivers to explore the emerging concerns about challenges the student experiences. Establishing a working relationship rests on honest discussion, portraying the exploratory nature of the prereferral stage, involving family members in sharing their insights and concerns, and finding ways they can get involved in fostering changes for the student. It is helpful to keep phone calls brief, unless it is difficult to find a meeting time. Keeping the description of the concern short avoids confusions. Jotting down notes after each contact between the teacher and the parents/caregivers records information shared and allows for the review of and building on previous conversations. The Parent/Caregiver Contact Toolbox offers a checklist to structure the phone conversation and provides examples of ways to invite parents/caregivers to get involved.

Prepare for and Conduct the Conference

Preparing for and conducting a conference with parents/caregivers means facilitating a two-way conversation in which concerns are raised and defined and mutually agreed-on plans to address them are made. It is important to convey that the prereferral stage is characterized by explorations, which requires willingness to ask questions and try out possible solutions. This path for addressing the concerns does not ensure all the answers but rather are steps to uncovering what is interfering with student participation and progress in the classroom and documenting the effectiveness of modification efforts. This cooperative commitment cultivates comfort to pose questions, share information and suggestions, and listen to one another so further understanding of the student and in-class solutions will be uncovered. The Parent/Caregiver Contact Toolbox provides a suggested conferencing checklist for the general educator to structure this initial meeting with parents/caregivers.

At this conference, the teacher presents the concern(s) along with samples of student work to convey the challenge(s) to the parents/caregivers in a meaningful way. He or she listens for their responses, hears their questions, and provides supportive answers to reach a mutual understanding of what is happening for the student. The teacher then explains early attempts at modifications and how they worked while inviting input from parents/caregivers. Together, they generate additional ideas for in-class solutions. The teacher also introduces the options available to support the student through general education supplemental programs and prereferral support systems. Parents/caregivers are informed about the possibilities regarding referral for special education evaluation, indicating its value when concerns persist after interventions are attempted, documented, and evaluated.

A plan for ongoing communication is established to examine how well the additional modifications are working. The general educator and parents/caregivers make a commitment to continue to work together to determine student responsiveness to interventions, collecting and examining evidence of student progress, gathering feedback from the student as modifications are made, and weighing decisions for sustaining current efforts and/or pursuing others. Together, they develop ways to stay in touch and set timelines and criteria for reviewing the effectiveness of what is tried.

With limited evidence of responsiveness to in-class modifications and continued questions or concerns about student progress and how to meet needs more effectively, the general educator and parents/caregivers may opt to pursue the existing building-based prereferral support system. To make this decision, they organize and review data collected in light of modifications and interventions attempted. They summarize what they understand about the concerns and pose questions as they seek more productive solutions to meet the student needs.

Step 3: Access Supports Through Formal or Informal Prereferral Options

Building-based prereferral systems provide the vehicle for determining more targeted academic and social instruction and interventions to address persistent student challenges. The forms they take may vary across schools. As formal or informal collaborative problem solving, their intent is to guide, support, and assist the general education teacher with or without parents/caregivers to define the problem(s), brainstorm alternative solutions, construct plans, and design a system to monitor student responsiveness. The collaborative efforts focus on gaining further understanding of what is challenging the student, figuring out how classroom expectations impact performance and progress, and determining what types of explicit instruction, intensive modifications, behavior interventions, and/or supplemental programs are suitable for the student and the teacher. The different viewpoints and expertise of additional educators add perspective to sorting out what contributes to the challenges the student experiences. Greater clarity regarding the challenges the student faces leads to different levels of responses for addressing them. These ideas are enriched when options are the result of cooperative brainstorming.

A collaborative, building-based prereferral model is designed to encourage the general education teacher to take the following actions:

- Participate in a cooperative prereferral support system, collaborating with a team of colleagues, accessing resources, and/or meeting with a peer coach to gain a better understanding of the struggles, needs, and successes of the student
- Work within the prereferral support system to develop modifications, adaptations, tasks, and strategies that respond to student challenges and strengths while connecting with general education
- Create a plan that explains how to implement instructional modifications and behavior interventions, monitor and evaluate their impact on student performance, and distribute roles and responsibilities to those involved
- Review student responses to the instructional modifications and behavior interventions to determine appropriate next steps

Colleagues work together to add depth to understanding the existing concern(s). The general education teacher draws from what he or she, along with parent(s)/caregiver(s), has done thus far to articulate a description of the problem, reference classroom-based assessments, share attempted modifications and interventions, and pose questions about what has been observed and the struggles that persist. The teacher engages with colleagues in cooperative discussion to clarify the problem, making presented information explicit in ways that create as complete a picture as possible.

Colleagues then turn their attention to generating ideas for more in-depth, differentiated modifications, interventions, and instruction and their potential results. The team develops more individualized ideas to adapt, modify, or alter instructional approaches, materials, or assignments, respond differently to student behaviors, and rearrange the learning environment. The focal point is to find more targeted ways to address missing skills, adopt strategies and teaching techniques to facilitate student progress, and refine settings to enhance investment and engagement.

General educators need to be open and willing to try some of the brainstormed ideas. Making this commitment requires recognizing their own grasp of the subject matter, flexibility in making classroom changes, and confidence with modifying existing instructional materials and approaches, adopting different teaching strategies, and/or implementing behavior intervention plans. As a result of self-assessment, general educators indicate which ideas will or will not work in the context of their classroom.

Regardless of the level and focus of interventions, corresponding progress-monitoring tools and strategies are developed to gather evidence of student academic and social growth, and thus determine the effectiveness of modifications and interventions. Tools for continuous progress monitoring are developed with reference to grade-level curriculum and behavior expectations. Tools may include sampling specific skill sets across grade-level curriculum standards and benchmarks by using curriculum-based measures and authentic tasks assigned as part of instruction. These may consist of focused and/or timed tasks or work sample products to identify to what degree the student is mastering and/or applying skills or concepts being taught. Student behavior is tracked through observations, documented on checklists or as anecdotal or running records to provide data for conducting functional behavior analysis. These data help clarify what the student does, when, how often, what setting(s), and what purpose the behavior serves with reference to schoolwide and classroom expectations.

An action plan is then built to give a clear direction for how to implement recommendations in conjunction with general education experiences. It outlines suggestions for materials, teaching methods, and ways to work with the student along with how the teacher accesses in-class help, instructional resources, and/or supplemental programs. The action plan sets guidelines for what is going to be done in the general education setting, how student progress is documented, what and when the general educator and student receive supports, how contacts with other professionals are coordinated, and when follow-up takes place.

Following a problem-solving agenda provides a structure for proceeding through the prereferral meeting effectively and efficiently. The format guides the team to establish the meeting focus and collaborative tone. The agenda sets the process for defining the concern(s) systematically, prioritizing focus(es) for working with the student, brainstorming solutions, generating a plan of action, designing tools for monitoring student responsiveness to interventions, and scheduling follow-up. It is the agenda that helps build the team and keep dialogue productive.

Emphasis on Collaboration

Engaging in collaborative conversations around the agenda with a colleague or group of colleagues involves blending a systematic approach to problem solving with effective communication skills. This requires a supportive team effort that acknowledges the existing issues and challenges what the general education teacher faces. Collaboration means inviting the teacher to share his or her concerns and questions and participate in brainstorming ideas and to work together toward solutions. The collaborative process necessitates communicating mutual respect, posing questions nonjudgmentally, supporting open and honest exchange of perspectives, encouraging expression of beliefs, giving constructive feedback, and facilitating teamwork on and through related issues, concerns, and options.

Being cognizant of ways questions are asked, ideas are brainstormed, and messages are delivered creates a welcoming, nonjudgmental, collaborative tone in which colleagues feel at ease rather than vulnerable. The problem-solving agenda in Figure 2.1 offers guidelines for facilitating a supportive meeting. It includes

---

PROBLEM-SOLVING AGENDA

1. **Describe the Concern(s).** During this segment of the meeting we are going to identify problem area(s)/ issue(s)/ factor(s) warranting attention. As a team, we will work to generate descriptions of the student in the context of learning experiences in ways that lead us to developing classroom modifications or alternatives. As we engage in this part of the meeting, it is an opportunity for each of us to gain an understanding of the student in response to classroom demands.

   Please describe the problem(s) that prompted attention:

   - **What do you see the student doing?** Provide an overview of who the student is in the area(s) of concern.
   - **What is the student being asked to do?** Describe the tasks, materials, assignments the student is given.
   - **What else is taking place in the setting?** Describe how the student works in different settings and groupings with regard to the area(s) of concern.
   - **With what is the student struggling?** Identify the qualities and patterns of errors/ misbehaviors the student makes.

   Problem solving requires listening actively and reflectively, giving clear descriptive messages (includes I-messages), using open-ended questions, remaining open minded, and committing to working through the issues.

   Communicate open-mindedness to the situation and what colleague is feeling. Use door openers (open-ended questions or statements) to check on what he or she is experiencing and feeling and encourage conversation, sharing, and clarifications:
   - Tell me about . . .
   - Please explain . . .
   - What happens when . . .?
   - That sounds interesting.
   - I am interested in hearing about that.
   - How do you see . . .?
   - What are your views about . . .?
   - Sounds like you have strong feelings about . . .

FIGURE 2.1 Problem-Solving Agenda

Use active and reflective listening to respond to a shared concern for what is going on and to recognize challenges related to the situation:

- It sounds like . . . is . . .
- I am hearing that . . .
- It seems as if . . .

(Avoid stating how the teacher *should feel or how I would feel in this situation*)

2. **Focus and Summarize.** During this segment of the meeting, target the priorities that emerge as a result of discussion, highlighting the variables over which the teacher has control (aspects of instruction and environment). Acknowledge teacher perspective and additional information that has emerged.

- You've raised several issues or problem areas. Let's reiterate . . .
- What feels most pressing for you?
- How do the student and parents/caregivers feel about the priority?
- Over what aspects of instruction and/or the environment do you feel you have control and can alter?

Summarize and set goals:
- We have been talking about . . .
- Sounds like . . .
- You seem to be concerned with . . . but have also raised . . . What feels most pressing?

3. **Brainstorm Strategies** (list strategies to address the concern):

- You have identified _____ as your priority.
- Let's generate a list of possible approaches to address the problem(s). Remember, we are listing ideas, practical and outlandish, and not evaluating them. So please save comments until we are finished.
- Let's take three minutes and go around the table to share ideas.
- Now that you see the list, what additional ideas are there?

4. **Construct a Plan** (select options that fit the situation and meet both student and teacher needs, and design a specific plan to implement the decisions):

- Of the list of ideas brainstormed (point to or read the list), which options might work in your situation/setting? Which do you prefer?
- In what way(s) might the option be incorporated into your classroom?
- Let's explore using the option a little further. What material or types of help would facilitate trying it out?
- Now that you have the skeleton of a plan (reiterate), how can we help you get started? How can we help support implementation?
- What ways can we develop to judge the effectiveness of this alternative?

5. **Schedule Follow-Up Activities** to see how the plan works (collect data to document student progress and participation and effectiveness of plan):

- It would be helpful to receive feedback. How should we go about setting up a communication system to evaluate how effective the modifications are?
- You may need some time to sort your thoughts and try out your plan. Contact and communication are important in offering ongoing support. How soon would you like to meet again? When would be a good time to touch base?

some prompts and open-ended questions to create an inviting setting and generate practical information, where the teacher retains ownership of the concern(s), is given opportunity to set the course for interventions, and feels supported. When a clear agenda and cooperative discussion are followed, the general education teacher feels it is legitimate to have questions rather than answers, to accept or reject ideas, and to convey apprehensions and hopeful enthusiasm (Friend & Cook, 2000; Pugach & Johnson, 2002).

Step 4: Initiate the Special Education Process

The effectiveness of prereferral interventions are judged by the evidence the teacher collects regarding how changes support student growth, participation, and performance. The impact of different strategies and modifications attempted, the time period dedicated to these efforts, the support provided to ensure successful implementation, and the degree of satisfaction with the results is evaluated. The use of these data determines if the prereferral plan is working, whether alternative in-class modifications and interventions are needed, whether additional supplemental services may help, and/or if referral and more extensive evaluation are warranted. Despite the efforts, some approaches may not match student needs. Some may just not work. Others may require adjustments and extended perseverance. When questions continue about the suitability of interventions, they may justify in-depth evaluation information to further understand student needs and to design more differentiated, explicit instruction for access to general education and/or specially designed solutions (Bahr, Whitten, Dieker, Kocarek, & Manson, 1999; Gerber, 2005; Mamlin & Harris, 1998). The general educator, parents/caregivers, and prereferral team reflect on whether:

- Collected data reveal that the student continues to struggle to make substantive progress even with the attempted tiered interventions
- Student concern(s) need to be described with more specificity
- Additional modifications and interventions need to be designed and implemented to better address student challenges
- Questions persist

When uncertainty about the student and what to do to support him or her remains, even after collaborations take place and alternatives are attempted and reviewed, it may be time to pursue the referral process. Choosing the path of referral for special education evaluation means gathering more specific information that builds from what the teacher and parents/caregivers learn during the prereferral stage. This results in following the problem-solving process in more depth, with more assessment data, with greater attention to details, and with additional professionals contributing to the pool of information and the development of interventions. The referral process uses the information generated during the prereferral period to initiate the special education process and to proceed through the next RSVP stages and related steps.

The referral document is a written request for further evaluation of student status and formally activates the special education process. Its purpose is to report documented prereferral efforts and results relative to student progress. The narrative depicts the concerns, summarizes levels of interventions attempted, reports student responsiveness, and poses unresolved questions to inform the multidisciplinary team. The content of an informative referral document, regardless of format, prompts the next cycle of problem solving. The depth of information provided sets the stage for making deliberate decisions about the direction the evaluation takes and which assessment tools the multidisciplinary team uses.

The classroom teacher, typically the author of a referral, has a crucial role in this process, documenting and sharing what has been learned and stating concerns about the student in relation to general education curriculum standards and classroom academic and behavioral expectations. The more relevant the information included in the referral, the more it serves as a catalyst for authentic evaluation of and response to pressing student concerns. The more detailed and descriptive the information contained in the referral, the more likely special education evaluation builds on experiences of the prereferral stage and leads to relevant assessment data and eventual appropriate instructional planning and programming. Here are suggested guidelines for writing a substantive and informative referral:

1. Write the problem statement(s), telling the prereferral story:
   - Describe concern(s)/struggle(s), using observable language and offering teacher perspective; discussing *what to teach, how to teach, how to approach, under what conditions, and why teach* (Interaction Formula).
   - Explain what the student is expected to be doing (academically and/or socially) that he or she is not doing now.
   - Provide supportive evidence of student struggles *and* successes in the area(s) of concern:
       Highlight what the student says, does, produces in the context of academic and social environments, including examples
       Attach work samples, anecdotal records, and related documentation to illustrate academic struggles and inappropriate behaviors in typical and modified classroom tasks and activities
2. List and justify attempted academic and behavior modifications and interventions and the related results:
   - Explain each modification/intervention attempted, justifying why it was tried.
   - Provide the results of each, explaining why the modification/intervention did or did not work:
       Attach evidence of progress monitoring (completed work samples, charts, observational data, etc., that indicate level of responsiveness and persistent struggles)

Once the referral form is written, submitted, and approved, the specific path it takes varies from school district to school district and sometimes from building to building. However, in most instances, a team leader is assigned to coordinate the case, facilitate meetings, and delegate responsibilities. A multidisciplinary evaluation team composed of professionals who have expertise relative to the area(s) of concern, the classroom teacher(s), the parents/caregivers, and student, when appropriate, is then formed to process the content of the referral collaboratively and cooperatively. It is valuable to recognize the classroom teacher and parent/caregiver as resources and assets, people who can contribute additional data, perspectives, and ideas to team problem solving and decision making. By treating the referral as a request for evaluation to understand further what is happening for the student, members of the special education evaluation team now gather collaboratively to set the course for individualized assessment planning in stage II of RSVP.

Excerpts from a Case Study:
Teacher Referral for Special Education Evaluation

Paul, a sixth grader, often refuses to write in his reader response log or complete creative writing assignments. When given these tasks, he puts his head down on the desk, saying, "I have nothing to write." He is more likely to make an entry in his personal journal. When he does write in his personal journal or about a book he likes, he tends to use simple bare-bone sentences strung together to convey a main idea. He seems to produce more when he works on the computer, although ideas introduced are not well developed. He introduces a character and an event as isolated facts without tying them together. Similarly, in written responses required for social studies and science, he provides short answers that give little indication of what he understands.

His written work is most often printed with letters trailing off lines and spaces between words varying. Words are often misspelled but discernible as he represents the sounds. He does use end punctuation, commas for series, and capital letters at the beginning of sentences and for some proper nouns.

Paul does participate in morning meetings and classroom discussions; using vocabulary pertinent to the topic and adding personal insights and details. During literature circles, he talks fluently about the stories and shares opinions about what he reads in contrast to what he includes in his reader response logs.

Attempts to address these issues include these tiered-level strategies:

1. *Class was provided with direct instruction for how to use graphic organizers (story maps and webs), including key words of setting, characters, problem to solution events. When given graphic organizers, Paul enters single words that he then uses in his writing. These do not seem to help him expand his ideas.*
2. *When given small group instruction for "framing your thoughts," he verbally expands sentence ideas but does not translate those in his writing. He continues to use bare-bone sentences.*
3. *When given opportunities to dictate answers to questions (reader response, science chapters) to a buddy, he does seem to add details to improve the content. The buddy system is not always feasible.*

4. *Misspelled words on papers are circled and clues are given for filling in the missing letters.*
5. *When the teacher adjusts his spelling words to reflect topics of study, he does not include them in his written responses.*

Included writing samples from reader response logs, graphic organizer and corresponding story, spelling list and related work, and examples from "Frame your thoughts."

Chapter Review: Focus and Decisions

Stage I: Explore Prereferral Concerns and Options

❑ Figure out the challenges and successes the student experiences, collecting evidence through work samples, observations, and conversations with student. Make tiered adjustments to expectations, tasks or materials, environment, or interventions.

- What is interfering with student participation, progress, and performance in classroom instruction and activities? How does he or she engage in academic areas and social situations?

❑ Examine how tiered adjustments to expectations, tasks, or response requirements affect student performance, participation, and progress; collect evidence to show impact.

❑ Share concerns with parents/caregivers, offering documents to demonstrate student work/behaviors that represent issues and successes. Elicit their perspectives, observations, and suggestions.

- How will parents/caregivers hear and contribute to the descriptions of concerns and successes? How will their insights about their child be of value to instructional planning, modifications, and interventions? How does listening to their input and suggestions increase quality of home–school working relationships?

❑ Evaluate data collected (general educator) regarding student status to better understand his or her needs and to design modifications. Implement and evaluate the impact of whole-group modifications, small group or individualized interventions. Determine to what extent alternative approaches address student needs and offer support to his or her learning and behavior in the classroom.

- How well is student status understood as the basis for designing modifications and/or interventions? How well do adaptations work to support student progress and performance in the general education setting?

❑ When concerns persist, access prereferral supports by collaborating with colleagues formally or informally. Revise modifications or select different approaches or supplemental programs to address student needs within the boundaries of general education. Monitor to determine response to adaptations and interventions.

- If concerns persist, what colleagues might offer additional perspectives and ideas? What prereferral options exist to support efforts to accommodate the student? What additional modifications and/or interventions might be tried? How well do these modifications support student progress and performance?

❑ Maintain ongoing records of student performance and communications with parents/caregivers, student, and others involved in prereferral efforts. Ask questions, document evidence of performance, evaluate effectiveness of approaches, and assess the quality of student educational life. Decide to what extent modifications and interventions directly address student needs and provide needed supports.

❑ Determine whether formal referral for special education evaluation is warranted, and how additional perspectives and assessments promise support.

- How are decisions reached as to whether to continue to monitor student progress or make a formal referral for special education evaluation? What additional information would shed light on understanding what is happening with and for the student in learning and/or social situations? How would additional information reveal a deeper understanding of who the student is as a learner and what approaches, interventions, and adjustments would support him or her more?

❑ Write and submit a referral for special education evaluation. Include descriptive information that depicts who the student is, interventions attempted, and results documented.

- How will the special education evaluation team use the prereferral/referral data to proceed?

Stage I: Apply and Learn

1. Think about a general attribute you use to describe yourself or someone you know (e.g., organized–disorganized, amenable–stubborn, ambitious–lazy, etc.).
   - Brainstorm a list of what leads you to believe this attribute fits this person. What does he or she say or do?
   - Given the information provided in the chapter about *capturing concerns*, review the brainstormed list and highlight words you used to describe the selected attribute that are observable behaviors, tell what the person was doing, and give the context of the situation.
   - Review and redo your original statements to make the information objective by capturing unclear descriptions in observable terms.

2. Inviting parent/caregiver input is critical to understanding the struggles and strengths of a learner. Their perspectives help examine initial concerns.
   - Write a script of a phone call between a classroom teacher and a parent/caregiver to report concerns and raise questions to gather feedback from the family.
   - List questions you might use in an in-person interview.
   - Role-play the phone conversation or in-person discussion with a peer.
   - Reflect on what happens during the role play, paying attention to the kinds of questions posed and quality of responses given.

3. Interview a classroom teacher, special educator, and/or building or special education administrator to find answers to these questions:
   - What are the expectations and steps for general educators to follow prior to referral for special education evaluation (contacting parents/caregivers, collecting data, and/or attempts at in-class modifications)?
   - What types of supports are available to classroom teachers and/or parents/caregivers during the prereferral stage? How are prereferral systems structured within the school?
   - What factors are considered in making the decision to submit a referral for special education evaluation?
   - What information does the teacher include on a referral form?

4. Research the benefits and issues of *response to intervention* approaches to support the prereferral stage.

5. Obtain a referral form from a school district. Find out expectations that are made for filling out the form:
   - What information does the form require?
   - In what way does the referral form communicate expectations of the prereferral stage and invite sharing perspectives of the student challenges and prereferral modification attempts?
   - How do the questions on the form ask the person making the referral to convey information about the student in ways that guide further assessment decisions?

6. Obtain a copy of a completed referral in which all personal identifiers are removed. Make a list of what the completed form tells about student challenges and attempts to support him or her in the current setting.

7. Generate a list of pros and cons for submitting a referral for special education evaluation:
   - What are the purposes for submitting a referral for special education evaluation?
   - What factors enter into making the decision to refer a student for special education evaluation?
   - How do prereferral efforts inform making the decision to submit a referral for special education evaluation?

- Who should be involved in the referral decision? How should they be involved? What do you believe those making the referral are seeking to learn or do?

8. The following case studies reflect initial problem descriptions that contain minimal information about each student's struggles in general education settings. Select a student and use the preliminary questions raised in the Interaction Formula to develop the description in more detail. Suggest a set of tiered modifications and/or interventions to address student needs.
   - When Darla reads from grade-level materials (fourth grade), she does so with great difficulty and little understanding.
   - Rick has trouble with word problems. He has trouble reading them and cannot figure out what to do.
   - Lucy seems to disrupt classroom conversations continuously. She doesn't stop no matter what the boundaries.

Parent/Caregiver Contact Toolbox

Initial Phone Conversation with Parents/Caregivers

		NOTES
Initiate warm greetings:	Start the conversation with amenities, drawing on existing knowledge of the family or previous contacts.	
Invite parent(s)/caregiver(s) to get involved:	Identify the intention of the phone call as an invitation to meet together to learn from each other about the student's progress, existing challenges and successes, options for addressing the challenges he or she is experiencing, and ideas for ways to increase success. *Example: I am calling to make a time we can meet together. I have a few concerns about . . . 's (skills/participation . . .). At an informal meeting, we can share information, perspectives, questions, and ideas about what we see. We will also talk about options that are available to address our concerns.*	
Be positive:	Share a positive(s) about the child, describing an anecdote, an academic or social achievement, or contribution he or she made to the classroom community.	
Provide objective information about the student (an I-message gives a more objective presentation):	Make sure concerns are described objectively. Use observable behaviors. Identify when the behaviors are occurring. Provide specific classroom examples to explain what you mean. Keep the focus on student: what he is doing. Avoid educational jargon and placing or eliciting blame for performance or behaviors. *Example: I am concerned that the book we are reading is getting difficult for Jay. He seems to be stumbling over words (such as reading word for worse, or start for strap). These errors interfere with his gaining meaning from what he is reading. He can give an overview of the story when we take turns reading because he listens very well and understands what others read. But when he is on his own, reading out loud or to himself, he seems to have a hard time.*	
Request parent(s)/ caregiver(s) to share what they know:	Suggest that parents/caregivers think about evidence they see related to student struggles. *Example: It would be helpful for you to think about what you see or hear your child doing at home that may help us understand further what is happening so when we sit down to talk you have some specific examples.*	
Request a meeting day and time at convenient day/time:	Ask parents/caregivers about setting up a meeting, giving them opportunity to identify times that are convenient and available. If they are concerned about child care, offer to create a space in the classroom for the children to draw or look at books quietly.	

(continued)

37

Parent/Caregiver Contact Toolbox

Initial Phone Conversation with Parents/Caregivers	NOTES
Make an agenda to plan content prior to the meeting:	
The agenda helps keep the meeting focused and productive and supports setting time limits, giving everyone a chance to talk, share information, and listen to each other.	
Think-abouts: Make an outline of what is going to be covered. This is an opportunity to organize thoughts, check on how information is presented, and make reminders for ways to give parents/caregivers a voice.	
List the concerns, specific in-class examples that illustrate the concerns, questions related to the concerns, intent to learn from parents'/caregivers' input, possible questions to ask them, available options, and some plausible ideas for the next step.	
Make notations about student competence and struggles:	
Use these data as the starting point in the conversation: Note what the student does well. State concern in terms of what the behaviors or areas of needs are. Confirm that what you will talk about is stated in observable, everyday language. Make sure classroom-related examples serve as supportive evidence: • Identify what needs further attention and list persistent questions. • Generate a list of questions related to the area(s) of needs to gain parents'/caregivers' perspectives. Check to make sure these questions are open ended (how, in what way, what, where, when).	

(continued)

Parent/Caregiver Contact Toolbox

Conduct the Meeting with Parents/Caregivers		NOTES
Start the meeting:	Establish the intent of the meeting, explaining the purpose and procedures of prereferral and listing main topics of information to address. Get input from parents/caregivers as to amendments or satisfaction with the proposed agenda.	
	Inform parents/caregivers of their rights under special education legislation and their role in the proceedings. Review the referral process with parents/caregivers: their right to choose to submit a referral for further testing. Explain the form that documents the concerns and the attempts to address them whenever they choose	
Introduce options and propose process:	Discuss possible ways to approach the concern and cooperatively decide the most appropriate alternatives for the situation, how they will be carried out and monitored, and how and how often progress will be reported to parents/caregivers.	
	Offer an overview of in-class options, general education support options (additional services, prereferral supports for the teacher), and if deemed necessary, the formal referral process.	
Describe the student:	Start by telling what the student is doing well rather than launch into challenges. State student current skills and approaches. Ask some general questions about the student to acknowledge what parents/caregivers know.	
	State the concern(s) in terms of what needs further attention. Organize samples of student work and describe what is happening in the classroom, what has worked and what situations and activities are challenging.	
	Provide an objective description of the challenges the student is facing, using examples to give a clear understanding.	
	Pose questions to check for understanding and elicit their input surrounding what they see or hear at home. Give parents the opportunity to share how they view the concerns and pose the questions they have.	
	Ask for input:	
	– How do you see at home . . .?	
	– What suggestions do you have . . .?	
	– Tell me your opinion about . . .	
Generate ideas for in-class supports:	Describe the set of options that are available in terms of general approaches to modification and intervention in the classroom.	
	Ask parents/caregivers what they would like to see happen and what suggestions or opinions they have. Ask parents/caregivers about their understanding of student hopes and dreams (Forest & Pearpoint, 1992).	

(continued)

Parent/Caregiver Contact Toolbox

Conduct the Meeting with Parents/Caregivers		NOTES
Explain the prereferral system in the school:	When a prereferral support system is in place, the classroom teacher uses the conference with the parents/caregivers to discuss the student concern(s), explain this option, indicate its potential values, assure them that discussions are confidential, and, when available, give them a chance to participate and/or to be continually informed.	
	Highlight the identified support as an opportunity to seek additional opinions and resources for informally assessing the student's needs and designing instruction.	
	Frame accessing this avenue of collegial support in a positive light, looking at the possibilities of a collective examination of the challenges the student is experiencing and collaboratively brainstorming and adding to the list of ideas for modifications, adaptations, and interventions designed to address these needs.	
	If the option to pursue the prereferral support system is considered, explain the types of information hoped to gain and intended ways to work informally with professionals.	
	– What questions would you like explored?	
	– How do you see additional perspectives contributing to working with the student?	
Commit to cooperative plan:	Discuss the options and sketch out a plan with ideas and timelines. This may include identifying decision points, ways to gather input from the student, or times to reconsider formal referral for special education evaluation.	

Establish Ongoing Contacts with Parents/Caregivers		NOTES
Design mechanisms for ongoing contact:	Maintaining open lines of communication helps generate, review, and capitalize on the stream of valuable information conveyed between home and school.	
	Ongoing communication to evaluate how well modifications are working is important from the perspective of student, teacher, and parents/caregivers.	
	A commitment to work together to examine progress, listen to the student as modifications are made, keep communication open, weigh decisions, and stay in touch regularly is made at the end of the meeting.	
	Identify ways to keep in touch, check in on student progress, and keep each other informed. Figure out the ways to do so, be they designated times for phone calls, e-mails, homework notebook, and so on. Communication techniques should reflect the style and time constraints of the parties involved.	

Chapter **3**

Stage II

Design the Collaborative Individualized Assessment Plan

As you read through this chapter, *think about*:

- How prereferral efforts and referral information are used to initiate the special education process in ways that inform evaluation

- Why it is important to plan assessment to reflect referral concerns

- What is involved in planning assessment

- How assessment planning cultivates a collaborative approach to the special education process

Overview of Stage II

Stage II of RSVP provides a structure and way of thinking to support team members in cooperatively designing individualized assessment plans. It guides the team to listen and respond to referral concerns, establish the purpose and focus of evaluation, determine what data are needed about the student, and select and justify which assessment tools will yield that data. Members draw from preliminary descriptions and the results of tiered interventions to determine the direction for assessment and how to deepen their under-standing of the student in the area(s) of concern (Gallagher & Desimone, 1995; McLoughlin & Lewis, 2001; National Joint Committee on Learning Disabilities, 2005; Zigmond, 1997). To develop an individualized assessment plan, the team:

- Shares and organizes what is known about the student
- Identifies gaps in descriptions and raises questions regarding performance, participation, progress, and challenges to determine what additional data are needed
- Chooses assessment approaches that build on what is known, answer questions raised, and promise to yield instructionally relevant data
- Distributes responsibilities among members to ensure that assessments complement one another
- Maps out a schedule for administering and analyzing identified strategies

During this stage of the RSVP process, team members meet as coinvesti-gators to review the referral package as the basis for assessment planning. Special educators and related service providers join the general education teacher and parent(s)/caregiver(s) to discuss the identified area(s) of concern and results of prereferral interventions. They summarize existing information and generate questions that, when answered, provide insights into student challenges (Gottlieb & Gottlieb, 1991; Gresham & MacMillan, 1997; Soodak & Podell, 1994). The team then figures out which assessments to use based on how potential tools directly respond to questions, clarify current understand-ing, reveal missing information, and generate practical data to unravel what is happening for the student. The process sets the stage for developing more intensive, individualized learning experiences and interventions according to substantiated student needs. The plan promises coordinated evaluation efforts to generate relevant data that lead to constructive decisions around instruc-tion and behavior interventions. This, in turn, informs decisions about the services for which the student is eligible (Huefner, 2000; Kauffman & Hallahan, 2005; Mastropieri & Scruggs, 2000; Reschly, 1997; Stainback & Stainback, 1992).

The _K_now-_W_ant-_H_ow Structure for Assessment Planning

The approach to assessment planning begins with what members _know_ (K) about the student, moves to figuring out what they _want_ (W) to learn to enhance their understanding, and concludes with deciding _how_ (H) they will find out (Ogle, 1986). The outcome of this structure is an individualized assessment plan that builds on referral information, sets the direction for what data to collect, and proposes corresponding tools to produce desired evidence. Working through this _Know-Want-How_ structure connects student description with team questions to select assessment strategies, which ensure that evaluation is informative and results are germane to instructional planning (Harp & Brewer, 1996; Simmons, 2000). This requires making sure that assessment tools are grounded in general education and look directly at student performance in the area(s) of concern.

When team members adopt the _Know-Want-How_ approach to structure assessment planning, they commit collectively to making deliberate decisions around data collection. In developing the plan together, the team shares a common focus and creates a coordinated evaluation, synchronizing efforts to produce complementary information for learning about the student (McLoughlin & Lewis, 2001). The more collaborative the approach to assessment planning, the more thorough and authentic the evaluation, and the more likely the collected evidence will lead to cooperative and realistic decisions for instructional planning and programming (Kroeger, Leibold, & Ryan, 1999; Strickland & Turnbull, 1993). The _Know-Want-How_ Assessment Plan Form Toolbox at the end of the chapter helps guide team members' thinking.

Step 1: Start with What the Team _Knows_—Analyze Concern(s)

The first task in assessment planning is to establish and organize what is _known_ (K) about the student in the area(s) of concern based on information gathered and collated during the prereferral stage and reported through the referral. The intent is to center the description on depicting student challenges and competence with respect to general education standards, practices, and settings. Examining pertinent evidence provides the springboard for framing an instructionally relevant assessment plan based on current classroom demands, student performance, and desired outcomes (Gresham & MacMillan, 1997; Yell & Shriner, 1997).

As the team works to determine what is _known_, attention is paid to what the student says, does, and produces when asked to perform across learning tasks and situations (Clark, 2000; Soodak, 2000; Wray, Medwell, Fox, & Poulson, 2000). Information about the student is sorted according to what it means to be competent in the area(s) of concern with reference to the general education setting. Knowing how curriculum is structured and organized, what constitutes behavioral and academic expectations, what instructional approaches and materials are used, how learning environments are designed, and how the student is involved and invested helps clarify who the student is as a reader, writer, mathematican, and participant/member of the classroom community. The more detailed and organized the description in the *know* column, the more likely the team is to identify gaps in their understanding of the concern(s) and raise questions that explore what is interfering with student progress to guide the assessment planning.

Filling in the *Know* Column in the *Know-Want-How* Chart

The *know* column is used to record and capture how the student functions in the primary area(s) of concern. The classroom teacher and parent(s)/caregiver(s) outline concerns and provide supporting evidence of observations, work samples, and student responsiveness to interventions. The following questions help stimulate the initial discussion:

- Who is this student in the area(s) of concern?
- What is the student asked to do?
- What does the student do effectively?
- What types of challenges and errors does he or she exhibit? What appears to interfere with student effectiveness?

The five components of the Interaction Formula, described in Chapters 1 and 2, serve as an organizational tool for expanding and arranging the student description in the *know* column. Follow-up questions that concentrate on what to teach, how to teach, how to approach, under what conditions, and why teach are helpful to add detail, clarify information, maintain the reference to general education and account for factors that impact performance. The following questions related to the Interaction Formula assist in generating and organizing supplementary information about how the student performs:

- What skills per cluster does the student demonstrate in isolation and in context? (*What to Teach/skill clusters*)
- How does the student respond to expectations, requirements, tasks, instructional activity, and materials? (*How to Teach/formats for performance*)
- What problem-solving and thinking strategies does the student employ? (*How to Approach/strategic thinking*)
- How does the student interact in the instructional and social setting and physical environment? (*Under What Conditions/context for participation*)
- How does the student invest in related activities and tasks? (*Why Teach/investment*)

The Guidelines for Describing the Student Toolbox, organized around the components of the Interaction Formula, is located at the end of this chapter to help the team hone in on the student as a reader, writer, mathematician, and/or participant/member in the classroom community. The questions offer ways to think about student struggles and achievements as they apply to each key area of concern.

To proceed to the next step in the assessment planning process, the team reviews the _know_ column description of the student. Members examine how information is documented, summarized, and organized. More than likely, gaps in understanding student difficulties are revealed that warrant more in-depth inquiry. As a result of reviewing the _know_ column, the team moves to the _want_ column to formulate questions that will help make assessment decisions intentional and relevant.

Step 2: Determine What the Team _Wants_ to Learn—Raise Questions

When team members recognize gaps in the student description, they shift their focus to identifying what they _want to learn_, asking questions to set the course for choosing productive assessment tools and strategies. This requires figuring out what information is missing, using the _know_ column and the area(s) of concern as reference points. Corresponding questions are framed to further explore student status, enhance the existing description (Bradley, King-Sears, & Switlick, 1997), and contribute to developing a comprehensive assessment plan.

The team brainstorms questions about the _interactions_ among the student, teacher, instructional activities, and learning environments to identify competence, challenges, and needs. This inquiry leads to justifying the selection of authentic assessment tools, grounded in general education standards and relevant to classroom instruction. It is this process that results in gathering relevant data about the student in the area(s) of concern to establish proposals for substantive individualized programming and sound eligibility decisions (Daly, Witt, Martens, & Dool, 1997; Etscjeodt, 2006; Reschly, 2005).

How the team brainstorms and organizes questions is pivotal in making the assessment planning process meaningful. The ways in which questions are worded influence the evidence the team sets out to collect, the assessment strategies it selects, and how it plans to analyze data gathered. Using an open-ended format (What . . .?, How . . .?, How often . . .?, When . . .?, In what way . . .?, etc.) when posing questions about the student leads to instructive and descriptive information about what he or she knows, does, says, and produces. In contrast, yes-or-no questions (Does . . .?, Is . . .?, Are . . .?, Can . . .?, etc.) result in sizing the student up as a "has or has not" and "is or is not." Closed questions produce general information with limited supporting details that do not fill in gaps in what is _known_. They offer insufficient direction to make assessment and instructional planning constructive.

Filling in the _Want_ Column in the _Know-Want-How_ Chart

The team engages in open discussion to keep the focus on what questions will help identify missing information based on what they now know. The team first uses a set of overarching questions to investigate what they _want_ to learn.

Given what is written in the *know* column, they think about the following:

- What questions will lead to further understand and describe the student in the area(s) of concern?
- What questions will help figure out what is interfering with student progress and participation in the area(s) of concern?
- What questions does the team want the evaluation to answer?

Team members then refer to the five components of the Interaction Formula to systematize their inquiry for understanding the student in the area(s) of concern. They center their questions on examining who the learner is with reference to competencies per skill cluster, responses to instruction, use of thinking and problem-solving strategies, involvement in settings, and investment in learning. Adjusting the following sets of Interaction Formula questions helps focus on portraying the student in the area(s) of concern as a reader, writer, mathematician, and/or participant/member of the classroom community:

What to Teach (skill clusters)

- What skills per cluster are problematic for the student in isolation and in context? What skills per cluster does the student use effectively in isolation and in context? How do student skills compare with academic and behavior expectations and standards in general education?

How to Teach (formats for performance)

- With what types of tasks and activities does the student struggle? How does the student respond to levels of materials, teaching and questioning approaches, and types and formats of instruction and assignments (introduction, practice, mastery)?

How to Approach (strategic thinking)

- How does the student work through academic/social tasks; identifying the ways he or she prepares, engages, and self-monitors? When faced with academic/social challenges, what thinking strategies does the student use in his or her attempts to problem-solve?

Under What Conditions (context for participation)

- How do the use of time, amount of work, instructional arrangements, and space impact the way the student attends, engages, and performs?

Why Teach (investment)

- How does the student feel about his or her performance and participation in the area(s) of concern? What is the student's sense of purpose, sense of self, interests, and responses to expectations, feedback, and incentives?

The Guidelines for Describing the Student Toolbox can also be used as a resource to prompt open-ended questions specific to identified academic and social concern(s).

Members review the questions raised to determine whether they are adequate to select and justify assessment strategies that will capture the student in the area(s) of concern. If the *want* inquiry is sufficient, the team moves to the *how* column of the *Know-Want-How* chart to decide which assessment tools will generate the data to answer the questions raised.

Step 3: Propose *How the Team Finds Out*—Select Assessment Tools

RSVP prioritizes the careful selection of assessment tools to generate authentic data that informs instructional decisions (Fountas & Pinnell, 1996; Zigmond et al., 1983). The process of determining what information about the student is missing and asking corresponding questions provides the rationale for proposing assessment tools and tasks that yield the data needed to explain student status in the area(s) of concern. Determining *how* to find out completes the individualized assessment plan. The intent is to select the assessment tools and strategies that generate relevant information for instructional purposes, leading to identifying factors that impact learning and providing objective criteria for eligibility determination and program planning (Choate, 1992; Coles, 1989; Ysseldyke, 2001).

Based on the questions raised, the team determines which assessment tasks, instruments, and methods to use. The choice depends on what information is needed and what tools reveal, to capture what is at the heart of the struggles or successes the student faces. Members commit to employing realistic and direct measures to sample student performance in the area(s) of concern, ones that approximate the demands of general education. The selection process draws on team members' understanding of the following:

- What constitutes a student description that leads to designing individualized instruction and program plans
- What comprises grade-level general education standards, curricula, and instructional experiences with respect to the student
- What it means to function effectively and with challenges in the area(s) of concern
- What assessment strategies produce the desired instructionally relevant data (Clark, 2000)

Members explore what types of tasks and methods give examiners direct, relevant, and authentic pictures of the student in the area(s) of concern. They create opportunities for him or her to demonstrate competence and struggles in response to varying task demands and across learning environments and situations. These assessment tasks include observing the student under a variety of conditions, sampling performance while adjusting qualities of materials, recording miscues/errors, watching responses to teacher prompts and corrections, examining the use of isolated and contextualized skills, and documenting student pre-during-post thinking, problem-solving strategies, and self-perceptions. The more opportunities team members have to sample student performance in authentic ways, the more evidence they generate to draw realistic conclusions about student effectiveness and the barriers that interfere with success (Wray et al., 2000).

Filling in the _How_ Column in the _Know-Want-How_ Chart

The _how_ column of the _Know-Want-How_ chart specifies tools and approaches that will generate data in response to the assessment questions raised. The team is reminded to draw from what-they-_k_now and what-they-_w_ant-to-learn columns to justify the selection. In this column, they identify (1) the focus of planned observations, defining the intended type(s) to be conducted, settings in which the student will be observed, and the number of observations needed, and (2) the types of informal and formal assessment activities/tasks to be structured, identifying surveys and probes to be administered. Treating this step as an organized brainstorming session invites team members to contribute evaluation ideas rather than the group relying on the same battery of tests for every referral. The team uses the following questions to support the assessment selection process:

Given what is written in the _Know-Want_ columns,

- What tools and tasks will provide direct measures of the student in the area(s) of concern?
- What will the student be asked to do to gather further evidence that helps learn more about him or her?

Based on the list, prioritize which tools and strategies to use:

- How will the tools help learn about the student in the area(s) of concern?
- Which tool(s) will generate the needed data to answer the questions?
- How will findings from the tool(s) contribute to a comprehensive evaluation and description of the student?
- Which tools does the team prioritize? Why?
- How will student performance on the different tasks be evaluated and analyzed?

The team selects which evaluation methods to use to complete the _how_ column of the _Know-Want-How_ chart. Members choose from the variety of informal and formal tools brainstormed to narrow down and decide on which combinations of tools will be used to generate the desired data and answer their questions. The team evaluates the completed assessment plan in terms of how well the proposed tools systematically complement one another to sample student performance, probe skills and approaches, study use of strategies, examine effects of the physical and instructional setting, and describe investment. They further determine whether the tools give the student opportunities to demonstrate success and struggles with reference to area(s) of concern. They commit to generating data that describe, define, pinpoint, and target who the student is as a learner with reference to qualities of instruction and the learning environments. To offer a starting point for brainstorming ideas for informal evaluation, one Assessment Plan Form Toolbox per area of concern is outlined at the end of the chapter. The approaches to authentic assessment are described next.

Survey-Level Tasks

Survey-level tasks (Zigmond et al., 1983) create opportunities to evaluate how the student performs in the area(s) of concern. These tasks afford the examiner opportunities to take a broad look at student performance with regard to applying a range of skills across levels and features of tasks and material and the use of process and strategies (McLoughlin & Lewis, 2001). Student performance on survey-level tools provides an overview of the skills and evidence of competence, struggles, comfort, and frustration. Survey tasks are often based on a sampling of requirements of in-class assignments. The student may be asked to read and retell a narrative, write a story, solve word problems, discuss topics, or respond to social dilemmas. By adjusting the demands of the task, the examiner learns about what conditions enhance or detract from student performance. For example, one may ask a student to hand-write, dictate, and/or word-process a story. The change of demands may impact the quality of what the student produces.

Probe-Level Tasks

Probe-level tasks (Zigmond et al., 1983) are important supplements to the survey-level assessments. Their intent is to generate a more detailed look at student competence and struggles in the area(s) of concern. Probes are designed to isolate specific skill sets and strategies and begin the process of scrutinizing student awareness, practice, and mastery levels, rates of response, and qualities of errors. They examine student competence systematically with specific isolated skills that contribute to overall performance or products. The detailed information generated by probe tasks helps decipher what contributes to the errors the student makes as he or she performs on survey-level tasks. These tasks are designed to correspond with each assessed skill cluster in the area(s) of concern. This requires creating tools that include multiple items for addressing comparable skills through different formats. The student may be asked to read a list of sight words that correspond with grade-level trade books, to respond to an open-ended character map to convey ideas for creating the key figure in the story he or she is to write, or to respond to flashcards with multiplication facts with multipliers to five.

Observation

Observation offers opportunities to watch and document student responses to classroom demands, adult and peer contacts, and different types of expectations, instruction, activities, materials, and environments (VanDeWeghe, 1992; Ysseldyke & Olsen, 1999). The information serves as an objective record of what the student does in the context of the instructional setting, providing evidence of what affects performance and participation and what patterns of behaviors and errors occur across situations. Regardless of the type of observation proposed (anecdotal records, running records, ethnographic study, functional assessment, use of checklist, frequency or duration counts), make sure the following information is included in record keeping: time of day, place, people involved, type of activity in which the student is involved, and student responses/behaviors during the time observed. The observer may keep notes in a notebook, set of index cards, journal, or on prepared checklists or charts of behaviors or errors. Setting up times to watch what the student does allows for recording student performance in relation to teacher and task demands in a variety of academic and social situations. When it is possible, asking the student about his or her perspective on what is seen may also be helpful.

Also, keeping observation notes regarding student behavior during assessment situations adds perspective on performance. Such records document and keep track of the responses the student makes to challenging materials, ease with assignments, amount of time tasks require, input from examiner, environmental demands, and other variables impacting the situation. Asking follow-up questions about performance on assessment tasks provides data regarding student attitude, approach to task, sense of purpose, and confidence.

Informal Interviews

Conducting an informal interview with the student provides opportunities to gain a perception of who the student is in the area(s) of concern, his or her preferences, how he or she uses strategies for engaging in tasks and solving problems, and how he or she views performance and challenges. The conversations are designed to give the student voice. A structured set of questions opens the door for gaining perspective about student sense of purpose, self-perception, approach, interests, and view of challenges. However, interspersing them in informal conversations as follow-up questions tailored to the student may help generate more usable information. Asking how the student arrives at answers, goes about problem solving, and/or works through different situations helps make his or her thinking audible. Recording student responses, making notes or tapes, or asking the student to write answers to questions ensures that critical information is documented.

Commercial Assessment Instruments

Commercial assessment instruments can serve as resources for survey-level and probe-level tasks. The value of these tasks depends on the extent to which they represent the academic standards and demands of the classroom. Examine tasks carefully, looking beyond the name of the test or subtest to understand what skills are being assessed and what the tasks are expecting the student to do. Many commercial assessments involve quantitative scoring. Be vigilant in looking at how scores inform the description of the student or whether a more qualitative analysis of performance is necessary to respond to the individualized assessment plan. As you examine what is being assessed, make sure the number and variety of items per skill are sufficient to give a realistic representation of what the student does and does not know. Criterion-referenced tools and curriculum-based measures systematically assess the isolation of skills from a variety of clusters. These tools may generate some interesting baseline or explanatory information about the student when they are grounded in his or her instruction.

Figure 3.1 offers an example of the **K**now-**W**ant-**H**ow assessment plan. The chart builds on the prereferral data collected in Stage I and reports on the referral to propose direction for assessment.

What the team *knows*	What the team *wants* to *know*	*How* the team finds out
Extracts relevant information from prereferral data, student files, and referral descriptions	Asks open-ended questions that draw on information presented to gather data to fill in gaps	Identify assessment tools
WHAT TO TEACH/Skill clusters		
Idea Generation Presents information related to topic, although not well developed	**Idea Generation** • What does Paul include in his writing? • What does he identify as key components of a story, research report, paragraph, journal?	**Idea Generation** • Give picture or topic and have Paul create a web or tree to identify ideas • Examine what prewriting tools he uses on own and those assigned • Ask him to talk through how he went about figuring out what to include in story • Given a topic, picture, and/or choice, have Paul write a story and journal entry
Sentence Structure Tends to use simple sentences with no descriptors or details	**Sentence Structure** • What types of sentences does Paul construct, when given a topic, asked to dictate, given a set of words? • What does Paul do when asked to enhance a bare-bones sentence? • With what descriptive words does Paul have familiarity? • What does he use to describe objects or actions in isolation (verbally . . . and in writing)?	**Sentence Structure** • Ask Paul to tell and write about a character or situation (What? How?) • Show a picture and have him write a sentence to convey what is happening, what is depicted (mix action and objects). • Give sets of words to arrange in complete sentences (start with simple and move to complex and compound).

(continued)

FIGURE 3.1   Excerpt from a Case Study: Paul as a Writer—An Example of *Know-Want-How* Assessment Plan

What the team _knows_	What the team _wants to know_	_How the team finds out_
		• Give sets of few words to use in own sentences.
		• Give sentence starters and have him complete them.
		• Give bare-bones sentences and ask him to ask questions and/or add description.
		• Given an object, ask him to write down as many describing words as he can think of.
Grammar	**Grammar** • What types of grammar errors does Paul recognize (e.g., noun-verb agreement, consistency of tense) in isolated sentences and his own work? • What types of corrections does Paul make to sentences containing grammatical errors?	**Grammar** • Give Paul sentences containing errors with tense, word order, use of pronouns to correct. • Ask him to fill in blanks for sentences, looking for use of tense, pronouns, etc.
Spelling Written work: contains misspelled words that are discernible in that sounds are represented	**Spelling** • What phonics rules does Paul apply to one- and two-syllable words in and out of context? • What sight words does he spell correctly in and out of context? • What specific types of errors exist?	**Spelling** • Dictate a list of phonetically regular spelling words to Paul, starting with one syllable and moving to two—make sure of opportunities to examine each of the rules. • Administer a list of sight words consistent with independent reading and some reach words. • Ask him to edit sentences with words with spelling errors.
Handwriting Prefers printing, although spacing and use of lines seem to detract from work	**Handwriting** • What does Paul's handwriting look like when writing words in isolation, in sentences, and/or paragraphs?	**Handwriting** • Give Paul a sentence to copy from distance and near to see how reading, availability of model impact handwriting.

FIGURE 3.1 _Continued_

What the team knows	What the team wants to know	How the team finds out
	• How does his handwriting change when copying from board or his own draft?	• Ask him to print and use cursive and compare. • Compare his writing samples.
Conventions of Print Uses capitalization for beginning of sentences and some proper nouns Uses end punctuation and commas for series	**Conventions of Print** • How does Paul distinguish proper nouns from common nouns verbally and in his writing? • How does Paul use apostrophes for possession and contractions?	**Conventions of Print** • Show Paul the different punctuation marks and ask to identify and tell function. • Have him edit sentences containing errors with each of the marks and explain why. • Give him sentences containing proper nouns and ask to explain why capital letters appear in the middle of the sentence. • Ask him to sort words that require capitalization from those that do not.
HOW TO TEACH/formats for performance Verbally shares ideas and details, using complex sentence and pertinent vocabulary when engaged in discussion around a topic of interest. Produces more when uses computer.	How do the qualities of stories change when Paul: • Talks about his ideas for writing? • Uses prewriting to plan out his ideas? • Is given a picture or starter prompt to which to respond? How do the qualities of content, organization, vocabulary usage, sentence variety and structures change when he: • Uses prewriting? • Word-processes his "freewrite"? • Hand-writes his "freewrite"? • Dictates a story? • Illustrates the story first?	Collect a number of writing samples from Paul: • Give choice writing and observe him as he generates the sample. Have him read what he wrote. • Ask him to select a topic, discuss it (tape record), and tell a scribe what to web. • Structure a writing situation in which he is asked to prewrite, draft, revise, edit, and produce a final copy. Make comparisons from prewriting through final copy. Have student read draft and final copy aloud.

FIGURE 3.1 *Continued*

What the team _knows_	What the team _wants to know_	_How the team finds out_
	How do the qualities of content, organization, vocabulary usage, sentence variety and structures change when writing in • journal entry? • story? • research report? • focused paragraph? How does his spoken language compare with what is written? How do errors in his writing reflect the way he talks?	• Ask the student to word-process a sample. Have him read what he wrote.
HOW TO APPROACH/Strategic thinking	• How does Paul use the stages of the writing process? • How does he get started, maintain focus, and complete assignments? • How does the use of webs or story frames impact the content and quality of his writing? • How does he go about revising work? What strategies does he use to figure out coherence of story, idea development, quality of description? • How does he go about editing his own work? What strategies does he use to correct for spelling, grammar, sentence structure, conventions of print?	• Compare what Paul does when given the opportunity to write on his own with use of writing process. • Structure a writing situation in which he is asked to prewrite, draft, revise, edit, and produce a final copy. Make comparisons from prewriting through final copy. Have student read draft and final copy aloud. • Ask questions as he goes through each of the stages to encourage sharing his thinking.

FIGURE 3.1 _Continued_

What the team *knows*	What the team *wants* to *know*	*How the team finds out*
UNDER WHAT CONDITIONS/ Context for participation	• How does Paul respond to writing conferences with teacher and/or peer? • How does he participate in writer's workshops? • Where does he opt to be during writing time?	• Observe what Paul does during different writing situations in the classroom, one-to-one situations, when involved with peers. Evaluate the writing he produces as a result of each situation.
WHY TEACH/Investments Interest waivers/refusal: seems to prefer to write expository pieces (journal about self) and struggles with fictional stories and content-related responses	• How does Paul feel about himself as a writer? • What purpose(s) does he attribute to different types of writing? • With what aspects of writing does he feel successful? • With what aspects of writing does he struggle?	• Observe as he engages in different tasks, writing down what he does and produces, how he accesses help, and the types of questions he asks and behaviors he exhibits. • In working with him, interview him about his views of himself as a writer and purposes he attributes to the values of writing.

FIGURE 3.1 *Continued*

Step 4: Distribute Assessment Responsibilities and Map Out the Plan of Action—Schedule

Once a listing of assessment tools is identified, team members indicate how they will contribute to the systematic collection and analysis of data (Clark, 2000). This requires designing an assessment action plan. Each member of the team considers the list of approaches and instruments and determines availability, perspective, and comfort with the prescribed tasks. Members then indicate how they will work with the student, document performance, and report back to the team (Cramer, 1998). A master schedule allows the general education teacher to maintain student involvement in the critical aspects of his or her day and frees up time for assessment. Both the parent(s)/caregiver(s) and the general education teacher are encouraged to think about opportunities they have to jot down notes about specific incidents, collect work samples, and examine what they are seeing in even more detail than previously. Preparation for implementing the assessment plan includes answering these questions:

- Who will conduct which assessments? When?
- Who will present the assessment plan to the student in ways he or she can understand?
- How will team members apply the _want_-to-learn assessment questions to guide their analysis of data collected?

It is important to support the student through the special education process. The first task of implementing the assessment plan is to designate someone to talk with him or her to convey what is going on and why. This is a way to share concerns and questions while discussing the intent of assessment. Giving the student an overview of what led to referral, how assessment decisions were made, and what he or she is being asked to do invites the student's active participation in the assessment process and beyond. For students who require transition planning, this discussion engages them early in the decision-making process.

Mapping out a schedule for conducting observations and administering assessment strategies provides the vehicle for implementing the individualized assessment plan. Using the list of assessments and distribution of assignments, the team devises a plan for implementing assessments, keeping in mind the teacher's weekly schedule. Preparing this schedule gives the classroom teacher voice surrounding _when_, retains the focus on cooperative efforts, and keeps all members informed. Keeping the agreed-upon schedule in a central location or sending out group e-mails serves as a task reminder and communicates when revisions are necessary. Critical to this entire process is remembering to refer to the student in ways that maintain confidentiality.

The Collaborative Perspective: Planning Assessment as a Team

The assessment planning discussion sets the stage for the ways the team works together throughout the special education process. Assessment planning is an opportunity for the team to establish a common focus and make a commitment to cooperative efforts. The process creates a shared starting point, based on a discussion of existing information about the student and an acknowledgment of pressing concerns and questions. Developing a collective picture of what is currently understood about who the student is as a learner and what questions remain helps build a collaborative approach to assessment planning.

Establishing a clear purpose for the team's work lets members know how their perspectives and contributions lead to the ultimate goal of developing and delivering learning experiences that promote student progress and success (Cohen, Thomas, Sattler, & Voelker-Morsink, 1997; Friend & Cook, 2000). IDEA 2004 reaffirms the importance of the general education teacher and parent(s)'/caregiver(s)' active participation in the special education process (Bateman & Linden, 1998; Friend & Cook, 2000). This assessment planning time is critical in keeping them engaged in the process, comfortable with the directions taken, and informed about the proposed actions and outcomes.

During the planning session, the referral is treated as the initiation of collaborative efforts and an introduction of the student to the team. Treating the referral as such leads the team to work together to gain increased understanding of student learning, pursue instructionally relevant assessment data, create a cooperative approach to evaluation, and develop effective and usable IEPs (Gresham & MacMillan, 1997). Consequently, the general education teacher and parent(s)/caregiver(s) are asked to take lead roles and introduce the rest of the team to the student, summarizing their concerns, experiences, observations, and current understanding of student status and struggles (Huefner, 2000; Rock, 2000). Using that information as the basis for developing the individualized assessment plan gives credence to their input and sets the stage for how vital their roles are throughout the special education process (Huefner, 2000; Turnbull & Turnbull, 1997). Using the information from the general education teacher and parent(s)/caregiver(s) as the basis for developing the assessment plan also maintains attention to the realities of classroom demands, the role of the general education curriculum, and the needs of the student to acquire particular skills and strategies, develop flexibility to handle different formats for instruction, participate in a variety of contexts, and invest in learning (Conderman & Nelson, 1999).

Oftentimes special educators and related service providers are asked to be a part of a team because of their expertise and experience. However, their perspectives need to be juxtaposed with the validity of all the members' input (Bauwens & Korinek, 1993; Walther-Thomas et al., 1999). This conversation provides time to develop an understanding of member roles and the potential values that multiple perspectives offer in terms of different ways to think about the challenges the student experiences. Members are asked to monitor vocabulary during discussions, making sure descriptions of the student have clear connections to classroom demands, observable behaviors, and qualities of student performance so everyone understands what is said. Keeping discussion focused on who this student is in the area(s) of concern helps avert tangents, finger pointing, or other nonproductive uses of time.

It is important to maintain a collaborative tone among the messages, activities, and interactions of this team meeting (Friend & Cook, 2000; Pugach & Johnson, 2002). Quality interactions ensure each member a role and voice throughout the process, establish parity among the members, and convey the value of input, ideas, perspectives, and shared visions. Given that the focus is a proactive response to the referral, it is particularly important for team members to listen to existing descriptions nonjudgmentally, pose questions that invite exploration, and adopt inclusive approaches to brainstorming. Attention to the style of communication is critical as members work to:

- Recognize the quality of information, the frustrations, and worries parent(s)/caregiver(s) and general education teachers have (active listening)
- Ask clarification questions without blaming, imposing one's own interpretations, or judging (use open-ended questions)
- Work to build on existing descriptions of the student without disregarding or discounting information
- Listen objectively and intently (reflection, active listening)
- Use language describing what the student does, being cautious about words that may need clarification

Identify the Assessment Planning Agenda

A clear agenda (Doyle & Straus, 1976) directs members to stay on task and proceed systematically through assessment planning. To engage the team, the agenda previews what the whole session looks like, ensures that people know each other, and establishes a sequence for accomplishing the goals of the meeting. The agenda guides members through the _Know_-_Want_-_How_ process to formalize the individualized assessment plan. Team members engage in problem definition, describing student struggles, and brainstorm to raise questions and identify tools for assessment. The cooperatively designed assessment plan ensures that comprehensive and complementary data are collected and the subsequent work of team members is coordinated. The agenda supports making efficient use of time and promotes a mutual understanding of and investment in what is happening (see Figure 3.2).

With an understanding of the focus of the meeting, members prepare by first reviewing the referral package to learn about the student and related concerns. They may access the student's file as another source of information, including a history of grades, observations, commentaries, and/or reports. Members may also examine general education expectations by reviewing school curricula or state standards relative to the age and grade level of the student

Time in minutes	Topic	Who	Process	Expected Outcome
10	• Welcome • Special Education Process Overview • Expected Outcomes for Meeting • Agenda Overview	Facilitator	Presentation • Overview chart • Agenda handout	• To explain how this meeting fits in the process • To clarify why meeting is taking place
5	Introductions • Who are you? • Role take during meeting and throughout process	Facilitator		• To begin to get to know members of the team
10	Step 1: What you Know about who the student is as a reader, writer, speaker, listener, mathematician, participant in the learning environment, and/or member of the classroom community? *Status report and concerns related to student (summary of existing info)*	Classroom Teacher and Parent Rest of Team	Presentation Q & A	• To clarify current understanding of the learner • To create a common starting point
15	Step 2: Raise questions as to What else needs to be learned.	Facilitator Full team	Brainstorming	• To generate a list of questions and missing information
5	Summarize key questions	Recorder	Presentation	• To ensure agreement regarding areas to assess • To check on what was heard

(continued)

FIGURE 3.2   Assessment Planning Meeting Agenda

15	Step 3: Choose How to collect additional information.	Facilitator Full team	Quick-write Brainstorm Evaluation	• To identify ways to collect information to round out understanding of student
10	Step 4: Delegate responsibilities for assessment to team members.	Facilitator Full team	Quick-write Round robin	• To divvy up assessment tasks
5	Step 4: Map out a tentative schedule for conducting assessments and follow-up meeting.	Facilitator Full team	Round robin	• To clarify who does what when • To schedule follow-up (Phase IV)
	End			

FIGURE 3.2 *Continued*

to gain perspective. Getting ready in this way promotes staying focused on the current dilemmas rather than rehashing the student's history so the team is productive in constructing the assessment plan.

Understand the Roles of the Team Members

It is important for the team members in attendance to come to the planning session with an understanding of how they will participate and contribute to the process. Preparation entails making sure that all team members understand the intent of the assessment plan, the roles they are expected to take, and the tasks they are to complete. The roles of team members are dictated by their relationship to the student and the meeting agenda. A clarification of roles allows members to recognize what each person is expected to do and share (Johnson & Johnson, 1987). Identification of responsibilities further gives value and credibility to all members' contributions (see Figure 3.3).

Organize Through Note Taking

There is a lot of information to hold on to during the meeting, making the task of the recorder critical. Note taking on poster boards, flip charts, overhead projectors, or with a projected computer screen helps keep team members engaged, ideas organized, and efforts documented while planning assessments. Given the interconnections of the agenda items, it is helpful to take notes in a

---

Tasks of Team Members

Parent/caregiver: Source of information and concerns based on observations and experiences; active participant in brainstorming questions and assessment ideas

Classroom teacher: Source of information and concerns based on analysis of work samples, observations of student performance in different learning activities, and interactions; direction provider, suggesting ways "specialists" may contribute perspectives, and active participant in brainstorming questions and assessment ideas

Special educator, related service providers, and administrator: Listeners and reflectors of the challenges student faces, competencies acquired; clarification seekers, asking questions to bring information to light; participants in brainstorming, posing questions and sharing ideas; resources, identifying assessment strategies and sharing perspectives on factors impacting development in the identified area(s) of concern

[*Student:* Contributor to the ideas generated by the team during assessment planning; either by being present at the meeting or sharing views through parents/caregivers, teachers, or designated liaison.]

Roles of Team Members

Facilitator of the meeting: Reviews roles and responsibilities of team members, goes over agenda, ensures the flow of information and adherence to the agenda, awareness of time allocation, and connections among members.

Recorder: Keeps notes that are visible to the full group to allow members to check on communication, make sure their points are heard, avoid repetition, and process what is being said. There may be one recorder who also keeps notes that are reproducible for the group. Notes may be recorded on large sheets of paper or projected on a wall (either on overhead transparencies or a laptop computer). In some instances this requires two recorders, one person to record information on easel paper and another to maintain the ideas on smaller size paper.

FIGURE 3.3 Tasks and Roles of Team Members in Assessment Planning

Know-**W**ant-**H**ow chart or web format. The chart or web may also include the Interaction Formula components as headings to help the facilitator guide the team and the recorder sort out what is presented or brainstormed in an organized fashion. Individuals may also opt to take notes as they listen to help understand the discussion.

Group note taking gives team members something concrete to review as they proceed through the meeting. When the team views their discussion framed in the **K**now-**W**ant-**H**ow chart, they better understand the descriptors of the student and their relationship to assessment questions and strategies. As a result, there is more understanding and consensus with the final assessment plan and how to proceed. When note taking is visible and represents team input, the meeting progresses forward because members are heard, recognized, and understood.

Chapter Review: Focus and Decisions

Stage II: Design the Collaborative Individualized Assessment Plan

❏ Draw on prereferral data and referral for special education evaluation information to determine the focus for assessment.

❏ Acknowledge the concerns of those who made the referral. Listen to and record the information presented by team members in describing the student and the challenges he or she experiences.

- What is the current understanding of the student in the area(s) of concern?
- What are the instructional and behavioral expectations for the setting?

❏ Evaluate the preliminary description of the learner to determine the gaps in understanding and what contributes to participation and progress or lack thereof. Generate questions regarding what additional information is needed to figure out what is happening with the learner in the instructional setting.

- With what questions is the team wrestling? How do these questions relate to learning more about this student in the area(s) of concern?

❏ Brainstorm and select assessment strategies that help understand the learner, address the gaps in information, and respond to team members' questions and concerns.

- What authentic assessment strategies will provide the data necessary to describe the student in the area(s) of concern? What types of assessment data will be informative? What assessment procedures and instruments will yield meaningful information that is valuable to parents/caregivers, classroom teachers, special educators, and related service providers?

❏ Connect reason for referral, purposes of assessment, and expected results with tools for collecting data. Design an assessment plan that leads to a comprehensive description of the student to justify instructional planning.

- How will the data be collected? How will assessment data enhance existing information about the student, be relevant to making informed decisions about future learning experiences and interventions, and the types of services and/or program options that will support the student? How will data help determine eligibility for services?

Stage II: Apply and Learn

1. Refer back to the Interaction Formula in this chapter. Using the five areas of the framework listed here, think of yourself as a reader, writer, mathematician, or participant in the learning environment/member of the classroom community. Write a brief description of who you are in the chosen area of learning relative to:
   - What to teach (skills per cluster)
   - How to teach (formats for performance)

- How to approach (strategic thinking)
- Under what conditions (contexts for participation/environments)
- Why teach (investment)

2. What are the benefits of constructing a **K**now-**W**hat-**H**ow chart to plan assessment?

3. Obtain a copy of a completed referral in which all personal identifiers are removed, or use one of the descriptions here. Develop a **K**now-**W**hat-**H**ow chart to respond to questions following the student descriptions.

   - **Reader**: Darla is in fourth grade, struggling to keep up with the literature books the class is reading. Even on the days she appears to read for the entire time, she only gets a portion of the assigned chapter completed. When she is assigned a "reading buddy," she follows along with her peer and rarely offers to do the reading. She does, however, key in on chapter titles and make predictions about what she thinks is going to happen, often asking her partner's opinion. As a listener, she seems to pick up key information or ask her buddy or the teacher for explanations of what is happening. When Darla does read from grade-level materials, she reads with hesitancy, word by word, recognizing one-syllable and some two-syllable words, attempting to sound out unfamiliar words as she goes. On those occasions, she picks up scattered information but loses the story line.

   - **Mathematician**: Rick is a third-grade student who appears to put random numbers down in response to timed addition and subtraction tasks. When given the time to calculate, he uses his fingers to add sums to 10 and subtract. At that time his work is accurate with sums to 10 and differences from up to 10. Rick is beginning to calculate multiplication and division and continues to rely on manipulatives to solve equations. When word problems are stated in a single sentence, he sets up the problem, choosing the appropriate operation. However, when there are extraneous facts and numbers, he tends to get confused. He seems to have a limited sense of time because he asks about lunch early in the morning and about going home midday.

   - **Participant in the Learning Environment**: Lucy is a fifth grader whose behavior fluctuates from barging into conversations among her peers to interrupting teacher-led lessons with off-topic statements to refusing to join cooperative groups to crying as she gets frustrated with independent work.

*K*now-*W*ant-*H*ow assessment plan questions:
   - In the **K** column, respond to *what you know* about the student as a learner: List key information about the student in the area(s) of concern. Organize descriptions around the Interaction Formula according to *what to teach* (skills per cluster), *how to teach* (formats for performance), *how to approach* (strategic thinking), *under what conditions* (contexts for participation/environments), and *why teach* (investment).
   - In the **W** column, generate a list of questions to indicate what you **w**ant to learn about this student, referring back to the **K** column, that come to mind

as you read through the presented referral data. To learn more, use the Interaction Formula elements to organize your questions, referring to the Guidelines for Describing Toolbox in this chapter to support focusing on the reader, writer, and so on.

- In the **_H_** column, respond to **_How_** you will learn more about this student. Identify assessment strategies designed to answer your questions, drawing from the Assessment Plan Form Toolbox in this chapter.

Guidelines for Describing the Student as a Reader

Overview

Who Is This Student as a Reader?

Profile the student reading. Provide an overview of how the accuracy and flow of student oral reading impacts understanding of what is read:

- Include description of effective interaction with text (fluency and understanding). Identify level of text and genres with which student has facility.
- Include experiences with different approach(es) to reading instruction (top down, bottom up, balanced) and describe responsiveness.
- Describe qualities of interactions with text in which student commits some errors/is challenged. Identify level of text and genres with which the student has difficulty reading with expression, commits errors, and loses understanding of parts or whole of the story.
- Identify patterns of errors (word recognition/miscues and missed information) and begin to account for them by looking at how they change meaning in the story, represent difficulties solving unfamiliar words, reflect tendency to move through text without monitoring for meaning.
- Describe student "sense of story" and how that knowledge plays a part in reading and reporting on what was read.

Supporting Detail

What to Teach/Skill Clusters

- What skills has the student mastered that enhance effectiveness as a reader?
- What challenges does the student face?
- What is the interrelationship among difficulties, experience, and skills with which challenged?
- What errors occur as a result of skill gaps?

Language Skills

- How does the student use language (primary) to communicate, express needs, engage in conversation, and tell stories?
- Under what conditions does the student express himself or herself through oral language (Cambourne, 1988)?
- In what ways does he or she make links between personal oral language and print?
- To what extent do student reading errors reflect his or her spoken word?
- What type of language cues (word patterns, meaning, sentence structure) does the student use to decipher an unfamiliar word, sentence, paragraph?

Fluency Skills

- How fluently does the student read story? Describe how the student reads continuous text. What skills support fluency?

- How does the student use punctuation to guide reading expression and fluency? What rules does he state? Apply to passage reading? Apply to reading individual sentences?
- What is the student's silent and oral reading rates? How is the rate when reading a passage or a single sentence?

Word Recognition

- What sight words does the student read correctly? In isolation? In context?
- How does sight vocabulary influence reading rate, fluency, and comprehension?

Word Solving

- What **phonics** rules does the student state and apply to one-, two-, and multi-syllable words? In isolation? In context? How effectively does the student segment words into parts to apply rules? How well does the student blend sounds together to make a word? How does the student use word knowledge to check on application of phonics?
- How many sounds, syllables does the student blend together to make a word? When said to the student? When the student says them?
- What types of words or word families does the student rhyme? How does the student use small words or word families to help decipher words?
- How does the student **use context** to aid in word recognition? What types of information does the student use? What types of **language** (meaning, sentence structure) cues does the student use to decipher an unfamiliar word?
- How does the student **use pictures** to aid in word recognition?
- What types of miscues does the student make when reading words in isolation? What types of miscues does the student make when reading words in text? What are the patterns?

Retell/Comprehension Skills

- What does the student include in his or her retell of stories read?
- What is student sense of story? How does student retell reflect an understanding of beginning, middle, and end of a story or connections among problems, events, and solution?
- How does the student identify the function of character, setting, events, problem to solution in story?
- How does the student respond to structured questions of who, what, when, where, how, in what way?
- What details does the student retain from what was read?
- What types of connections does the student make among facts presented in a story?
- What kinds of inferences does the student make from reading the story?
- How does familiarity with the topic influence student understanding of the story and retention of supporting details?
- How does familiarity with the topic influence student understanding of concepts, connections among facts, and importance of information?

- How is retell influenced by the qualities of miscues the student makes as he or she reads?
- How does retell of expository pieces reflect student understanding of that structure—presentation of concepts, supporting facts, and usefulness of information?

How to Teach/Formats for Performance

Qualities of Materials

How does the way stories or information is presented impact student understanding?

- How does the quality of student understanding vary or remain consistent when he or she reads aloud, reads silently, or listens?
- How does the quality of student understanding of what is read vary when the story has pictures versus text only?
- How does the level of material impact the quality of student understanding? How does the level of material make a difference when it is text only or has pictures, when the student reads silently, reads aloud, or listens?
- What differences are there among different types of books (genre, picture vs. chapter) in student fluency and comprehension?
- In what types of materials does he or she invest? How do interests play a part in investing in reading?
- How does asking questions at specific points during the story rather than at the end help the student understand what is read?
- How does the level of the text or topic impact fluency and comprehension?

How to Approach/Strategic Thinking

How does the student engage in the reading process? How strategic and effective are the techniques the student uses to engage in reading?

- How does the student approach and engage in the reading process? What steps does he or she take when left to own resources? What steps are effective and ineffective?
- How does the student go about choosing a book to read? How does the student manipulate a book?

Prereading

- What previewing strategies does the student use when first given a book? How does the student go about preparing to read?
- What information does the student gain from the cover? How does the student use that information to prepare for reading the book?
- What types of prompts direct the student to use title, pictures, chapter titles, and prior knowledge? How does preparation to read influence fluency and comprehension?

- What types of predictions does he or she make? How do the predictions connect with information gathered as part of prereading? How do initial predictions reflect an understanding of story?

During Reading

- What strategies does the student use to decipher unfamiliar words? How do reading errors (e.g., miscues, substitutions, omissions) impact level of comprehension? How do reading errors reflect the way the student talks?
- What evidence does the student offer that indicate engagement with the text/story?
- What evidence does the student offer that he or she is monitoring understanding of what is being read?
- What does the student gain from reading stories?
- What types of predictions does the student make as he or she reads? How well do these predictions reflect information presented as reading?

Postreading

- What does the student highlight when asked to summarize what was read? How does retell reflect an understanding of story?
- What supporting evidence does the student use from reading?
- What process does the student use to recall what was read?

Under What Conditions/Context for Participation

Instructional/Social Aspects

How does the environment impact attention and involvement in reading?

- How does the student engage in reading tasks when working independently, with a peer, in groups with and without adult support?
- How do the amount of work, pace, and expectations impact student performance, commitment, and attention to task?
- What structures support student use of time and completion of tasks (agendas, to do lists, picture cues, assignment sheets, etc.)?
- What available resources (e.g., word wall, word sorts, leveled readers, talking books, Internet and computer-related programs) enhance student performance?
- What physical setting(s) support(s) student attentiveness and responsiveness to reading tasks?
- What type of space encourages the student to read independently, monitor comprehension, and take constructive breaks when attention wanes?
- How does the student respond to reading conferences, readers' workshops, readers' theater, and literature circles?

Why Teach/Investment

How do sense of purpose, self, interests, and responses to expectations and feedback play a role in effectiveness as a reader?

- How does the student see self as a reader?
- How does sense of self as a reader impact performance?
- What does the student find hard? Understandable?
- How does the student ask for and/or respond to help, prompts? What types?
- How does the student tolerate frustration when it comes to:
  - Reading aloud in class, small group?
  - Reading in a one-to-one situation with a peer or teacher?
  - Reading independently?
  - Reading material at an independent level?
  - Reading material with which he or she is having difficulty understanding?
- Overall, what type of attitude does the student exhibit during reading? How do levels of materials impact attitude? How do situations (oral, silent, independent, listening, small group, large group) impact his or her positive or negative attitude toward reading?

Guidelines for Describing the Student as a Writer

Overview

Who Is This Student as a Writer?

Profile the student as a writer. Provide an overview of the qualities of student written communications in conveying sense of story or reporting an event:

- Describe student use or lack of use of the writing process and impact on the qualities of products.
- Include description of what characterizes student written pieces.
- Describe the development and flow of ideas with reference to different types of writing assignments (e.g., distinguish journals, story, essay, persuasion).
- Describe patterns of errors that detract from the effectiveness of written pieces.
- Describe proficiencies that contribute to quality of written pieces. Include patterns of competencies.
- Describe student sense of story and expository structures and how those play roles in the products he or she develops.
- Give an indication of how products mirror the student's oral language.
- Describe the impact of spelling, handwriting, conventions of print on the quality of written pieces. How does the quality of written communications represent levels of competence in spelling, handwriting, conventions of print?

Supporting Detail

What to Teach/Skill Clusters

- What skills has the student mastered that enhance effectiveness as a writer?
- What challenges does the student face that impede effectiveness as a writer? [How do sight vocabulary and phonics skills relate to spelling errors? How do handwriting difficulties relate to rate of producing work, completing writing tasks? How are language skills reflected in what and how the student communicates in writing?]
- What error patterns exist in writing pieces, and how do these impact the effectiveness of written work?

Ideas, Content, and Organization

- What is student sense of story? How does the student begin, develop, and end a story?
- How does the student identify the function of character, setting, events, problem to solution in story?
- How does the student respond to structured questions of who, what, when, where, how, in what way?
- How does the student develop premises, arguments, support assertions or perspectives, etc.?

Expression of Ideas

- How does the content of student writing reflect the purpose of the writing task?
- How is the writing responsive to the intended audience?
- What does the student include in his or her stories?
- How do ideas progress and connect? What is the sequence like?
- How does the student develop character, setting, events, problem to solution in a story?
- How does the student identify the function of character, setting, events, problem to solution in a story?
- How does the student begin, develop, and end a story?
- How does the student use transitions between segments of writing?
- What does the student include in his or her essays?
- How does the student develop a thesis and make pertinent connections in an essay?
- How does the student identify the function of the thesis, introduction, and supporting details in an essay?
- How does the student begin, develop, and end an essay?

Grammar

- What type of vocabulary does the student use in his or her writing (slang, informal, variety of words)? How does vocabulary used in writing compare with that used in conversation?
- How effectively are words used? How are words misused?
- How does the student correct for agreement among nouns and verbs, nouns and pronouns, tense, singular versus plural?
- How does the student use complete sentences and vary length and structure?

Conventions of Print/Mechanics

- How does the student use capitalization, punctuation?
- With what rules is the student familiar? Under what conditions does he or she apply them?

Spelling

- What types of spelling errors does the student make? What about the spelling errors make the words discernible or confusing? Of what developmental level are spelling errors indicative?
- What sight words does the student spell correctly?
- What phonics rules does the student apply to one-syllable and multisyllable words?

Handwriting

- How does the student write in manuscript or cursive?
- How does the student form circle or line letters? Use lines on papers and put spaces between words and sentences?
- How does letter formation, use of lines, and spacing of letters and words contribute to or detract from legibility of written work?

How to Teach/Formats for Performance

Qualities of Assignments (Different Types of Writing, Use of Prompts, Explicit Requirements)

How do different options for presenting ideas impact the quality of written pieces?

- What differences are there among the quality of student writing when producing stories, journals, reader responses, reports, essays?
- How does the quality of student stories vary when given the opportunity to choose the topic, dictate a story, respond to a story starter or set of pictures or structure for writing (e.g., graphic organizer, make own pictures first)?
- How do the requirements related to a written composition impact the quality and quantity of piece?
- How does handwriting, word processing, or dictation impact the quality of story, idea development?
- How does the message to disregard spelling, or access a dictionary or adult for help impact the quality of written work?
- How are grammatical errors representative of student's spoken language?

How to Approach/Strategic Thinking

How does the student approach and engage in the writing process? How does use of a step-by-step approach impact the quality of written products?

- What steps does the student take when left to own resources? What steps are effective and ineffective?
- How strategic and effective are the techniques the student uses to engage in writing? What affects productivity?

Prewriting

- What does the student do when given a writing assignment?
- How does the student consider audience?
- How does the student go about choosing a topic about which to write? How does writing change when assigned a topic, given a picture, or given choice?
- How does the student generate ideas? What strategies are used to spark and develop ideas?
- How does the student go about organizing ideas and preparing to write?

Drafting

- How does the student use graphic organizers (if applicable)?
- How does the student use freewriting to get ideas down?
- How does the student remind self about the intent of the task, audience for whom writing, and organization of ideas?
- How does the student take ideas and develop a draft of writing?

- How long does it take to get a draft on paper?
- What types of supports (e.g., Franklin speller, word processor, personalized dictionary, etc.) does the student use to facilitate getting ideas on paper?

Evaluation of Draft

- How does the student go about evaluating the content for flow of ideas, description, detail? What does the student do to revise work?
- How does student self-check for parts of story (beginning, middle, and end), order, details, clarity, and accomplishment of goals?
- What does the student do to edit writing? How does the student go about evaluating writing for grammar and mechanics/conventions of print? How does the student go about spelling words (asks for help, represents sounds, etc.)?

Final copy

- How does the student go about copying, formatting, and publishing his or her writing?

Under What Conditions/Context for Participation

Instructional/Social Aspects

How does environment impact attention and involvement in writing?

- How does the student engage in writing tasks when working independently, with a peer, in groups with and without adult support?
- How do the amount of work, pace, and expectations impact student performance, commitment, and attention to task?
- What structures support student use of time and completion of tasks (agendas, to do lists, picture cues, assignment sheets, etc.)?
- What available resources (e.g., webs, peer conferencing, spell-check tools, Internet and computer-related programs) enhance student performance?
- What physical setting(s) support(s) student attentiveness and responsiveness to writing tasks?
- In what way is writing treated as an opportunity for the student to share his or her personal interests, knowledge of a subject, or imagination?
- What type of space encourages the student to work independently, focus on his piece, and take constructive breaks to deal with *writer's block*?
- How does the student respond to writing conferences? How well does the student hear compliments and constructive criticism? When (during what part of the writing process) are conferences effective for him or her?
- How does the student access support from peers or teachers to work on content development, word choice, revision, or editing?
- How does the student participate in writer's workshops and author's sharing?

Why Teach/Investment

How do sense of purpose, self, and interests play a role in effectiveness as a writer?

- How does the student see self as a writer?
- How does sense of self as a writer impact performance?
- What types of writing tasks does the student choose to do on own (e.g., letter writing, diary, memos, stories, job applications)? What purpose does the student attribute to writing (pleasure, function)?
- About what does the student like to write? How does the student feel about writing on an assigned topic?
- In what types of writing tasks does the student invest, struggle, perform?
- How does the student view the writing process? What commitments does he or she have to prewriting, drafting, revising, and editing?
- How does the student ask for and/or respond to help, prompts? What types?

Guidelines for Describing the Student as a Mathematician

Overview

Who Is the Student as a Mathematician?

Describe student proficiencies as a mathematician. Provide an overview of effectiveness in problem solving, concept development, and computation. Include patterns of accuracy, thinking, reliance on prompts, and qualities of errors.

- How does the student think and perform in math?
- What evidence do errors provide regarding student thinking in math, understanding vocabulary, fluency with symbol system, accuracy of recall and/or work, use of operations, problem solving?
- What setting (e.g., proximity of teacher, partner tasks, quiet space) supports student responsiveness to tasks?

Supporting Details

What to Teach/Skill Clusters

- What skills has the student mastered that enhance effectiveness as a mathematician?
- What challenges does the student face?
- How does the language of math impact student understanding of concepts? How does recall of operation facts affect quality of response to assignments? What is the interrelationship among difficulties, experience, and skills with which challenged?
- How does the student use math concepts and other skills in everyday life?
- With what types of math does he or she perform effectively?

Number Concepts

- How does the student use:
  - One-to-one correspondence?
  - Count bys . . . ?
  - Numberline, manipulatives, "touch math"?
- How does the student present math ideas through manipulatives, drawings, written work, and talk?
- How does the student read and construct graphs and charts?
- How does the student use estimation to figure out the sensibleness of a math solution (checking correctness of answer, approximating purchase costs)?

Computation: Add or *Subtract* or *Multiply* or *Divide*

- What operations has the student mastered by rote?
- What types of equations does the student read? How does the student respond to them?
- What vocabulary does the student use when reading equations?

- What evidence has the student shown that he or she has mastered operations in terms of
  - Concept(s)
  - Vocabulary
  - Reading equations
  - Representing and/or solving with manipulatives, words
  - Calculating
  - Responding by rote

Problem Solving

- What steps does the student take in solving word problems?
- What vocabulary does the student associate with which operations?
- How does the student write out equations to correspond with the questions asked in a word problem? How do the equations represent the information presented? Steps involved?
- What skills does the student have to support problem solving:
  - Read problem
  - Proceed with X number of steps
  - Translate actions to operation(s)
  - Write corresponding equation(s)
  - Solve
  - Check answer
- How does the student use drama, models, pictures, diagrams, tables, charts, patterns to solve problems?
- How does the student use everyday situations as a source of constructing problems to solve?

Life Skills

What characterizes student understanding and use of:

- Money concepts (e.g., label coins, state values, make change)?
- Measurement skills (e.g., use of ruler, dry and liquid measures, state equivalencies)
- Time (e.g., read clocks, make schedule, calculate elapsed time)
- Applying mathematics to daily activities (e.g., collect and organize data to create and read mathematical representations such as graphs, tables, charts, equations, symbols/ dollars and cents)?
- Probability to predict events?

How to Teach/Formats for Performance

- How does student accuracy and quality of responses change when there are manipulatives, opportunity to talk through, steps, or prompts provided? How does accuracy change when asked to compute mentally?
- How does the student respond to an emphasis on functional math versus isolated skill and drill approaches to math?

- How does the student understand mathematics concepts—when they are represented in a table, on a chart, embedded in sports statistics, on a menu, in children's literature?
- How does the student do when asked to represent thinking in math through words (writing, speaking) versus symbolically (graphs, tables, charts, manipulatives, equations)?

How to Approach/Strategic Thinking

- How does the student approach mathematical equations and problems? What steps does he or she take when left to own resources (look for patterns, rely on what knows, examine properties or relationships)?
- How does the student use understanding of concepts, procedures, and connections to solve mathematical problems?
- How does the student approach math tasks (structured, timed, manipulative based)?
- What differences are there among calculations, word problems, daily living problems, etc.?
- What prompts (e.g., use of graph paper, multiplication charts) enhance student performance?
- How does the student go about solving a word problem? What steps does the student take (state the problem, determine what need to do, write out equation(s), use tools to figure out, write or state answer, check to make sure answer makes sense)?
- What are typical errors the student makes when solving word problems?
- How does the student go about solving an equation/calculating $+, -, \times$? Single digit? Two digit? with and without regrouping?
- What are typical errors the student makes when solving equations? How does the student go about checking work?
- What types of supports (teacher prompts, manipulatives, calculators, charts) help cue the student to enhance accuracy or memory of facts?

Under What Conditions/Context for Participation

Instruction/Social Aspects

How does environment impact attention and involvement in mathematics?

- How does the student engage in math tasks when working independently, with a peer, in groups with and without adult support?
- How do the amount of work, pace, and expectations impact student performance, commitment, and attention to task?
- What structures support student use of time and completion of tasks (agendas, to do lists, picture cues, assignment sheets, etc.)?

- What available resources (e.g., calculators, white boards, manipulatives, picture clues, Internet and computer-related programs) enhance student performance?
- What physical setting(s) support(s) student attentiveness and responsiveness to math tasks?
- What type of space encourages the student to work independently, monitor accuracy of thinking and work, and make constructive use of breaks?
- How does the student organize space to work with materials (e.g., manipulatives, calculator, measuring devices, etc.) and paper and pencil tasks?

Why Teach/Investment

- How does the student see himself or herself as a mathematician?
- How does sense of self as a mathematician impact performance?
- What does the student view as challenges in mathematics? To what does the student attribute the challenges?
- How does the student judge the value of learning math?
- How does the student respond to an emphasis on functional math versus isolated skill and drill approaches to math?

Guidelines for Describing the Student as a Participant in the Learning Environment/Member of the Classroom Community

Overview

Who Is This Student as a Participant in the Learning Environment and Member of the Classroom Community?

Profile student participation and interactions. Describe what the student does, his or her behaviors. Provide an overview of the ways the student works in the learning environment and the ways the student relates with peers and adults. Generate a description of the patterns of errors/misbehaviors and links among antecedents-behaviors-consequences to indicate the functions that behaviors serve for the student.

A Way to Think About Describing Behavior

Describe the appropriate behaviors and misbehaviors in terms of *topography* (what they look and sound like), *frequency* (how often they occur), *duration* (how long the behaviors last), *latency* (amount of time elapses between antecedent and behavior), *magnitude* (force or power of behavior), and *locus* (where behavior occurs).

Participant in Learning Environment

- Describe what the student does and says during instructional situations that are appropriate, conducive for gaining from experiences, productive in terms of meeting expectations and requirements, and consistent with the rules and structures of the setting.
- Describe what the student says and does during instructional situations that might be considered behavior errors (misbehaviors, misjudgments). Identify qualities of the situation with which the student has difficulty attending to task, responding to rules and structures, understanding expectations, making effective choices and decisions, expressing feelings and thoughts appropriately. How do the situations pose challenges to the student?

Member of the Classroom Community

- Describe student behavior as he or she relates to others. How are the behaviors appropriate, engaging, and effective in terms of supporting interactions, cooperative activity, and community environment? Identify responsiveness to work situations, levels of activity, teacher and peers, subject matter.
- Describe qualities of interactions in which student commits some errors (misbehaviors, misjudgments). What does he or she do? Identify qualities of situation with which the student has difficulty expressing in words what he or she wants, waiting for his or her time, and being a part of give-and-take. How do the situations pose a challenge? What do behaviors tell about the challenges the student faces, the function they serve, impact of context, specify contaminants, effect of consequences? How are student

self-perceptions consistent with his or her behaviors as a participant of the learning environment and member of the classroom community?

Supporting Detail

What to Teach/Skill Clusters

What are the skills the student brings to being a participant in the learning environment and being a member of the classroom setting? **and** *What are social/ inter- and intrapersonal skills required for effective participation and membership in the classroom setting?*

- What skills has the student mastered and with what skills does he or she struggle? How consistently does the student demonstrate appropriate or inappropriate use of skills? In what ways do attending, self-control, decision making, reading a situation, reading the faces of others, taking on other's perspectives impact participation, willingness, flexibility, and acceptance by others?
- What skills does the student have to engage in social interactions? What challenges does the student face? What is the interrelationship among difficulties the student experiences and the skills with which he or she is challenged?
- What errors/ misbehaviors occur as a result of skill gaps?

Awareness of Self

- What feelings does the student identify and label? How does he or she express personal feelings and values? How does the student take into account the situation, timing, and appropriateness to share feelings and desires?
- How does the student connect feelings-thoughts-behaviors? How does the student assess situation to understand feelings (e.g., anger, frustration) and figure out ways to address (e.g., ways to keep self engaged)?
- What are the topics, activities the student identifies as holding his or her interest?
- How comfortable is the student with sharing views and feelings? Under what conditions does he or she do so?
- In what ways does the student deal with challenging situations? What choices does he or she see in those situations? How does the student make choices about behavior that indicate foreseeing consequences of behaviors?
- How does the student use self-control strategies to acknowledge feelings but also find ways to calm down, move out of a situation, etc.?
- How does the student monitor responses to feedback from others (e.g., accept consequences or listen to accusations, difference of opinion, correction)?

Communication: Participation in Conversation/Discussion

Participates in Conversations or Discussions

- How does the student use greeting behaviors to introduce self or signify hello?
- How does the student go about initiating conversation?
- What characterizes that the student is listening (eye contact, head shaking)?
- How does the student respond to the give-and-take required of conversation or discussion (e.g., takes turns, responds to questions, builds on what others say,

encourages others to contribute ideas, acknowledges the contributions of others)?

- How does the student show he or she is making an effort to understand what is said? What does the student do (e.g., paraphrases what hears, uses active and reflective listening, asks questions to help clarify, responds to verbal and nonverbal behavior of others)?
- How does the student stay focused on topic? What does he or she do (e.g., checks with speaker to make sure ready to "move on," have tools for attending)?

Shows Awareness of Others

- How does the student recognize and show understanding of the feelings of others?
- How does the student do in situations that require taking the perspective of someone else?
- How does the student express own feelings of concern, anger, affection, fear, etc., while acknowledging those of others?

Interacts with Peers and Adults in Community Situations

- What is the student's preferred mode of engagement ((cooperative ventures, parallel, isolated)? How does he or she establish self to ensure these types of situations?
- In what types of interactions does the student establish connections with others? How?
- How does he or she act as a part of group situations (e.g., makes a suggestion, suggests an activity, negotiates/compromises)?
- What does the student do to be a part of the group (e.g., takes on roles to contribute to completion of joint activity, completes task to which commits to contribute to group project)?
- How does he or she work through issues with group members (e.g., deals with group pressure, addresses conflicts)?
- How does he or she offer support to others (e.g., shows appreciation, distinguishes types of positive gestures (compliments, kindness), says thank you, responds with "random acts of kindness," gives and receives compliments, rewards self and others for accomplishments)?

Reads, Initiates, Engages, and Responds to Social Situations

- How does the student use verbal, nonverbal, rhythm cues of a social situation to determine how and when to ask questions, appropriateness of comments and questions, when to begin and end a conversation, how to bring closure to a conversation or activity?
- How does he or she pick up on cues of the situation and gauge timing to determine when to ask to join an activity, ask a favor, ask for help, offer help, express concern, examine the impact of one's own behavior or words to discern when or if to do . . . , apologize?
- How does the student find ways to avoid confrontation/trouble/fights?
- How does he or she assess situations to determine own role/responsibility or causes of the "problem"?

Engages in Work Behaviors That Support or Detract from Effectiveness

- How does the student follow written or oral directions? What types of questions does the student pose when directions feel unclear?
- What does the student do to help self focus on and stay with assigned task through to completion (e.g., break up tasks into small increments, take breaks as needed)? How does the student focus on assignments, ignore distractions? What types? How does he or she complete assigned tasks?
- How does the student prepare for work times (bring or access materials needed for task)?
- When and how does the student ask for assistance after trying to complete task?

How to Teach/Formats for Performance

How do the demands of work or activity support or challenge the student and impact behavior? In what ways does the student participate as an individual in the learning environment: conditions under which complies, makes choices, responds to structures, attends to task, avoids disrupting, engages in listening (eye contact)?

- What differences are there among different types of activities and demands in relation to student behavior?
- How does behavior change or remain constant when expectations and rules are explicit versus implicit?
- How does behavior change or remain consistent when expectations for how to interact with peers, participate in an activity, access support are made explicit versus implicit?
- How does the structure of activities, materials impact behavior and investment in performing?
- Under what conditions does the student demonstrate appropriate and inappropriate ways to engage with peers, work on assignments, access support, and deal with own frustrations? What are the appropriate and inappropriate behaviors?
- What types of activities, materials does the student reject? Feel challenged? Act overwhelmed? How does breaking directions into small increments, assigning tasks one step at a time, giving choices facilitate student performance and behavior?
- What enhances student performance and behavior?

How to Approach/Strategic Thinking

How does the student approach and engage in learning experiences? What steps does he or she take to enter, maintain attention, be active in the learning experiences when left to own resources? What steps are effective and ineffective? How does the student go about choosing to participate in learning experiences? How is the student a part of the activity in the classroom (loner, parallel player, interactive, interconnected)? How is the student a part of the social network and fabric of the community (contribute, establish role, interrelates, cooperates, collaborates)?

Preparation for an Event

- What information does the student gain from transition periods (announcements indicating the next item on the schedule, think-abouts) or introductions to lesson? How does the student use that information to prepare for participating in the learning experience?
- What types of prompts direct the student to make appropriate behavior choices, ones conducive for the learning experience? How does preparation for a situation influence behavior?
- What types of predictions does he or she make about an upcoming event/learning situation? How do the predictions connect with information gathered from student observations of setting, listening to announcements? How is accuracy of anticipation reflected in behavior?
- What triggers inappropriate behavior? When in the process do these occur?
- How accurate is the student in reading the social situation in the classroom?

During Learning Experience

- What strategies does the student use to maintain attention to activity in which he or she is supposed to be involved? How does student reading of the situation influence behavior? How do misbehaviors reflect student "impulse control," investment in what is going on?
- How does the student cut out the extraneous activity in the setting?
- What evidence does the student offer that he or she is monitoring behavior during the activity?
- What function do misbehaviors serve during the lesson? How do different types of lessons impact the behaviors the student exhibits? What does the student say?
- What do student interactions show about his sense of belonging and affiliating with others (ways makes connections, types of relationships cultivated, approaches to getting attention, qualities of attention seeks)?

Postsituation

- What does the student highlight when asked to reflect on appropriate behavior and misbehavior? What does he or she own about behavior? What does the student believe is the function of the behavior? What qualities of the situation does he or she believe contribute to what happened?

Under What Conditions/Context for Participation

Qualities of Situations

How does the environment impact behavior? What does the student do in different situations? How are behaviors consistent or different? When are the behaviors appropriate or inappropriate? What are the appropriate and inappropriate behaviors? How does the student respond to different structures in the classroom? What structures are used to guide behavior, promote learning?

- How does structure (e.g., explicitness of rules, schedule, procedures) of a situation impact the quality of student behavior? To what types of prompts does the student respond (e.g., posted rules, written agenda, nonverbal reminders)?
- How does availability of choices/options impact the way the student participates in the learning environment? With peers? In activities?
- How does behavior change or remain constant when working in project-based learning, direct instruction, teacher-directed large group, teacher-directed small group, cooperative activity, in a one-to-one situation with a peer or teacher, independently? What social situations (paired, small group, large group, choice, teacher directed) are comfortable and uncomfortable for the student? What are behaviors like in those situations?
- How does behavior change or remain constant when the pace of the activity is "fast moving," reflective, self-regulated? In what situations (drill, discussion, question and answer, independent work) is the student comfortable and uncomfortable with the pace as evidenced by attention to task? What are behaviors like in those situations?
- What physical setting supports student responsiveness and attention to tasks? How so? What types of spaces, work areas, decor optimize or detract from productivity? In what way(s) does the student respond to activity level and noise in the classroom? In what way does behavior change or remain constant when in proximity to peers and adult?
- Identify and describe social situations in the classroom in which the student exhibits appropriate responses, effective communication, self-control, behaviors consistent with expectations. What is it about those situations that are conducive to appropriate behaviors? What skills are required to be a part of those situations? What does the student do, say in those situations?

Why Teach/Investment

How does sense of purpose, self, belonging, and investment play a role in the way the student participates in learning experiences and classroom community exchanges?

- Describe student sense of self as a participant in the learning environment and member of the classroom community. Identify how he or she understands the learning environment, is aware of own internal and external "controls," understands language as it relates to appropriate behavior in the setting.
- What do student behaviors show about his or her sense of self; comfort being on own or alone; awareness of own attributes, interests; being realistic about what is within own grasp? What do student behaviors indicate about feelings of competence: willingness to take risks, share opinions, and contribute ideas? What evidence is there that the student gets satisfaction from personal accomplishments? How does the student establish and act with a

sense of purpose: sets reasonable goals, takes responsibility, and/or follows through on plans?

- How does the student see self as a participant in the learning environment and member of the classroom community? How does the student see self engaged, interacting, handling social demands of the learning environment and classroom community? How does the student recognize his or her control over behavior? What does the student identify as contaminants in the environment?

- How does student "attitude" impact behavior? What does "attitude" look and sound like that promotes student effective participation in the situations? How does the student enter those situations? What does "attitude" look and sound like that detracts from student effective participation in the situations? How does the student enter those situations?

- What values does he or she attribute to social amenities that contribute to creating a safe, constructive, and caring classroom environment?

- How does sense of self as a learner impact performance and behavior? How does the student use own values as filters for what he or she says and does? How does the student use own values as filters for judging the impact of the behavior?

- How does the student see the value of activity taking place in the classroom setting?

- How does the student see activities designed for learning social skills and strategies? What connections does he or she make with the focus of instruction and self?

- To what does the student attribute misbehavior? What role do control and responsibility play?

- What are the standards the student holds for being part of the experiences (how mediates self needs, group needs, situational demands)? What does the student find hard? Understandable?

- How does the student ask for and/or respond to help, prompts? What types?

- How does the student tolerate frustration and monitor personal needs when it comes to:
  - Working in a large group?
  - Working in a small group?
  - Working in a one-to-one situation with a peer or teacher?
  - Working independently?
  - Waiting for attention?
  - Dealing with material he or she is having difficulty understanding?

- Overall, what type of attitude does the student exhibit during independent and interactive work times? What type of attitude does the student exhibit during "play"/ less structured (choice, recess, lunch) times? How do levels of materials impact attitude? How do situations (oral, silent, independent, listening, small group, large group) impact positive or negative attitude toward participating?

Collecting Assessment Data: Reader

Rules of Thumb

- When listening to a student read continuous text or words in isolation, have a copy of what the student is reading and write down exactly what he or she says and does.
- For each story a student reads (orally or silently) or hears, have him or her retell it in own words *before* you ask specific questions. Retell documents the meaning student gains from reading, emphasis placed on content, and organization given to story. Record what he or she tells you on a tape recorder, take notes, or write anecdotes.
- For each student a student reads or hears, construct questions to *follow-up* retell, giving the student another chance to demonstrate understanding of material and indicate personal connections and interpretations of text. Use open-ended questions to prompt student rethinking and recapping the story with what he or she gained.
- Make observational notes about student fluency, use of voice/expression, or if reading continuous text, look at how the student keeps his place, the rate of recognition—keep notes objective.

Survey-Level Reading Tasks

Survey-level reading assessments examine how the student interacts with continuous text and reveals what he or she gains from the experience (Beaver, 2001; Goodman, Watson, & Burke, 1987). Choose from a variety of stories, essays, or poems that afford opportunity to examine student performance relative to grade-level instruction to figure out independent, instructional, and frustration levels. Note how the student performs and comprehends when is read at different levels, giving opportunities to make minimal errors and read above level (6–7 errors per 100 words):

- Keep running records of oral reading to have a record of the way the student uses word recognition and solving skills, sentence structure to string words together in fluent phrases, use of expression and/or *side* conversation to make meaning of what is read.
- Keep a record of student *retell* of selections read, to evaluate what he or she gained from experience with text.
- Develop follow-up structured questions that may prompt the student to share more or differently what he or she understands, comparing with content of retell. Listen for connections among information, pertinent detail, awareness of setting, mood, characters, events, problem(s) to solution, information stated in text, and inferences made based on what transpired.

Vary **How to Teach/Formats for Performance** to identify reading behaviors under various conditions. Ask the student to read text orally and silently to examine how different types of demands contribute to or detract from responsiveness to print. Compare with student listening and responding to narrative for another opportunity to examine sense of story or expository writing and understanding when not responsible for deciphering what is on the page:

- Compare retell and response to comprehension questions following student reading of comparable stories, collecting data when the student reads silently and orally or is read to.
- Examine performance with different level books, illustrated stories, and text only.
- Compare retell and response to comprehension questions following student reading of story written at independent level versus instructional level versus frustration level, examining the rate of reading, detail of retell.
- Use a wordless book to observe and record student sense of story (particularly helpful when students are early/emergent or *non*readers).
- Keep running records (including what the student says, substitutes, omits) as student reads text, word cards, or phoneme cards aloud, comparing response to isolation of versus contextualized skills.

Observe **How to Approach**/**Strategic Thinking** and structure situations to determine how attention to reading process impacts effectiveness. Design tasks to provide opportunity to observe student approach/strategies, and use of process, observing the ways the student prepares, engages, and self-monitors throughout the reading process:

- Observe student with a *new* book to evaluate orientation to book. Record comments student makes as previews the book. If student does not preview book, take one at lower level than reads and structure the situation asking a set of questions to evaluate how the student uses title, cover, pictures, etc., when prompted.
- Compare two situations in which the student reads a story. If the student processes the story as he or she reads, connecting to own life, making predictions, and acknowledging new information, then only necessary to do once. If the student does not process the story as he or she goes along, ask questions at different junctures to look at how the student is using information and how the questions impact the quality of interaction with text and retell. Note how predictions and retell change when actively engaged pre-during-post reading.
- Note how the student handles difficulties, ways/attempts to discern unfamiliar words, and attention to meaning. Describe how student monitors own miscues, difficulty with text, and meaning by writing down questions, raises concerns.

Watch and listen for the **How to Approach**/**Strategic Thinking** the student uses to problem-solve related to (in isolation, passage reading helps give information in context) deciphering unfamiliar words when reading passages. Compare with performance on probe tasks.

Examine the impact of the **Under What Condition/Context for Participation:**

- Observe the student working independently, in instructional groups, in cooperative groups to determine how the student engages in reading, works with others in reading-related activities.

Assess **Why Teach/Investment** in terms of comfort, sense of self, awareness of how approaches, and impact of challenges on risk taking and performance:

- Interview the student, asking how he or she feels about reading, choices makes about books, relevance seen to life, what makes it hard/easy, tricks uses to help self (decipher unfamiliar words, remember what the story is about).
- Observe student in various reading situations (DEAR/SSR, reading group, cooperative group involving reading, etc.) and record behavior (e.g., look for patterns of attending to task, participating, volunteering to perform/respond).

Probe-Level Tasks

Probing skills and strategies involves isolating and concentrating on what contributes to reading with fluency and interacting with the text for meaning. Probe tasks are organized to get at rules related to sounds and sentence structures, hone in on language competence and challenges, identify sight word vocabulary and word-solving skills, and evaluate skills extracting and attributing meaning relative to story elements of narratives or thesis and supporting details in essays.

Focus on **What to Teach/Skill Clusters,** creating opportunities for student to demonstrate sight vocabulary, phonics skills and phonemic awareness, use of context, comprehension—sense of story, prediction skills, understanding of problem to solution, response to who/characters, what/problem and events, when/setting, where/setting, how/solution. Develop materials to study specific skills involves referring to graded word lists, sequential arrangements of phonics rules, different types of sentences organized from simple to complex, and different aspects of comprehension (elements and literal vs. inferred meanings).

- Create an array of tasks to help evaluate phonemic awareness and use of phonics rules to decipher and build words is one part of probing reading; using flashcard, letter tiles, rhyming tasks, word-sorting, and word-building games and activities offer opportunities to probe the specific word-solving skills the student brings to reading fluency and accuracy.
- Probe specific **phonics** rules student applies. Ask the student to listen to set of sounds and blend them together to make a real word, read phonetically regular words presented on flashcards or with letter tiles (systematically examining phonemic awareness prerequisites/sound blending and word rhyming, vowel and consonant patterns in single syllable and then multisyllable words, depending on grade level).

- Design tasks to look at how the student uses pictures, sentence meaning, and sentence structure to figure out unfamiliar words; offers another view of what the student brings to reading, drawing from various forms of CLOZE procedures (omit designated words from text, leaving a blank) to look at how the student uses the meaning of words, phrases, and pictures to fill in missing words or ideas.
- Focus on use of **context clues** by designing cloze sentences or passages, eliminating words that are cued by the surrounding meaning.
- Wordless or early reading books help focus on use of pictures and sense of story. Choose books, sentences that focus on character, setting, problem, and so on to isolate story elements.
- Have student arrange pictures, sentences, paragraphs to indicate what cues he or she uses to sequence information; asking why the student chooses a particular order.
- Concentrate on **use of pictures** by constructing cloze sentences or passages with picture clues, eliminating words cued by the illustrations. Compare with student reading a wordless book or performances with picture books versus text only.
- Assess language the student brings to reading situation. Have student dictate and read own story. Compare reading errors with conversation and reading own story.

Analysis of Data

Once samples of student performance across survey- and probe-level tasks are collected, sort through the evidence and work to extract descriptors about the ways in which the student engages in reading, decipher patterns of errors, and determine how the information fits together to describe the student as a reader. A sampling of charts for analysis is included in this section. Systematically look at how the student reads text materials at different levels to evaluate the relationship of fluency to comprehension, use of word recognition and solving skills with varying difficulty levels, and the qualities of comprehension that exist when text is at independent, instructional, and frustration levels. Use charts to:

- Extract descriptors about the ways in which the student engages in reading; decipher patterns of errors
- Evaluate the quality of student reading and retell and the impact of levels of materials, types of assignments and student's language, word recognition, and word solving, understanding of story or expository writing elements on performance
- Determine how the information fits together to describe the student as a reader

Collecting Assessment Data: Writer

Rules of Thumb

- When a student writes a story (sentence, web, journal entry), have him or her read it to you. It is helpful to have your own copy of student product. Record what the student reads and compare with the product, taking notes. You may use a tape recorder or write notes.
- When assessing student writing, gather any prewriting, drafts, revisions, conference notes related to the final copy. Looking across the process offers perspective on how the student thinks through and develops pieces. Note how the task(s) is assigned, prompts supplied to the student, and input given by peers.

Survey-Level Tasks

Survey-level tools provide the opportunity to observe the extent to which the student uses the recursive process (Duncan, & Griffiths, 1992; Murray, 1998) to formulate and organize ideas and express them on paper; examining the impact of language, handwriting, and spelling. These survey-level tasks should generate evidence of the thinking process and priorities the student adopts when writing. The evaluator looks at how thinking is represented through topic selection and development, recognition of audience, form/genre of writing, structure that ties the piece together, order, use of language features, and use of voice/ownership/investment (Lane, 1992).

- Make comparison of different types of writing that appear in writing folder and journals (creative stories, personal stories, response to books, letters). If these do not exist, set up times to engage in various writing activities with student. If using existing pieces, ask the teacher what the assignment was.

Vary **How to Teach/Formats for Performance** to identify writing behaviors under various conditions. Ask the student to write, dictate, or word-process to examine what demands contribute to or detract from written products. Ask for different types of writing (e.g., narrative, expository, persuasive) to figure out with what the student is comfortable, has voice, and conveys ideas. Compare what the student produces when he or she is given choice or a prescribed topic and whether the student is guided through the writing process or responds with a *freewrite*.

- Use a *freewrite* to observe student approach to choosing a topic, executing his or her process, and producing a piece.
- Give the student a set of topics, questions, pictures and/or story starter sentences or passages from which to choose. Make sure such materials prompt the student to do the types of writing being sought. A picture of an object promotes descriptive or expository writing, whereas a picture(s) depicting action or a dilemma is more apt to suggest a story with a sequence of events. Similarly, it is important

to determine what types of writing the verbal stimuli invite. A prompt about a hobby may lead to expository writing, whereas a problem a fictitious character faces may lead to a story. Examine how quality of products are consistent or vary when the student is given the different prompts.

- Evaluate the quality of products when the student hand-writes, dictates a story, produces one on computer, and/or talks into tape recorder. The different formats help analyze how handwriting and spelling, in particular, influence word choice, sentence structure, and grammar used.

Observe **How to Approach**/**Strategic Thinking** and structure situations to determine how attention to writing process impacts effectiveness. Design tasks to provide opportunity to observe student approach/strategies, and use of process, observing the ways the student prepares, engages, and self-monitors throughout the writing process and where *breakdowns* occur that might account for the quality of work:

- Examine how different types of graphic organizers affect student preplanning. A student may prefer a web format over a more linear story frame.
- Observe how the student uses prewriting devices, noting whether the student is more responsive to key terms or questions that suggest development of a story (e.g., audience, setting, or where and when the story takes place, characters or who is in the story).
- Compare how the student talks about or webs what he is about to write with the product.
- Interview the student regarding approach to writing a story or journal and views of self as a writer (open-ended questions and possible follow-up questions).
- Observe how the student goes about writing a story (puts pencil to paper and writes, uses prewriting approaches—outlines, webs, flowcharts, guideline questions) when he or she has a choice of how to proceed.
- Observe the conditions under which student uses the writing process—when teacher makes a requirement or on own. Note impact on organization, inclusion of story elements, development of elements, application of editing skills.
- Observe, evaluate, and compare the content and mechanics of student products during the different stages of the writing process.

Examine the impact of the **Under What Conditions**/**Context for Participation:**

- Observe the student working independently, in instructional groups, in cooperative groups, when writing is embedded in activities to determine how the student engages in writing.
- Observe how the student responds to writers' workshops and authors' chair experiences.

Assess **Why Teach**/**Investment** in terms of comfort, sense of self, awareness of how approaches, and impact of challenges on risk taking and performance:

- Interview the student, asking how he or she feels about writing, relevance the student sees to life, what makes it hard/easy, tricks uses to help self (how to spell words, remember to include parts of story).

- Observe the student during writing and related (spelling, handwriting, grammar) instruction, independent work time, activities that embed writing requirements.

Probe-Level Tasks

Probing written language often resembles direct instruction or practice activities. It is an opportunity to look at the specific language, thinking, grammar, conventions of print, spelling, and handwriting skills that support effectiveness as a writer.

Focus on **What to Teach/Skill Clusters,** creating opportunities for student to demonstrate idea generation/sense of story, grammar, conventions of print/mechanics, spelling, handwriting. Developing materials to study specific skills involves referring to graded expectations with regard to use of different sentence structures, level of description, use of story elements, application of sight and phonics rules to spelling, application of punctuation and capitalization rules, and use of script and manuscript:

- Give the student a web and a topic to examine how he or she brainstorms and develops concepts.
- Give a set of sentence strips or a paragraph out of sequence to evaluate how the student organizes the flow of ideas.
- Give the student a sentence or paragraph to edit; may be used to examine use of punctuation, capitalization, grammar rules, or spelling.
- Evaluate use/knowledge of sentence structure by asking the student to complete sentence starters, put together cut-up sentences, fill in the blanks of different types of sentences with varying complexity. Ask the student to arrange a set of words into a complete sentence or take two similar sentences (e.g., declarative, exclamation, interrogatory, simple, compound, complex) and combine them into one. Ask the student to add description to an otherwise bland sentence or paragraph.
- Ask the student to correct grammar errors to ensure agreement or consistency.
- Probe spelling to determine how the student approaches phonetically regular and irregular words or applies rules for prefixes and suffixes. Conduct *spelling* tasks (sight list and phonics, rule-driven lists). Dictate words in isolation and have student write them down. Have student use letter tiles to make the dictated words. Have the student look at words and sentences containing misspelled words and correct what he or she believes need correction. Check to make sure student has the skills to analyze a word into component sounds.
- Have the student copy sentences and write ones from dictation to examine handwriting and/or keyboarding without the need to generate own ideas.
- Administer DOL (daily oral language) sentences for specific editing skills (punctuation, capitalization, conventions of print, and also word use/misuse).

- Analyze how oral language (sentence structure, word choice and order) impact quality of writing by having the student talk about a picture, use words in a sentence, fill-in blanks orally.

Analysis of Data

Once samples of student performance across survey- and probe-level tasks are collected, sort through the evidence and work to extract descriptors about the ways in which the student engages in writing; decipher patterns of errors and determine how the information fits together to describe the student as a writer. A sampling of charts for analysis is included in this section. Systematically look at how the student responds to different types of writing assignments and evaluate the relationship of idea development, sense of story or reporting, language, grammar, conventions of print, sentence structure, use of descriptors, spelling, and handwriting/word processing. Use charts to:

- Extract descriptors about the ways in which the student engages in writing, decipher patterns of errors
- Evaluate the quality of student written work and the impact of conditions and language, handwriting, spelling, and tasks on performance
- Determine how the information fits together to describe the student as a writer

Collecting Assessment Data: Mathematician

Rules of Thumb

- When a student completes a word problem or calculation of an equation, have him explain how he arrived at the answer. Record what he or she tells you either on a tape recorder, with notes or anecdotally.
- Capture student thinking. Observe what the student does as he or she calculates. Look beyond the answers—collect the student's thinking by getting the work on scrap paper and watching the ways he or she uses talk, manipulatives, or prompts.
- The development of probe activities in mathematics should offer the student the opportunity to try solving mentally, using paper and pencil, manipulatives, or concrete objects, or talking aloud. It is important to have the student share thinking as he or she works.

Survey-Level Tasks

Survey-level mathematics assessments examine how the student thinks in terms of and uses the language of mathematics to solve equations and problems. Create situations in which the student is asked to work with objects to represent numbers and operations, manipulate numbers to respond to equations and calculate prescribed operations, and work with numbers, shapes, or objects to solve problems. Document how the student thinks and talks to explain procedures and answers. Giving the student opportunity to describe his or her numerical thinking and problem solving and represent them with objects, numbers, graphs, and words (NCTM Standards; Tucker, Singleton, & Weaver, 2001) offers perspective on performance as a mathematician. Designing survey-level tasks in mathematics involves constructing tasks with a mixture of different types and levels of equations and problems (Zigmond et al., 1983).

- Design a set of mixed equations from single digit and two- to three-digit examples, with and without regrouping and written vertically and horizontally, looking at understanding of operations and shifting among them. Watch as the student works through the variety. Be careful to avoid overwhelming the student with too many items. Consider asking the student to read equations; rewriting them in ways that are more comfortable or blocking out the number of items on the sheet may be ways to further examine performance.
- Select a variety of word problems, using a direct if-then question to more subtly embedded problems involving one to three steps, different operations, and different types of questions or use of language.
- Follow up student work by selecting examples with both correct and incorrect responses and asking, "What steps did you take? How did you figure that out?" to discover how the student thinks through math concepts, is adept with the related language, and goes about solving equations and problems.

Vary **How to Teach**/**Formats for Performance** to identify mathematical behaviors under various conditions.

Ask the student to solve equations with and without manipulatives, number lines, charts, timed and untimed. Ask the student to solve problems read aloud, silently, with and without illustrations. Compare how the student performs as supports are and are not available:

- Ask the student to calculate math facts of one operation using flashcards, worksheet, in timed, untimed situations, with and without manipulatives or number line.
- Ask the student to calculate math facts of mixed operations using flashcards, worksheet, in timed, untimed situations, with and without manipulatives or number line.
- Ask the student to calculate equations of one operation (without and/ or with regrouping) in timed, untimed situations, with and without manipulatives or number line.
- Ask the student to calculate equations of mixed operations (without and/ or with regrouping) in timed, untimed situations, with and without manipulatives or number line.
- Present student with word problems in single-question format, illustrated literature (Burns) or story, one-step operation to multiple step. Observe how the student goes about solving and presenting response.
- Present student with word problems in single question format, illustrated literature (Burns) or story, one-step operation to multiple step. Observe what the student does when presented with props to act out the problem versus paper and pencil.
- Observe what happens when the student reads the problem versus student listens to the problem in terms of how he or she sets up equation(s) on own.

Observe **How to Approach**/**Strategic Thinking** and structure situations to determine what process/approach the student uses and how it impacts effectiveness. Design tasks to provide opportunity to observe student approach/strategies, and use of ways of thinking, observing the ways the student prepares, engages, and self-monitors throughout solving equations and problems:

- Observe the student as he or she goes about solving a word problem, the different prompts used (e.g., use of fingers, tally marks, count up) when left on own and the effectiveness of those prompts. Ask the student to talk you through different types of problems to hear his or her thinking and approaches.
- Observe the student as he or she goes about calculating single and multiple digit numbers, and so on, and the different prompts used (e.g., use of fingers, tally marks, count up) when left on own and the effectiveness of those prompts. Ask the student to talk you through different types of equations to hear his or her thinking and approaches.
- Ask the student to present *how to calculate equations* or *how to figure out word problems* by acting out, using manipulatives or drawings, written work, or talk. Listen for student use of language related to math, and record.

Examine the impact of the **Under What Conditions/Context for Participation:**

- Observe the student working independently, in instructional groups, in situations that embed mathematics, in cooperative groups to determine how the student engages as a mathematician.

Assess **Investment** in terms of comfort, sense of self, awareness of how approaches, and impact of challenges on risk taking and performance:

- Interview the student, asking how he or she feels about math, relevance to life, what makes it hard/easy, tricks uses to help self (e.g., figure out what operation to use in a word problem, calculate answers, to know when to carry or not).

Probe-Level Tasks

Probing skills and strategies involves isolating and concentrating on what contributes to competence as a mathematician. Probe tasks are organized to examine what the student knows by rote; how he or she understands concepts, solves mentally, talks aloud, and how he or she uses paper and pencil, manipulatives, concrete objects, or pictures. Probes allow for exploring how the student reads equations, rewrites them in ways that are understandable, and the language and cues to which the student responds.

Focus on **What to Teach/Skill Clusters,** creating opportunities for student to demonstrate number concepts, operations, computation, problem solving, and life skills. Develop materials to study specific skills involves referring to grade-level expectations and work with figuring out sums, differences, products, quotients, and working with whole numbers and fractions/decimals/percentages, and geometric shapes and formulas:

- Observe the student as math assignments are completed, interviewing him or her as to how the student proceeds through equations and problems and what helps him or her recall facts and check work.
- Design probes to examine rote memorization of facts per operation (those at automatic level), using flashcards and/or precision teaching/mad minutes (timed math worksheets).
- Interview student, asking for explanations of how he or she solved examples, asking the student to explain how to calculate single-digit examples for each operation using manipulatives, number line, and with words.
- Construct tasks in which the student is to use manipulatives to solve equations, actions to demonstrate understanding of concepts, and explain what the student did in his or her own words.
- Give the student the opportunity to write equations that represent an action, question, and story.
- Ask student to match vocabulary words with operations and explain why or give an example of why.
- Give different types of story problems, changing language of question and ask student why he or she chose particular operation(s).

- Give the student a set of problems that correspond to each operation ($+, -, \times, /$), varying the number of steps involved and the types of calculations (e.g., operations, fractions, time, money).
- Simulate use of math in daily living/ life skills and observe how the student uses money, rulers, scales, and geometric principles to solve.
- Ask to solve an array of problems that involve calculations, use of time, measurement, money, and so on (design to be completed with and without prompts)—establishing student explanation and observation as part of assessment.

Analysis of Data

Once samples of student performance across survey- and probe-level tasks are collected, sort through the evidence and work to extract descriptors about the ways in which the student engages in mathematics, decipher patterns of errors, and determine how the information fits together to describe the student as a mathematician. A sampling of charts for analysis is included in this section. Systematically look at how the student solves equations and problems at different levels to evaluate the relationship among his concept understanding, fluency with arithmetic facts, reliance on manipulatives or pictures for support, use of calculators or charts for answers, responsiveness to different types and levels of problems. Use charts to:

- Extract descriptors about the ways in which the student engages in solving equations and problems; decipher patterns of errors
- Evaluate the quality of student problem solving, understanding of language and related concepts, types of assignments, and the level of questions and calculations
- Determine how the information fits together to describe the student as a mathematician

Collecting Assessment Data: Participant in the Learning Environment/Member of the Classroom Community

Rules of Thumb

- When observing a student, use objective descriptions to depict what the student is saying and doing. Separate out subjective language, reflections and opinions. These statements may be used to help you consider hypotheses but also detract from the legitimacy of data you collect. Keep track of qualities of the situations in which appropriate and inappropriate behaviors occur.
- For as many social situations as possible, those in which the student is involved and recaps and those "fictional" ones he or she retells or answers related questions, encourage use of own words. Record what the student tells you on a tape recorder, or take notes or write anecdotes.
- When analyzing observations, make sure there is an understanding of what skills are required to be a part of the learning environment and classroom community.

Survey-Level Tasks

Survey-level assessments regarding challenging behaviors examine how the student responds to and interacts with the expectations of participating in the learning environment and being a member of the classroom community. Use objective observations as primary sources of data, supplementing with input from the student about specific situations in which he or she is involved and perspectives on situations with which the student can take distance:

- Keep anecdotal records or more structured functional assessments to gain authentic surveys of what the student is doing, in what context, and under what conditions (Sugai & Horner, 1999). These offer opportunities to identify what constitutes appropriate and inappropriate responses to situations, examine how behaviors escalate, document the contexts in which those behaviors occur, and evaluate the sequence of events that contribute to or maintain student behavior.
- Follow-up observations with questions to ascertain student perspective on the different situations (What did you do? What was in it for you? What might you do differently to get what you want? Meisels, 1974). Student perspective may corroborate the hypotheses generated with regard to intent, missing social skills, impact of antecedents and consequences, reactions to teacher and/or peer behavior, and understanding of options in the situation.
- Use simulations, social stories, or literature to get at student responses to different social situations when the student is calm. Ask, *What would you do in this situation?* and follow with *What do you think . . . might feel?* or *How might you deal with . . . ?* to help figure out what the student understands about appropriate and inappropriate behavior and the social demands of situations and interactions.

Vary **How to Teach/Formats for Performance** to identify intra- and interpersonal skills/behaviors under various conditions. Observe the student in a range of in-class, recess, and specialist situations to examine how the student responds or what behaviors are exhibited when there are different types of expectations, activities, and focuses. Look for what it is about situations that are conducive to appropriate behavior or act as deterrents, figuring out conditions under which the student complies, makes choices, responds to structures, attends to task so as to avoid disrupting, engage in listening, and so on:

- Collect anecdotal records following incidents of misbehavior and events of appropriate behavior. Describe what the student says and does. Record demands of the situation, antecedents and consequences. Analyze anecdotal records, attending to qualities of alone time/ independent work, structured/ adult-mediated groups, structures (schedule vs. choice, rules, directives), and ways the student handles continuity-transitions-changes-spontaneity.
- Compare and contrast social situations in which the student exhibits misbehaviors and appropriate responses. Evaluate the behaviors that comprise student attending, responses, communication, self-control, etc., with regard to expectations. Examine the qualities of the situations regarding structures, explicitness of rules, expected performance, types of interactions.
- Observe student during choice time, cooperative learning groups, small group instruction, morning or classroom meetings. Note where and how the student sits, engages in activity, relates to peers, uses materials. Consider how observation substantiates the ways the student attends, contributes, establishes role, interrelates, cooperates, collaborates. Consider how observation sheds light on the way the student is in terms of being a loner, an isolate, a parallel player, an interactive person, and whether that way of being accounts for inappropriate behaviors in some social situations.
- Use literature and ask the student to predict outcomes of both internal and interpersonal conflicts. Ask questions regarding the feelings, thoughts of pictured characters as well as narrative. In this way, you can hear how the student picks up on both verbal and nonverbal cues of others. Write down what types of information the student shares (attribution of feelings, intentions, thinking about others, problem solving, using information, etc.). Compare and contrast the degree to which the context of the incident changes student response. Ask the student to rewrite the story or ending and evaluate the emphasis or shifts in setting.

Observe **Why Teach/Strategic Thinking** and structure situations to determine the student is a part of activity in the classroom and part of the social network or fabric of the community. Design tasks to provide opportunity to observe student approach to different situations, observing the ways the student prepares, engages, and self-monitors throughout the reading process. Also, ask the student questions regarding getting ready, precipitating factors, involvement, and monitoring his or her own behavior in different situations:

- Consider how observation substantiates the ways the student contributes, establishes role, interrelates, cooperates, collaborates. Identify the defining behaviors.
- Consider how observation sheds light on the way the student is in terms of being a loner, an isolate, a parallel player, an interactive person and whether

that way of being accounts for inappropriate behaviors in some social situations. Identify the defining behaviors.

- Ask student to revisit situations you observe and describe his or her perspective.
- Show illustrated situation cards (comparable to those that might occur in school and classroom) and ask the student to tell or write what he or she thinks the main character is thinking, feeling, and going to do. Use follow-up questions to have student evaluate the effectiveness and appropriateness of the character's behavior choices.
- Ask the student to read narrative situation cards (comparable to those that might occur in school and classroom) and ask the student to share what he or she thinks the main character is thinking, feeling, and going to do. Use follow-up questions to have student evaluate the effectiveness and appropriateness of the character's behavior choices. Take notes as the student reports information.
- Use literature and ask the student to predict outcomes of both internal and interpersonal conflicts. Ask questions regarding the feelings, thoughts of pictured characters as well as narrative. In this way, you can hear how the student picks up on both verbal and nonverbal cues of others. Write down what types of information the student shares (attribution of feelings, intentions, thinking about others, problem solving, using information, etc.).

Examine the impact of the **Under What Conditions/Context for Participation:**

- Make note of the different characteristics (seating arrangements, teacher proximity, peer proximity), expectations (rules, directions), types (e.g., instructional, independent, cooperative, competitive) and focus of groupings (e.g., academic demands, social activity) for each of the situations observed. This information is key to examining the when and how of challenging behaviors.

Assess **Why Teach/Investment** in terms of comfort, sense of self, awareness of self and environment, and impact of challenges on risk taking and behaviors:

- Interview the student, following incidents, when things are going well, and with regard to a general overview of how the student sees self in school gives perspective to hypotheses professionals make.
- Interview the student, asking how he or she feels about behaviors, choices he or she has and makes, relevance he or she sees of involvement in school and classroom to life, what makes it hard/easy to *stay in control*, tricks uses to help self add voice. *How does the student see self engaged, interacting, handling social demands of the learning environment and classroom community? How does the student recognize his or her control of behavior? What does the student identify as contaminants in the environment? To what does the student attribute misbehavior? What are the standards the student holds for being part of the experiences (how mediates self needs, group needs, situational demands)?*
- Keep a collection of *incident* interviews. Maintain notes regarding student self-report regarding what the student did, wanted, viewed the situation to be, and what he or she is willing to try next time. Listen for extent to which student assumes responsibility for behavior, examines options for what to do in the situation, is aware of own triggers, has a sense of own intent for behavior.

- Observe student in various social situations (choice time, cooperative learning groups, small group instruction, morning or classroom meetings) and record behavior (e.g., look for patterns of attending to task, participation, volunteering to perform/ respond). Use observations to corroborate student perspectives, looking for patterns of attending to task, participating, volunteering to perform/ respond, exercising *controls*, etc.
- Document what "attitude" looks like and listen for what it sounds like. Record what student's participation is like in those situations. Try to note whether student enters situations with "attitude" or whether there are events or qualities of the situation that trigger the "attitude."

Probe-Level Tasks

Probing skills and strategies involves isolating and concentrating on what contributes to desirable behaviors and appropriate engagement in classroom activity and with peers. Examining skills pertaining to participant in the learning environment or member of the classroom community may involve asking the student to identify rules for specific situations and role play what they mean or show how he or she is expected to behave in different activities. A variety of activities focusing on specific intra- and interpersonal skills offers opportunity to hear student perspective and cue into what he or she values relative to demands placed on him or her.

Focus on **What to Teach/Skill Clusters,** creating opportunities for student to demonstrate awareness of self and others, skills expressing feelings, getting involved in situations, addressing issues, making choices, and exercising controls. Developing materials to study specific skills involves looking at social skills curricula, social scripts materials, and relevant activities in and out of the classroom:

- Ask the student to "read" pictured faces and label feelings, describe what the expectations are for behaving when having those feelings, or share words to express those feelings.
- *Play what-if* with simple examples of feelings or situations, requiring the student to state or draw what he or she might do or say also focuses in on specific social skills and responses.
- Ask the student to share what he or she would say in different situations, listening for communication skills, such as listening or delivering *I-messages*.
- Ask student to illustrate a booklet of feeling words. You might consider having the student write sentences "I feel . . . when . . ." to correspond to pictures. Or you might ask students to write a story about a character who experiences several types of emotions (might give a set of words from which to choose).
- Show a set of face pictures and ask student to label with feelings. You might follow up with questions regarding the student identifying situations in which he or she feels that way and what he or she does.
- Show a set of feeling words and ask student to show what those look like and what they mean. You might follow up with questions regarding the student identifying situations in which he or she feels that way and what he or she does.

- Read stories (fables) with specific morals and ask the student what the messages are and how he or she lives by them. Or ask what do those look like in the way you act in school.
- Interview the student regarding specific behaviors (e.g., What does it feel like when . . .?).
- Show photographs or illustrations of situations in which character confronted with challenges (sitting in a class with bored look, hesitating to raise hand to contribute, looking embarrassed, gleaming with accomplishment, etc.). Ask student to identify what is happening, what the character is feeling, and what the student would do if he or she could change places with the character.
- Ask student to write or illustrate a book or story "About Me." Use prompts to examine student sense of self (comfortable being alone, awareness of attributes, interests, realistic about what is within own grasp), competence (takes risks, shares opinions, contributes ideas, satisfaction from personal accomplishments, uses own values as filters), purpose (realistic, sets reasonable goals, takes responsibility, follows through on plans).
- Read scenarios, narratives, or picture books that focus on a specific skill.
- Collect "conference" notes from follow-up sessions with student after exhibits misbehavior/acts out. Evaluate how expresses emotions (deal with personal frustrations, anger) in the moment versus in the follow-up discussion. Note how the student talks about and when he or she does exert control, finds appropriate outlet for emotions versus acts on the emotions.
- Show photographs or illustrations of situations in which character confronted with interpersonal situations that depict situations which support and challenge a student sense of belonging and affiliating with others (e.g., ways makes connections, types of relationships cultivated, approaches to getting attention, qualities of attention seeks). Include scenarios that invite the character to cooperate (ways works with others, shares, offers and receives, initiates-engages-draws closure to conversation, play, exchanges; verbalizes feelings, thoughts, ideas at acceptable times; takes on the perspective of others, appreciates difference of opinion, acknowledge other points of view; uses wording and timing according to the demands of the social situation; objectively discusses events and enters into problem solving process to resolve conflict, mediate issues with group. Ask student to identify what is happening, what the character is feeling, and what the student would do if he or she could change places with the character.
- Read scenarios, narratives, or picture books that focus on a specific skill.

Analysis of Data

Once samples of student performance across survey- and probe-level tasks are collected, sort through the evidence and work to extract descriptors about the ways in which the student engages learning and community activities; decipher patterns of errors, and determine how the information fits together to describe the student as a participant in the learning environment and member of the classroom community. A sampling of charts for analysis is included in this section. Systematically look at how the student behavior varies or is consistent across situations, what student signals or situational triggers exist, how do responses help or exacerbate behavior, and when and how does the student make appropriate and inappropriate choices. Use charts to:

- Extract descriptors about the ways in which the student engages in learning situations; decipher patterns of misbehaviors
- Evaluate the quality of student behavior and impact of setting qualities, antecedents, consequences, tasks, and peer and adult behaviors
- Determine how the information fits together to describe the student as a participant in the learning environment and member of the classroom community

Assessment Plan

	K What _K_now	W _W_ant to Learn	H _How_ Find Out
	Extract relevant information from referral and files	Ask open-ended questions	Identify strategies for gathering assessment data
What to Teach/Skill Clusters Determine the student skill competencies/repertoires.			
How to Teach/Formats for Performance Describe how the student responds to tasks, materials, and activities.			
How to Approach/Strategic Thinking Determine the thinking, problem solving, and pre-during-post strategies the student uses.			
Under What Conditions/Contexts for Participation Determine how the student engages in the instructional and physical setting.			
Why Teach/Investment Determine when and how the student feels confident, competent, and committed to learning.			

Stage III

Collect, Chart, and Analyze Assessment Data

As you read through this chapter, *think about* how to:

- Use the <u>Know</u>-<u>Want</u>-<u>How</u> plan to prepare evaluation tools, activities, corresponding record-keeping forms, and analysis charts

- Schedule, organize, and implement the set of assessment tools, documenting student responses, products, behaviors, and the settings in which they occur

- Chart, collate, and analyze assessment data

- Analyze student performance, charting and collating data within and across tools to uncover patterns of competence and challenges

- Synthesize findings to draw conclusions and hypothesize what accounts for student successes and struggles in preparation for the IEP meeting

Overview of Stage III

Stage III provides a methodical approach for gathering, charting, and analyzing authentic assessment data to reveal a comprehensive picture of the student. Team members access and design data collection tasks, record-keeping forms, and analysis charts based on the _**K**now-**W**ant-**H**ow_ plan developed in stage II. *Implementing the assessment plan* involves preparing the proposed evaluation tools to collect evidence of student performance in the area(s) of concern. Members implement the set of tools and document student responses and then display, sort through, study, cross-reference, and evaluate the findings. As an outcome of their work, team members have usable and meaningful data to better understand and explain student competence and struggles. During this stage, team members:

- Translate the _**K**now-**W**ant-**H**ow_ plan into distinct assessment tasks, activities, and record-keeping forms
- Set up testing time, location, and materials
- Establish relationships with the student to support his or her performance during assessment
- Administer assessment tasks and gather observation and interview data
- Develop charts to examine student performance, using objective criteria that allow for a comprehensive analysis of each tool and across tools
- Chart and collate data within and across tools to describe the student as a learner, hypothesizing what contributes to or interferes with successes
- Prepare to integrate assessment data with information collected by other team members

Translating the _**K**now-**W**ant-**H**ow_ into a working assessment plan consists of developing and administering authentic tools to produce substantive samples of student performance. Constructing direct measures of *who* the student is in the area(s) of concern involves selecting or developing authentic tasks, materials, and activities to closely resemble the demands of general education. Corresponding record-keeping forms are designed to prompt documentation of student successes and challenges: what the student says, does, and produces in various situations and in response to different tasks. Figuring out what the data indicate requires a thorough analysis. To make assessment data useful, team members articulate qualitative criteria to chart and examine student performance, responses, and behaviors, and thus determine where the student is at, account for struggles, and develop constructive plans to address needs (Bateman & Linden, 1998; Daly et al., 1997; Dykeman, 2007; Johns, Crowley, & Guetzloe, 2002; Layton & Lock, 2007; Wilson et al., 2005).

The more authentic the assessment tools, the more they approximate academic and social requirements of learning, the more relevant the data produced. The more detailed the record keeping, the more comprehensive the documentation of student responses and behaviors with respect to task and setting demands. The more substantive the criteria for evaluating the evidence, the more likely analysis of data offers insights into student performance, proficiencies, and challenges. The more complete the evaluation, the more likely the team is to construct a thorough description of the learner, articulate competencies, and account for factors that interfere with effectiveness and growth. The more comprehensive the description of the student in the area(s) of concern, the more likely the team is to design a constructive individualized education program (IEP) that supports student progress (Dykeman, 2007).

Step 1: Access and/or Develop Assessment Tasks, Tools, and Activities

Data collection is the process of capturing student performance, behavior, and thinking in response to a range of assessment tasks, instructional activities, and learning situations. Translating the _**K**now-**W**ant-**H**ow_ into action means making decisions about which particular assessment tools to access and develop to obtain the desired data. If information gathered is to be used to construct a functional description of the student and subsequently inform instructional planning and eligibility decisions, a comprehensive set of direct measures of student performance in the area(s) of concern is required.

Understanding what contributes to becoming readers, writers, mathematicians, and participants/members in the classroom community (Wiggins, 1997) guides evaluators in establishing assessment focuses, designing related tasks, and defining criteria to judge performance. If assessment is to inform instructional planning and programming, the tools need to be constructed to represent the nature of the area of concern and to hone in on the variables that impact performance. Consequently, the results of direct and authentic assessments allow for appraising the student against academic standards and behavioral expectations of the general education curriculum and classroom (Daly et al., 1997; Horner, 1994; Sugai, Lewis-Palmer, & Hagan-Burke, 1999–2000; Reschly, 1996). The measures yield evidence for examining skills the student employs, responsiveness to task formats, use of problem solving and strategies for thinking through performance, interaction with instructional settings, and how investment plays a role.

Team members develop a combination of tools to balance the assessment packet, deliberately organizing a complement of informal and commercial survey- and probe-level assessment tasks and tools. Survey-level tasks create opportunities for the student to demonstrate how he or she uses the aggregate of skills required to function in the area(s) of concern. Probe-level tasks provide supplementary data that examine discrete skills per cluster, zeroing in on what the student knows in isolation and how he or she applies them in context. They focus in on evaluating student competence with reference to what is initially revealed through survey information. Interviews and direct observations are other tools used to enhance the data collected and discern what factors impact student effectiveness.

Developing the set of survey-level tasks requires finding assignments and materials to study student thinking and performing and coincide with the demands and activity related to the area(s) of concern. This involves asking a student to read and retell a narrative, write an essay or story, speak a monologue, engage in dialogue around a topic of interest, listen to and take notes from a lecture, solve a mixture of mathematical equations or word problems, and/or participate in a social situation. Presenting the student with such tasks gives the examiner the opportunity to observe, investigate, and document the ways in which the student plans, mediates, and executes tasks, applying skills, using strategic thinking and problem solving, and monitoring his or her own performance. Adjusting the levels of difficulty, task and response formats, types of materials, and kinds of questions on survey assessments helps uncover competencies and challenges that may otherwise be masked (Ysseldyke, 2001).

For example, assessing the student as a reader requires asking the student to read aloud and then retell the story to track and document how fluency and miscues impact understanding content. Asking the student to read comparable narratives silently offers an additional opportunity to evaluate a range of comprehension skills and strategies based on retell and follow-up questions. The levels of difficulty of questions asked may begin an open-ended request for retelling the story and be followed up with more focused questions of who, what, when, where, how, in what way, and why regarding problem to solution, key events, characters, and setting. Additional adjustments to reading materials involves changing the levels of narratives and story lines, using text with and without pictures, varying genres and topics, controlling vocabulary, and/or using text resources that are sight, language, or phonetically based (Simmons, 2000; Tucker & Bakken, 2000; Wilson et al., 2005).

Regardless of area(s) of concern, the examiner strives to discern the independent, instructional, and frustration level(s) at which the student works by systematically adjusting the difficulty of materials, concepts, and questions. Tasks can also be altered for other variables that may impact performance. Altering formats of comparable tasks provides samples of how the student engages in reading, writing, mathematics, or social situations to respond to different demands. When comparable tasks change the level, modify specific requirements, alter format used, or vary the pace of task or amount of work, the examiner has opportunities to discover when or how the student demonstrates proficiency and/or indicates challenges in learning and behaving (Choate, 1992; Zigmond et al., 1983).

Probe-level tasks differ from surveys because they narrow the focus to isolate and assess specific skills in an in-depth sequential fashion; drawing on skill hierarchies, scope and sequences, and curriculum standards and benchmarks, relative to general education expectations and requirements. The design of probe-level tools centers on separating out sets of skills per cluster and using focused tasks to assess what the student knows and does with the skills out of context. In constructing probe tasks, provide the student with a range of format options to demonstrate his or her skills (e.g., timed–untimed, dictated–written, use of word banks, include manipulatives), taking into consideration how he or she is asked to respond and possible supports to enhance performance.

For example, the evaluator assesses a student's understanding and facility with multiplication facts by giving a timed pencil-and-paper task and/or using a set of flashcards at a prescribed rate. Comparisons are then made with what happens when the student is asked to calculate equations untimed. Related probes involve the student reading several equations, representing them with manipulatives or on a number line, and stating the product. He or she is asked to write and compute equations in response to prearranged manipulatives. The probes target multiplication facts/concept from multiple perspectives, isolating the skill while also varying the task. Similarly, the evaluator might examine spelling phonetically regular words by dictating single words for the student to write or arrange letter tiles or giving him or her a prepared list of misspelled words on a paper to correct.

Student performance on probe tasks provides the basis for cross-referencing evidence to understand the kinds of errors made, difficulties experienced, and/or inconsistent responses given on survey-level tasks. The examination of skills offers an understanding of what prerequisites the student has, determining the extent to which he or she uses or applies specific skills and/or strategies compared with what it means to be effective in the area(s) of concern. There are commercial instruments that give evaluators opportunities to examine how the student performs on survey- and probe-level tasks. For examples of survey and probe ideas, refer to the Assessment Plan Form Toolbox in Chapter 3 and Construction of Assessment Tools Toolbox at the end of this chapter.

Step 2: Prepare to Conduct Assessments

Preparation is a key component to collecting assessment data. The evaluator is required to organize materials, arrange the setting, and track the qualities of the situation in which the assessment takes place. Being prepared for assessment frees the evaluator to take in and record a range of information to describe student performance and account for the conditions and context to which the student is asked to respond. Record-keeping devices are an important part of organizing assessment materials and data. They help the examiner account for the range of situational factors—who is involved, when the assessment takes place, what the setting is like, the qualities of materials with which the student is asked to work, what the student is asked to do, and the directions and cues given. Being prepared for assessment also frees the evaluator to "be in the moment" with the student, to listen actively, make adjustments, and respond to him or her, noting the comments made and outcomes of prompts. The beauty of such detail is that it allows the evaluator to gather useful information to describe the student and evaluate the impact of a variety of factors, which eventually justify considerations and decisions regarding instructional plans.

It is helpful to consider the logistics of conducting assessments as well as the construction of the tools. The evaluator engineers the assessment activities to produce useful information. He or she takes into account use of time, organization of materials, and building a relationship with the student. The context for conducting assessments is enhanced when the examiner has materials organized and keeps the flow of the session going to involve the student. A comfortable environment and experience depends on being informed about the events of the session(s) and feeling heard as he or she works. Readiness for the different assessment tasks allows the evaluator to attend to the quality of interactions and thus offer the student chances to show what he or she knows and does. Figure 4.1 provides a checklist to guide an evaluator through the preparation and administration of assessment.

Figure 4.2 provides some ideas for thinking through final preparations for assessment, answering these questions: What am I planning to do with this student? What order makes sense? What materials do I need to conduct assessment? How much time do I need? How do I ensure a comfortable setting?

Prior to conducting assessments:

☐ Confirm that parental/caregiver permission is granted
☐ Access and construct the tasks to use with the student, making sure there is a connection with the **_Know-Want-How_** plan, balancing survey and probe tasks
☐ Organize and package materials needed for each task
☐ Work with classroom teacher to identify times and activities appropriate for observations and individual assessment
☐ Design record-keeping devices to assist in taking notes about student performance, responses given, questions raised during assessment
☐ Arrange for space conducive to conducting assessments
☐ Double-check on scheduling
☐ Develop charts, checklists, rubrics to analyze student performance on the different tasks, using common criteria (Interaction Formula components) to support systematic comparisons across tasks

During administration of assessments:

☐ Establish rapport with student (note how student transitions to testing situation)
☐ Set ground rules for interactions during assessment activities, explaining purpose of tasks and note taking
☐ Engage student in assessment tasks
☐ Maintain distance during observations unless following a participant-observer role
☐ Record student responses, questions, behaviors during assessment tasks
☐ Keep activity moving during sessions
☐ Attend to transitions between tasks and give the student breaks as needed

Following administration of assessment tasks:

☐ Add to notes taken during assessment session, recording objective information and jotting down impressions
☐ Analyze student performance on each task administered and identify key descriptors
☐ Synthesize data from analysis on charts/checklists/rubrics to allow for cross-referencing across assessment tasks
☐ Extract themes (Interaction Model components), draw conclusions, and make tentative hypotheses
☐ Prepare to share charts and findings with members of the team

---

FIGURE 4.1 Logistics: Sequence of Assessment Responsibilities

☐ Make a to-do list of tasks, materials, time estimates that will constitute the logistics of assessment.
  • List the tasks and observations you propose.
  • Review the list of tasks and give them a sequence. Consider moving from survey to probe, easier to more difficult, and varying the types of tasks to maintain student interest and investment in assessment.
  • Schedule student-evaluator contact times and observations.

☐ Set up a filing system that maintains confidentiality. Use folders and/or envelopes to hold testing materials, evaluator notes, samples of student work/documents, recording devices, analyses, charts together. Include a task sheet so other members of the team may take a look at the data collected. Store tapes, sets of documents, responses to flashcards, discussion notes, or records of observations. Here are some materials to include in a file folder, pocket folder, or manila envelope:

Note card or task observation sheet with an assessment, objective, brief description of the task, and directions for student

Paper
  • Interview questions with space to record responses
  • "Scrap" paper for taking a break with the student (e.g., tic-tac-toe), giving the student something to work on (e.g., decides to create own web for prewriting, illustrates the story read, uses for working out arithmetic equations, uses to doodle as listens)

Assessment tools
  • Copies of books, webs, worksheets, manipulatives, flashcards; packets for student and evaluator (makes recording student response easier)
  • Tape recorder, computer disks
  • General observation forms to record student response to tasks
  • Design interview tool so when information arises spontaneously, there is access to it

☐ Develop form for data collection.

☐ Consider having "things to do" while the student is performing independently:
  • Have sheets of paper or forms for observation notes
  • Identify recording strategies per task

☐ Consider available space and how to arrange it for working together or encouraging independence:
  • Seating arrangement: Determine where (across from or side) you prefer to sit on in terms of observing the student as he or she works and jotting down notes
  • Placement of materials: Determine how materials are stored, placed when in use and not in use; avoiding overwhelming student, cluttering work space, or being threatening when you choose not to use some things
  • Room for student to work and you to record

☐ Develop an agenda for each session with the student. Start with a nonthreatening task.

☐ Organize file folders or manila envelopes to allow sorting through and comparing and contrasting what and how the student performs on individual tasks and across tasks.

FIGURE 4.2 Logistics: To-Do List for Evaluators

Developing Forms for Data Collection

The actual gathering of materials, figuring out a reasonable way to document what happens during the session(s), and articulating criteria for analysis requires understanding what the assessment process is about. Planning not only involves constructing tools but also designing record-keeping devices to facilitate recording what happens during the assessment sessions and developing the analysis charts to examine findings thoroughly and systematically.

Setting up record-keeping devices to support note taking during a session helps retain those qualities of student responses that are key to figuring out what is going on for him or her in the area(s) of concern. Documenting student responses, talk, and nonverbal behaviors can be challenging and pose a dilemma of determining the *important* information. The pace of tasks may add to the difficulty of jotting down what the student says and does. However, documenting these data, rather than merely checking whether he or she is right or wrong, makes a difference in the quality of information gathered and how his or her status is understood.

The advantage of informal assessment tasks and activities is that even with predetermined questions and directions, there is flexibility to reword confusing information and engage in conversation to hear what is unclear and acknowledge how the student is feeling. The student's comfort level is more readily established when exchanges are casual versus scripted. When the examiner is obligated to use prescribed talk, responsiveness may be stilted and the student may feel more apprehensive.

The materials can be organized, directions written out, the setting arranged, and there are still going to be factors that are unforeseen. For this reason, establishing places to note the unaccounted-for factors, the qualities of student responses, ways the student deals with difficult tasks, and observations of successes help with analyzing the data collected. The dilemma is how to write down all that the student says and does during the situation and still be responsive. Clearly, the as-much-as-possible rule fits here. Use a tape recorder when the student okays it and it is feasible. Write notes as reminders of what happens, and then take time directly after the session to fill in as much as you can remember. Keeping written records of student responses (verbal and nonverbal) contributes to how the assessments are analyzed. Designing record-keeping devices and having duplicate copies of materials used with the student help track responses, observations, and questions to capture key information. Think about:

- What types of data does each task generate and not generate?
- What types of forms would be helpful to capture student performance on each assessment?

Task Records

Prepare an outline on which to record information about task, directions, setting, the qualities of the assessment situation, and student responses to the task. This is the place to record comments the student makes as he or she proceeds through each task. This sheet is also a reminder to note conditions that surround student performance: (1) questions posed at the outset, during, or at the end of the activity; (2) questions and comments the student makes at different points, and (3) assistance offered or prompts suggested when the student is stuck, confused, or frustrated. In addition, space might be included to elaborate on what the student does and the evidence collected to define his or her approach and understanding of process, use of strategies, impact of attitude/investment, and response to directions, prompts, or error corrections. Figuring out a format that is suitable for the individual evaluator ensures the information is gathered in detail. Forms may include the following:

1. Student name
2. Date task administered
3. Title for task or brief description of it
4. Directions for the task
5. Space to record student:
   a. Entry into the situation
   b. Behaviors during the session
   c. Response to directions
   d. Approach to and execution of the task
   e. Handling of challenges (e.g., ask for help, skip items, use strategies)
   f. Investment in the task and impact
6. Teacher's prompts or cues and student responses to them

Evaluator's Copies

Keep duplicate copies of prepared materials with which the student is asked to work. It is easier to record his or her responses to materials or specific items directly on a prepared copy. This makes it easier to consider task demands, make notations of help offered, record student errors, and include other factors that arise. For example, when using flashcards, list the words or facts on a sheet of paper in the order they are presented. Recording directly on the prepared copy of material allows for writing specifically what the student says or writes in response to the stimuli and the impromptu remarks and questions you both state. Remember to include some of the basic information of date and setting.

Step 3: Conduct Assessments

Preparation for assessment requires you as the evaluator to think about how you relate interpersonally and build rapport with the student. Gathering a genuine picture of the student rests on establishing a working relationship. In addition to preparing the logistics of assessments, getting ready also involves thinking about how you present yourself at the outset of assessment, the ways you respond to the student during sessions, and the explanations you offer for tasks, note taking, and behavior. Treating evaluation as the opportunity to get to know the student and involve him or her in the process shifts it to a more congenial tone. As the student proceeds through the survey- and probe-level tasks, use pauses to pose some of the prepared interview questions so they are more a matter of conversation. In this way, you are more apt to get at student viewpoints. Figuring out how to approach assessment means asking yourself these questions:

How does your demeanor impact student performance? What explanations are you planning to offer about the assessment situation? How is support provided throughout the assessment process?

Introductions. How will you

- Introduce yourself to the student?
- Set the tone for the assessment activities?
- Empower the student through your presentation of the intent of assessment?
- Explain the intent of the tasks and activities you are using? What rationale for working with the student do you offer? What do you say?
- Present an icebreaker to help create a comfortable situation?

During assessment sessions, different tasks serve different purposes. There are times where you will take a more strict approach to maintaining distance, whereas other times you will work with the student. How will you

- Work with the student during informal assessments?
- Prepare the student for independent tasks?
- Distinguish tasks with which you are willing or not to help?
- Intend to destress the situation, particularly when the tasks are more difficult for the student?
- Take breaks during a longer stretch of time?
- Address student concerns regarding what is being missed in the classroom?
- Respond to errors? When?
- Ask the student to go back and revisit some of his or her errors? When?
- Record student behavior and responses?
- Explain why you are taking notes?

Bringing closure to assessment. How will you

- Determine appropriate stopping points?
- Give the student the opportunity to reflect on his or her performance?
- Share initial findings with the student?
- Give real *positives* to the student?
- Put assessment in perspective and explain how the team will use the information?

During the assessment planning (meeting), the team designates a person to sit down with the student to explain what is going to happen over the course of weeks. It is helpful to designate someone with whom the student is familiar and comfortable to be in charge of mapping out the assessment process so he or she is prepared for new faces, being separated from class and missing what is going on, and investing in the assessment activities. How the intent of assessment is framed depends somewhat on the age of the student, but the bottom line is that he or she gets the message the team wants to figure out what is making learning challenging, determine "best ways" to teach him or her, and help make learning more enjoyable and successful. Each evaluator echoes the intent of assessment, giving the student a sense of purpose for the time spent, an awareness of genuine concern, and a message of commitment to making his or her educational life better.

Offering the student an explanation for assessment is one opportunity to invite him or her into the IEP process to sort through what is going on, express how he or she is feeling, and share what might be helpful, giving the student a voice in sharing experiences in the area(s) of concern. Setting up the process in this way lets the student know the value of his or her input in figuring out the challenges faced. The message communicates that assessment is a vehicle to demonstrate realities with regard to the area(s) of concern. The use of authentic tasks helps confirm the stated intentions of assessment. So when it is suggested that the intent of authentic assessment is to figure out what makes the area(s) of concern challenging, the student sees the connection between what he or she is asked to do and what is being said.

Some students are preoccupied with the accuracy of their responses. Others are curious about what the evaluator is writing. Part of preparing the student for working in the assessment situation is to explain the reasons for recording information—to help remember what is going on and to make notes about the different tasks. Students are more apt to be receptive if recording the information is tied in with the explanation for conducting the assessments.

Explaining what the student may expect in terms of some tasks being comfortable and others being difficult helps establish an honest working relationship. Let the student know that there are times during assessment when you may offer help but other times when he or she is expected to work independently. Further, caution the student that at times he or she will be asked to work alone, so how problems are solved and how the student works independently may be closely observed. These are expected in situations in which the more standardized psychometric approach to administering assessment are used: The task is set up, directions given, student responses observed, and what he or she says and does is recorded. Interaction is limited to acknowledging through "hmm, uh huh, okay," or encouragement of "give it a try, this seems hard, you are doing fine, give it your best shot," and so on. However, when the student is finished with such a task, it is okay to switch gears and process performance by going back and asking the student to rethink an item or section, explain how the student did something in his or her own words, or describe what he or she was thinking: "When you said/ wrote/ answered . . . , what were you thinking?" Or, "How did you arrive at that answer?" On informal assessment tasks, questions, prompts, hints, error corrections, and suggestions may be used at the outset of the task or in the midst of it to examine the impact of using prereading or writing strategies that encourage the student to self-check, and so on. This more interactive approach can be challenging for you in drawing the line with how much help to offer. It requires keeping in mind what factors are being studied and balancing supporting the student rather than infiltrating his performance.

Step 4: Chart and Analyze Student Performance and Products

The focus of charting and analyzing assessment data is to study products and behaviors systematically to extract descriptive information about the student and move beyond scores. An in-depth analysis of documents gathered depends on how authentic the tools were and how systematically the assessment plan was carried out. A qualitative description of competence and challenges in the area(s) of concern is necessary to address student needs and develop a usable individualized education plan. Such a description comes from the methodical study of the data by sorting, organizing, and displaying the information gathered through the surveys, probes, interviews, observations, and/or formal testing. A systematic analysis of the assessment results requires reviewing, grouping, and charting collected evidence to discern patterns of academic and social performance to draw conclusions and hypotheses with reference to general education (Garcia, 2007; Goodman, Watson, & Burke, 1987; Henk, Marinak, Moore, & Mallette, 2003; Henk, Moore, Marinak, & Tomasetti, 2000; Sugai, Lewis-Palmer, & Hagan-Burke, 1999–2000). To examine the data in constructive ways, answer the following questions:

- What is the purpose for using the assessment tool in relation to the general education expectations?
- Against what criteria is student performance judged?
- What evidence of competence and types of errors does the student make on individual tools?
- How is performance across multiple tasks going to be compared and contrasted to discern patterns of competence and challenges?
- What do the identified patterns suggest to account for student competence and challenges in ways that indicate academic and social needs with reference to general education?

Examining the data thoroughly involves a multistep process. You appraise student performance on each task, taking into account what the student is asked to do and how he or she responded. Criteria are derived from articulating academic and social standards, expectations, instructional experiences, task demands, and setting variables. They are established and applied to prompt the scrutiny of performance to provide a baseline. The information must be specific enough to determine starting points for instruction, effective approaches and interventions, and supportive learning environments. The evaluator examines what the student does and produces, sifting through evidence from individual tools and across tasks and/or situations to figure out what patterns of competencies, errors, and/or misbehaviors exist, what they indicate, and how they affect the quality of student performance. Resist skimming the data because key information may get lost.

To organize, connect, and use assessment data constructively, develop analysis charts and select a corresponding approach to coding the evidence. Adopt a system for comparing what the student does against expected performance on designated tasks and/or social situations. As you read through assessments, identify errors and areas of strength to highlight/color-code, group, and cluster similar skill- and behavior-related information. Extract descriptive information and enter it on charts to display and uncover patterns of errors and competence. Charting assessment results leads to understanding findings, generating hypotheses, and determining student needs. Ask, *How does what the student said, did, and produced tell about him or her related to the area(s) of concern?*

Move through the multistep process to examine the results from each assessment tool:

1. Develop an analysis chart for each tool according to a comprehensive set of criteria designed to capture what the task is asking the student to do with reference to the area(s) of concern.
2. Read through each sample of student work or record of behavior to code (highlight, shorthand, list, circle, sticky notes, etc.) each example of competence and errors.
3. Enter the evidence onto the chart to display examples of student performance.
4. Examine chart and groups of related descriptors/student responses to discern patterns of competence and errors with reference to task demands.
5. Compare and cross-reference evidence of student competence and errors across tasks and charts to evaluate findings, draw conclusions, generate hypotheses, and discern needs.

Charting Data and Analysis

Analysis charts provide a framework for displaying assessment data to examine systematically what the student said, did, or produced under different conditions and/or in response to defined tasks. The design of analysis charts involves identifying specific criteria to examine products, behaviors, and performance with reference to task and setting demands. The criteria incorporate an understanding of academic and social content to help guide you to identify, extract, and articulate student competencies and errors in the area(s) of concern.

Create charting devices that allow for a detailed study of performance and products on individual and related tasks concurrently. The purpose is to provide graphic organizers to represent student performance to discern patterns of errors within and across similar tasks. The matrices are set up to display each example of academic and social competence and errors/misbehaviors that are evident on the tool and define student status. Write headings across the top row and stems going down the column on the left side based on established criteria to designate spaces for entering and organizing data. Charts incorporate specific criteria for evaluating student performance around the following questions:

- What is the assessment task asking the student to do?
- What are the expected responses/behaviors?
- What does the student do effectively?
- What errors does the student make?

Charts are constructed to evaluate what the student is asked to do on assessment tasks with reference to variables that impact student performance in the area(s) of concern. One approach incorporates the elements of the Interaction Formula to help define criteria for creating headings and stems that will support analyzing and charting assessment data. This charting device is set up to present how skills per cluster, task formats and demands, strategic thinking and problem solving, qualities of situations and settings, and investment have their respective effect on student success and errors. The Interaction Formula for Analyzing Individual Tools Toolbox at the end of the chapter provides a skeletal framework for evaluating student responses to each assessment tool used.

Alternatively, charts may also be designed and organized to describe the student as a reader, writer, mathematician, and/or participant/member of the classroom community. Draw from resources to develop and articulate detailed criteria for describing student performance to generate thorough analyses. Consider the specific assessment tasks and desired performance with reference to the hierarchy of grade-level skills per area to establish specific criteria for the analysis chart. The criteria identify and list skills per cluster and problem-solving and thinking approaches as specific variables that serve as points of reference for examining student performance.

Figure 4.3 illustrates the process involved in creating detailed charting devices based on what skills per cluster are assessed in relation to how the student is asked to perform. The Sample Analyses Charts Toolbox at the end of this chapter illustrates the forms the charts may take. To develop charts to guide analysis, the Checklists to Guide Descriptions Toolbox at the end of Chapter 5 suggests specific criteria per area(s) of concern for creating detailed analysis charts while referencing the Interaction Formula elements. Also, related scope and sequence lists, grade-level expectations, state standards, and curriculum benchmarks offer supplements to the checklists.

Charting data prompts you not only to study and record, but also to analyze student products, responses, and performance holistically with supporting evidence. After you record the coded information within the chart, look for clusters of like competencies and errors with reference to task demands to figure out the existing patterns. Compare and contrast the patterns within the tool to draw some conclusions about what they indicate. The patterns and tentative conclusions per assessment tool are recorded in the margins of the chart, on sticky notes, or on separate paper. The descriptions of patterns derived from such analyses are concrete and constructive and provide the bases for comparing student work within and across different assessment tools.

Cross-Referencing Data

Once data have been charted for each tool, the next steps are to compare results, identify relationships among the data, pull information together, account for the discrepancies in student performance, and draw preliminary conclusions. Cross-referencing involves comparing the individual analysis charts of student

Who is this student in the area(s) of concern?	What is the task asking the student to do?	What are the criteria for evaluating student performance?
Reader	Read text fluently and gain meaning from content: • Recognize words and/or figure out word that makes sense and does not change meaning • Engage in prereading • Draw on information as read the story and interact as process • Summarize content	Description of: • Fluency: Pace of reading, phrasing, expression, qualities of errors • Word solving: Use of phonics skills to break up words, use of context, use of small words • Cues picks up from title and pictures, and feasibility of prediction • Types of evidence of being attuned to story (predictions of upcoming events, self-corrections) • Inclusion of key elements (setting, problem, solution, sequence, resolution)
Writer	Communicate ideas, information in an essay format clearly and coherently: • Select topic • Research facts • Prewrite • Arrange information by paragraph • Provide supporting detail to back up assertions • Revise • Edit	• Organization of ideas, giving "big picture" and related details • Use of introductory, supporting, and concluding paragraphs • Use of topic sentences, supporting statements, and summative sentence in paragraph • Use of effective sentence structure including connectors, consistent tense • Use of capitalization, punctuation, and accurate spelling
Mathematician	Select the operation, calculate accurately to solve a problem: • Read problem • Identify question • Explain action • Extract key information • Set up equation to correspond with question • Ask question to check on feasibility and label for answer	• Use of steps to come up with answer: Associate action with problem • Connect action with operation • Translate into number sentence • Calculate response
Participant in the learning environment	Read the demands of the situation and choose acceptable ways to contribute, work, engage with peers • Pick up on cues that indicate wants of characters • Ask self what choices are • Weigh options against standards for behavior • Justify actions	• Compare behaviors with expectations of the situation • Listen for consideration of others • Ask student to identify what wanted

FIGURE 4.3 Sampling of Thinking That Contributes to Design of Analysis Charts

performance and products across tasks and situations to sort related information. Information from analysis charts are grouped according to how assessment findings from the different tools typify student proficiency and struggles when demands vary. As a result of comparing statements of what the student says, does, and produces under various conditions, patterns of responses, errors, and competencies emerge to generate hypotheses that account for effectiveness and challenges in the area(s) of concern.

Clustering and integrating assessment data from the different tools means sorting like and disparate statements of findings and organizing them to contribute to a detailed picture of the student in the area(s) of concern. Examining performance across probe- and survey-level tasks allows for such comparisons. Contrasting what student performance is like when skills or strategies are aggregated on survey-level tasks versus isolated on probe-level tasks leads to developing initial conclusions about the challenges he or she faces. How the student uses skills in context versus isolation may provide indicators of his or her levels of understanding; what skills per cluster he or she may recognize, use, and/or apply. When a student does or does not generalize skills or strategies to other situations, it is possible that he or she does not understand their use in different contexts, does not resort to that approach, or is not yet automatic with their use.

Including interview data is an opportunity to reconcile what is observed and documented using the words and views of the student. Interviews may help shed light on the student's realities and insights relative to learning situations and social interactions, what appear as self-defeating approaches to the tasks, ways he or she deals with difficulty and frustration, sharing personal interests, and/or understanding/misunderstanding relevance for the area(s) of concern. The student's perspective offers a vehicle for taking some of the guesswork out of interpreting behavior or statements such as "I don't know" or "I don't care." There are times when the student gives the "expected" answers with regard to completing tasks and being effective and other times where *attitude* seems to be a factor. There are also times where the behavior speaks for the student who does not have the words or understanding of how he or she feels, thinks, or approaches the area(s) of concern.

Referencing observation data helps examine the impact of the instructional and physical settings, consisting of time on task, amount of work, schedule, pace, use of groupings, activity levels, noise, behavioral expectations, procedures, rules, and interactions with peers and adults. Observation data allow you to see how the student maneuvers through the array of factors as he or she performs in the area(s) of concern. The behaviors may corroborate self-report. The behaviors may offer perspective about student sense of self, attitude, and confidence when involved in the area(s) of concern in the context of the classroom. The behaviors may also give a different view of student use of strategic thinking. Regardless of how the observational data add to understanding the student in the area(s) of concern, they also offer perspective on the skills the student has when he or she is performing in the classroom setting or assessment situation.

How do student performance and behavior vary and remain constant across tasks and situations? You identify and list consistencies and discrepancies across patterns of performance and behavior with reference to task and setting demands. You extract, organize, and add examples from student responses, task products, observational data, and interviews to account for what is contributing to struggles. Comparing and contrasting student performance across survey- and probe-level tasks give an authentic view of his or her skill repertoires, responsiveness to task demands, and approaches to strategies and problem solving in the area(s) of concern. Blending observation data into the mix adds information about how settings impact performance. Filtering in interview data uses student report of his or her thinking and outlook to recognize how situations are understood, difficulties are framed, and responses are justified.

Cross-referencing assessment findings by the format provides a structure for merging analyses of the individual tools, using Interaction Formula elements to generate statements to describe student competence and untangle what contributes to the challenges he or she experiences. Collating these data involves fitting the qualitative descriptions of the student together, using a chart, pad of paper, sticky notes, and so on, to look across tasks to note patterns of appropriate responses and common errors that typify performance or products. Compiling cross-referenced information leads to discerning substantive statements with supporting details about the student.

Analysis of performance across the tools brings the jigsaw pieces of the student struggles into perspective. Returning to the <u>K</u>now-<u>W</u>ant-<u>H</u>ow chart to reference the original questions raised helps evaluate what has been learned, makes sure the referral is addressed, and determines how the information fits together to describe the learner relative to the area(s) of concern (McLoughlin & Lewis, 2001; Zigmond et al., 1983).

Drawing Statements of Conclusions

What explanations provide an understanding of student challenges? The goal of this step is making constructive statements that look at performance in terms of what the student accomplishes, with what he or she has difficulty, and under what conditions. Cross-referencing and synthesizing the data leads to making connections among findings and accounting for what is interfering with student performance, participation, and progress. Figuring out what factors contribute comes from what was learned as a result of data analysis and comparisons of patterns of competence and errors. Statements are made that evaluate what aspects of student status are indicative of and account for challenges or mismatches with performance and situation demands.

The following represent examples of statements of conclusions, drawn from cross-referencing data and examination of patterns of competence and errors:

Dorrie may skip unfamiliar words or ask for help when reading text-only stories. However, when she reads an illustrated book, she pauses, refers to the picture, reexamines the word, and makes a guess that fits the story line and begins with the correct first sound(s). Her retell indicates that she gains greater meaning when illustrations accompany the story and offer her a mechanism for self-monitoring.

When writing an original story, Paul may limit his word choice to those with which he feels comfortable spelling. However, he uses an extensive vocabulary (multisyllabic words in contrast to single-syllable ones) when he preplans the story with the teacher who writes down key vocabulary for him and when he dictates a story to a scribe or tape. During conversations, he uses multisyllabic words to label concepts, objects, and descriptions.

Rick extracts numbers from a written problem, assigning an operation, setting up a corresponding equation, and working out a solution. At times, his answers correctly respond to the problem's question, whereas other times a mistaken choice of operation or misuse of a number accounts for the difficulty. When Rick reads the problem aloud, talks his ideas through, and then sets up the example, he is more accurate in the use of numbers and choice of operation.

As you draw conclusions, retain a *strength-based* view of the student, holding on to what and when he or she does well, rather than solely dwelling on *limitations*. Conclusions link cross-referenced data to determine whether and how student challenges reflect gaps in skills and strategic thinking, issues responding to formats of learning tasks and experiences, demands of instructional settings, and difficulties investing in participation and learning. Draw explicit connections among the data by referring to the Interaction Formula to write statements about the relationships among patterns of errors and competence.

The process of charting and analyzing data against clear criteria allow you to study student status and struggles, organize supportive evidence, and create justification for eventual programming. The more substantive the criteria for evaluating student performance, the more likely descriptors will emerge to portray the student comprehensively. The more comprehensive the charts, the more likely analyses of student performance on surveys, probes, and observations are systematic. The more systematic the analyses, the more opportunity to uncover what the student does effectively, find patterns of errors, and begin to determine what interferes with learning (Goodman et al., 1987; Sugai et al., 1999–2000). The more consistent the criteria are for evaluating student performance on individual and across tools, the greater the insights into student experiences, proficiencies, and challenges. The more thorough the synthesis of data, the more attention paid to how the data substantiate student competence and struggles within or across different learning and social situations.

Each evaluator's thorough, systematic treatment of data is central to entering the team meeting in which members share their data to describe the student. Pulling descriptive data together as a team translates to characterizing student performance, identifying and hypothesizing about apparent struggles, and making connections with what he or she does. The collated assessment data provide an authentic perspective on what is happening for the student and prepare the team to take proactive approaches. This step is addressed in more detail in Chapter 5.

Chapter Review: Focus and Decisions

Stage III: Collect, Chart, and Analyze Data

❑ Use the *Know-Want-How* assessment plan to choose, access, and design specific instruments to assess the student in the area(s) of concern.
  • How do I translate the *Know-Want-How* into action? What specific assessment tools do I select and/or develop for use?

❑ Prepare assessment tools to gather information and analyze data to enhance understanding of the learner and challenges he or she faces.

❑ Figure out a system for analyzing assessment data that is responsive to *Know-Want-How* questions and provides a lens for examining student performance across different tasks.

❑ Arrange conditions for conducting assessments:
  • How do I prepare for and conduct assessments in ways that allow me to observe the student and maintain objectivity?

❑ Administer assessment tools to gather evidence of student performance under a variety of conditions and determine the quality of impact. Collect data that contribute to describing student skill repertoires, responsiveness to task formats, strategic thinking, participation in instructional contexts, and sense of purpose and self (Interaction Formula):
  • How do I keep track of information generated from assessment tasks? How do I organize the data I collect?
  • How do I evaluate performance on the different tasks to contribute to building a constructive picture of the student? How do I look at the different data individually and concurrently?
  • How do I analyze the student's performance on the different tasks to determine evidence of skill awareness, mastery, and/or gaps?
  • How do I evaluate how the student responds to different materials that involve the area(s) of concern?
  • How do I look at the student's responses as indicators of how he or she prepares, engages, and self-evaluates while performing in the area(s) of concern?
  • How do I evaluate how the student responds to different situations that involve the area(s) of concern?
  • How do I account for student demeanor when working in the area(s) of concern?

❑ Chart and analyze student performance to:
  • Describe what student performance tells
  • Chart student performance and behavior to display evidence of strengths and challenges, looking individually and collectively across tasks
  • Identify skills per cluster: skill repertoires and use of those skills to figure out factors that contribute to mastery and difficulty

- Describe formats for performance: responsiveness to different media, materials, and tasks
- Describe strategic thinking: ways student prepares, engages, and monitors self in performance
- Describe context for participation: responsiveness to instructional arrangements and social environment
- Describe investment: ways student demonstrates sense of self, purpose, and interests

❏ Determine whether there is sufficient evidence regarding student status in the area(s) of concern (repertoire of skills, strategies, challenges he or she experiences, and optimal conditions for promoting growth).

❏ Summarize the challenges the student experiences in the area(s) of concern and prepare to contribute findings to the team's collective understanding of the learner:
- How do I collate the assessment data to present information meaningfully and coherently? How do I use the data to begin to account for student challenges?

Stage III: Apply and Learn

1. Gather samples of student journal writing, math worksheets, and reader response logs, and/or collect anecdotal records of behavior. Practice analyzing student performance and behavior. Start with survey-level tasks and then use probe-level tasks. Examine student work in terms of Interaction Formula elements:
   a. Ask yourself, What is the task asking the student to do? What skills per cluster are tapped through the task?
   b. What format does the task take? How might presentation of the task impact on student performance?
   c. In what context was the student asked to perform the particular task? How does instructional and/or physical setting impact performance? What observation data confirm that?
   d. What evidence is there about student investment in the task?
   e. Create or adapt a chart (see the Sample Analysis Charts Toolbox) that helps you extract information systematically about student performance, attending to what the student does and what patterns of errors emerge. Remember to use the chart structure to look at errors against appropriate responses.
   f. Enter the information into the chart.
   g. Review the chart. Refer to the Checklists to Guide Descriptions that appear in the Toolbox in Chapter 5 under the respective area of concern(s). Write two to four sentences that depict what the student does effectively and two to four sentences that convey the challenges you documented. What other information would help you understand this student?

2. How do data collected, charted, and analyzed from each tool help answer questions raised in the KWH chart about the student in the area(s) of concern?

Construction of Assessment Tools Toolbox

Construction of Assessment Tools: Reader

Thinking That Guides Moving from *Know–Want–How* Plan to Assessment Tasks		
What constitutes an effective . . .?	**What specific assessment task/materials will generate the data?**	**What does the evaluator plan to observe? What are the criteria for examining performance?**
READER: To observe: • Student approach to *reading* new material • Student sense of story • How the student uses pictures to gain meaning • A sample of student "reading" or "storytelling" language • *How the student "reads" pictures when given questions (e.g., What do you think is happening? How does he feel?, What do you think will happen next?)*	"read" wordless books (*Rain* by Peter Spier, *A Boy, a Dog, and a Frog* by Mercer Mayer) (This task is helpful for a student reported to be a nonreader or an emergent reader. It may also be used as a means of gathering student dictation of a story.)	Analyze observation of situation in terms of: • How the student handles the book • Extent to which he or she examines cover, flips through pages first (engages in "prereading"/preparation for getting involved in the book) • Looks to examiner for help Analyze what the student says in terms of: • What descriptions student extracts from pictures and personal experiences he or she attributes when looking at more of an information book • What student includes in terms of a beginning, middle, end (b-m-e) • Ways in which b-m-e are connected • How student makes reference to information presented in the pictures • Extent to which student presents isolated information • How uses information to describe setting, characters, problem, events, resolution • *Difference between initial response to pictures and response when given questions* Evaluate the quality of spoken language: • Sentence length and structure, grammar, word usage

125

Construction of Assessment Tools Toolbox

Thinking That Guides Construction of Related Assessment Tasks

Survey	Alternative Qualities/Conditions	Probe	Alternative Qualities/Conditions	Observations
Read • Short story • Chapter from book • Poem(s) **With retell of what read**	**Vary materials** *To offer different levels, cueing systems as part of text materials:* • Picture books/illustrated story • Predictable book vs. narrative • Change level of text • Read silently vs. orally vs. being read to **Guide retell** *To give student structure to report on understanding of what reads (use following retell):* • Pose a set of questions (open-ended and if needed multiple-choice or fill-in-the-blank questions) • Give key pictures from story as prompts	**Fluency** *To focus on the flow and use of expression:* • Reading dialogue • Sentence or phrase reading *(vary punctuation)* • Sight word list **Cuing system** *To examine how the student uses context, sentence structure, phonics to decipher words and meaning:* • Cloze procedure with sentences, paragraphs • Read mixed sentences, some that contain erroneous words in terms of grammar and others with meaning	**Vary Materials** *To offer different levels of material, cuing systems as part of text materials:* • Give background information pertaining to what is being read • Use corresponding pictures as cues • Change the level of words used • Decrease the complexity of sentences • Read aloud to student and have student repeat reading	**Record:** • Description of how the student handles reading materials, independently or with prompts is involved in prereading • Each of the miscues student makes when reading passages, words in isolation • Student wording of retell, response to questions

Thinking That Guides Design of Analysis Charts

What is the task asking the student to do?	What are expected behaviors?	How do you judge the student's performance?
Reader: Read text fluently and gain meaning from content	• Recognize words and/or figure out word that makes sense and does not change meaning • Engage in prereading • Make meaning while reading to interact with text • Summarize content	*Description of* • Pace of reading, phrasing, expression, qualities of errors • Cues picks up from title and pictures, and feasibility of prediction • Types of evidence of being attuned to story (predictions of upcoming events, self-corrections) • Inclusion of key elements (setting, problem, solution, sequence, resolution)

Construction of Assessment Tools: Writer

Thinking That Guides Moving from *Know–Want–How* Plan to Assessment Tasks

What constitutes an effective . . . ?	What specific assessment task/materials will generate the data?	What does the evaluator plan to observe? What are the criteria for examining performance?
WRITER: To observe: • The process the student uses to generate a story and self-monitor product • The content of what writes • Student competence in sentence structure, spelling, handwriting, grammar, mechanics when asked to use skill clusters concurrently • *How student uses preplanning when asked to share what he might want to include on a web* • *What amendments the student makes when asked to read the story aloud*	Write a story, based on a picture the student chooses or draws on own.	Analyze how student: • Preplans, uses brainstorming, outlines, mapping, and what he or she includes • Free-writes (puts ideas on paper) • Produces a draft (sample of idea development, organization, handwriting, spelling, sentence structure, grammar, and word usage) and checks work (rereads work and checks for legibility, spelling, mechanics, content Compare: • *what included when reminded to preplan or ask self questions* • *content of revision versus initial writing* Evaluate the quality and errors of: • Content • Sentence structure • Grammar • Handwriting • Spelling • Mechanics

Construction of Assessment Tools Toolbox

Thinking That Guides Construction of Related Assessment Tasks

Survey	Alternative Qualities/ Conditions	Probe	Alternative Qualities/ Conditions	Observations
Compose • Journal entry • Original story • Essay • Response to literature **Follow up by asking student to read his or her work aloud.**	**Offer prompt** *To stimulate thinking:* • Picture(s) (depicting dilemma, character, sequence) • Question(s) • Quote • Topic **Provide Web/Map/Graphic** *to guide organization, preplanning, brainstorming:* • Blank web • Labeled web (containing elements of story, related questions, subtopics to consider) **Give support options** *To eliminate contaminants that may impact performance:* • Computer • Handheld spell-check • Dictate versus write	**Idea development** *To generate a list of related ideas, descriptors:* • Web a list of information related to a topic • Brainstorm a list of descriptions for an object • Write sentence for each idea **Sentence structure** *to construct individual sentences:* • Arrange a set of words into a sentence (moving from simple to complex) • Give simple sentences to combine into one • Give combination of legitimate sentences, sentence fragments, and run-on sentences and have student correct • Give student bare-bones sentences and ask student to make more descriptive	**Vary task** *To offer student option for generating ideas:* • Dictate ideas to scribe • Use a picture related to topic as resource • Offer a word bank to eliminate spelling issues **Sentence structure variations** *To construct sentences:* • Listen to two simple sentences and combine • Listen to sentences and tell if correct; change if incorrect	**Record:** • Description of how the student responds to writing tasks, way preplans or brainstorms on own, process uses as writes draft, and extent to which revisits content and/or mechanics of product • Each of the changes the student makes as he or she reads what was written • Student requests for help

Construction of Assessment Tools Toolbox

Thinking That Guides Design of Analysis Charts

What is the task asking the student to do?	What are expected behaviors?	How do you judge the student's performance?
Writer: Communicate ideas, information in an essay format clearly and coherently	• Select topic • Research facts • Prewrite • Arrange information by paragraph • Provide supporting detail to back up assertions • Revise • Edit	*Description of:* • Organization of ideas, giving "big picture" and related details • Use introductory, supporting, and concluding paragraphs • Use topic sentences, supporting statements, and summative sentence in paragraph • Use effective sentence structure including connectors, consistent tense • Use capitalization, punctuation, and accurate spelling

Construction of Assessment Tools Toolbox

Construction of Assessment Tools: Mathematician

Thinking That Guides Moving from *Know-Want-How* Plan to Assessment Tasks		
What constitutes an effective . . . ?	What specific assessment task/materials will generate the data?	What does the evaluator plan to observe? What are the criteria for examining performance?
MATHEMATICIAN: To observe: • The items to which student responds spontaneously • *How the student changes responses when asked to identify what each sign means* • What the student does to figure out answers does not know by rote • The errors in terms of reading equation, use of operation, recollection of fact, application of strategy to figure out • Student approach to worksheet • Student response to being timed • Student talk through his or her thinking of calculating several of the examples	Timed worksheet of mixed examples of single digits	Analyze student's work in terms of: • Responsiveness to signs of operations • *Responsiveness to signs once pointed out* • Use of rote to answer questions • Use of strategies to figure out facts • Understanding of written examples and operations, writing sums, differences, products, and quotients for facts Evaluate student's system for working and response to: • Being timed • Shifting among different operations • Working with a number of examples

Construction of Assessment Tools Toolbox

Thinking That Guides Construction of Related Assessment Tasks

Survey	Alternative Qualities/Conditions	Probe	Alternative Qualities/Conditions	Observations
Solve word problems containing single and multiple steps with and without extraneous information **Ask student to explain the process and procedures used.**	**Vary materials** *To offer different levels, cuing systems as part of text materials:* • Picture books/ illustrated story • Objects or facsimiles contained in problem available	*Place Value* *To identify the levels at which the student understands concept and applies:* • Calculate two-digit examples with and without regrouping (take each operation separately and expand to decimals if appropriate) • Ask student to read multiple digit numbers and represent them on a place value board with numerals and sets of objects • Ask student to look at a representation of multiple digit numbers on the place value board and write the corresponding numeral	• Have student calculate examples, using the place value board	<u>Record:</u> • Description of how the student goes about calculating (use of fingers, manipulatives, "Touch Math"), types of self-corrections, and sequence of solving examples • What the student says about how he or she proceeded to calculate examples or solve problems • Student requests for help

Thinking That Guides Design of Analysis Charts

What is the task asking the student to do?	What are expected behaviors?	How do you judge the student's performance?
Mathematician: Select the operation; calculate accurately to solve a problem	• Read problem • Identify question • Explain action • Extract key information • Set up equation to correspond with question • Ask question to check on feasibility and label for answer	*Description of:* • Use of steps to come up with answer: Associate action with problem • Connect action with operation • Translate into number sentence • Calculate response

Construction of Assessment Tools Toolbox

Construction of Assessment Tools for the Participant in the Learning Environment/Member of the Classroom Community

Thinking That Guides Moving from _Know-Want-How_ Plan to Assessment Tasks		
What constitutes an effective . . . ?	What specific assessment task/ materials will generate the data?	What does the evaluator plan to observe? What are the criteria for examining performance?
PARTICIPANT IN THE LEARNING ENVIRONMENT: To document: • The way the student sorts out feelings, thoughts, behaviors • How the student attributes behavior to the situation, peers, teacher, or own responsibility • The steps the student takes in reasoning a purpose for a behavior • What the student values as appropriate and inappropriate behaviors • What the student sees as alternative behaviors • _How responses to the scenarios change when given a set of structured questions_	"What do you do?" scenarios (description of in-class situations in which student asked to evaluate behavior and discuss appropriateness, explain why student doing what doing, and identify alternatives)	Evaluate student responses in terms of: • Awareness of feelings person experiencing, acknowledgment of the thinking and choice involved, and acceptance of responsibility for behavior • Acceptance of responsibility vs. blame for behavior • Criteria uses to judge the appropriateness of behavior • Degree to which student recognizes there is more than one way to get what want • _Extent to which student states each character's point of view, intention of behavior_

Construction of Assessment Tools Toolbox

Thinking That Guides Construction of Related Assessment Tasks

Survey	Alternative Qualities/Conditions	Probe	Alternative Qualities/Conditions	Observations
Observe student In situations that are considered challenging/volatile **With opportunity to process events with him or her**	**Observe student** In situations that are relatively calm **With opportunity to process events with him or her**	**Focus on specific social skills** Read a brief story with a dilemma (e.g., joining with a group, cooperating with peers, handling anger, etc.) Ask the student focused questions: • How the character is feeling • What he is thinking • What is the appropriate response in the situation • How he or she would handle the situation in comparison to the character	**Focus on specific social skills:** • Have student draw a picture, write own story about the skill/dilemma • Have talk about the skill/dilemma with connections to own life	Student attention to task Verbal and non-verbal responses

Thinking That Guides Design of Analysis Charts

What is the task asking the student to do?	What are expected behaviors?	How do you judge the student's performance?
Participant/Member Read the demands of the situation and choose acceptable ways to contribute, work, engage with peers	• Pick up on cues that indicate wants of characters • Ask self what choices are • Weigh options against standards for behavior • Justify actions	*Description of:* • Compare behaviors with expectations of the situation • Listen for consideration of others • Ask student to identify what wanted

Sample Analysis Chart: Reader

MISCUE ANALYSIS

1. Form is for passage/story reading.
2. Transfer the words with which student struggled. Enter the text (correct) words and the miscues/errors the student made while reading aloud.
3. Compare and contrast the word as student reads with the text word to determine graphic and semantic similarity (columns 3 and 4).
4. Read student error in the sentence in which it occurred to respond to the last two columns.

Text Word	Miscue	Note if Self-correct (SC) and when or how	Graphic/aural similarity: To what degree does the miscue *look* like and/or *sound* like the intended word?	Semantically correct? How close is the word read to the intended meaning of the text word (gave synonym, changed plural, etc.)?	Syntactically/ grammatically correct: How does the student use sentence structure to cue self (substitute same part of speech?)?	How does the miscue change intended meaning of sentence/story? How does miscue impact retell?

5. Compare the potential impact of errors with student retell and response to comprehension questions.
6. Compare the qualities of errors made while reading in context with the qualities of errors made when reading sight words and phonetically regular words in isolation.

Adapted from Goodman, Y., Watson, D., and Burke, C. (1987). *Reading miscue inventory: Alternative procedures.* Katonah, NY: Richard C. Owen.

Sample Analysis Charts Toolbox

This form offers a guideline for examining the qualities of a student telling the story in his or her own words. It is helpful to compare what the student includes with responses to structured questions.

STORY RETELL

Retell	Summarizes story; succinct highlights	Supporting detail included or available when prompted with open-ended question	Errors indicative of difficulties or unawareness	Supplies own information to fill in (indicates awareness of story)	Impact of reading errors on . . .
Key events identified					
Order/sequence					
Connections (sense of if-then)					
Supporting detail					
Highlights problem to solution					
Names characters; tells role in story					
Examines relationships among characters					
Indicates how the setting impacts the mood, events, and outcomes of the story					

Sample Analysis Charts Toolbox

Survey Level Reading Tasks

CRITERIA	FORMAT 1 INSTRUCTIONAL-LEVEL STORY Previews story with pictures, responds to questions as goes, predicts, summarizes		FORMAT 2 INSTRUCTIONAL-LEVEL STORY Orally, with pictures		FORMAT 3 INSTRUCTIONAL-LEVEL STORY Silently, with pictures	
	Assets	Errors/miscues	Assets	Errors/miscues	Assets	Errors/miscues
Quality of reading	Assets	Errors/miscues	Assets	Errors/miscues	Assets	Errors/miscues
• Fluency, phrasing • Expression • Rate						
• Accuracy • Impact of errors on meaning of story						
Quality of retell	Assets	Errors/miscues	Assets	Errors/miscues	Assets	Errors/miscues
• Summarizes story • Organization • Highlights key events • Highlights key message • Provides details to support description						
• Supplies details in response to questions • Shows awareness of story elements (when questioned) • Connects cause and effect and relationships						
Evidence of skills	Assets	Errors/miscues	Assets	Errors/miscues	Assets	Errors/miscues
Word recognition • Applies phonics • Draws on sight words • Uses pictures • Uses context • Uses combination						
Expression • Responds to punctuation • Uses sentence structure • Uses character						
Extracts information • Who in story/characters • Where and when/setting • Problem • Events • Solution						

Sample Analysis Charts Toolbox

Sample Analysis Chart: Writer

Development of Ideas		
Ideas	**Evidence**	**Errors**
Story Organization		
Beginning Middle End		
Character Development		
Setting		
Problem		
Events (sequenced)		
Solution		
Expository Writing		
Introduction Development Conclusion		
Thesis Statement		
Supporting Statements and Details		
Offers Narrative, Descriptive, Explanatory, and/or Persuasive Perspectives		
Productivity (number of words per sentence/sentences/paragraphs)		
Vocabulary (choice of words, use of descriptors, variety)		
Grammar (noun–verb agreement, consistency of tense, use of pronouns, appropriate referents)		

Sample Analysis Charts Toolbox

Handwriting		
	Description of Formation	**Errors**
Quality of printed letters		
Use of upper and lower case letters		
Use of lines		
Quality of cursive letters		

Conventions of Print			
	Rules Used	**Errors**	**Consistency**
Punctuation			
Capitalization			
Sentence Structures Varies ways begins sentences Uses different sentence structures (simple, complex, compound)			

Spelling					
Student's Spelling	**Correct Spelling**	**Sounds Heard Appear in Spelling**	**Word Looks Like Correct Spelling**	**Applies Rules**	**Developmental Level of Spelling**

Sample Analysis Charts Toolbox

Analysis of Survey-Level Writing Tasks

This is a sample form. It will probably be helpful to enlarge boxes in order to enter descriptive information. Pay attention to the conditions as they offer opportunity to examine the ways in which the quality of student writing changes when writing process is involved.

CRITERIA	FORMAT 1 FREEWRITE		FORMAT 2 WITH PRE-WRITING		FORMAT 3 DICTATED		FORMAT 4 WORD PROCESSED	
Quality of Product	Assets	Errors/ miscues	Assets	Errors/ miscues	Assets	Errors/ miscues	Assets	Errors/ miscues
• Organization • Development of ideas • Flow								
• Use of story elements to develop story line								
Evidence of Skills	Assets	Errors/ miscues	Assets	Errors/ miscues	Assets	Errors/ miscues	Assets	Errors/ miscues
Sentence structure								
Grammar								
Conventions of print • Punctuation • Capitalization								
Spelling • Application of phonics • Sight words								
Handwriting • Manuscript • Cursive								

Sample Analysis Charts Toolbox

Analysis of Survey Level Writing Tasks: Use of Writing Process

This is a sample form. It will probably be helpful to enlarge boxes to enter descriptive information. Pay attention to the conditions because they offer an opportunity to examine the ways in which the quality of student writing changes when the writing process is involved.

CRITERIA	FORMAT 1 PREWRITING TOOL		FORMAT 2 FREEWRITE		FORMAT 3 REVISION		FORMAT 4 FINAL COPY	
Quality of Product	Assets	Errors/ miscues	Assets	Errors/ miscues	Assets	Errors/ miscues	Assets	Errors/ miscues
• Organization • Development of ideas • Flow								
• Use of story elements to develop story line								
Evidence of Skills	Assets	Errors/ miscues	Assets	Errors/ miscues	Assets	Errors/ miscues	Assets	Errors/ miscues
Sentence structure								
Grammar								
Conventions of print • Punctuation • Capitalization								
Spelling • Application of phonics • Sight words								
Handwriting • Manuscript • Cursive								

Sample Analysis Chart: Mathematician

Analysis of Computation Across Different Types of Tasks				
	Timed vs. Untimed	Used manipulatives or number line	Talked through computation	Wrote an explanation of thinking
	$(+, -, \times, /)$	$(+, -, \times, /)$	$(+, -, \times, /)$	$(+, -, \times, /)$
Calculates single digit (what facts by rote?)				
Calculates two digits without regrouping				
Calculates two digits with regrouping				
Uses vocabulary of operation				
Explains concept behind operation				
Errors indicative of misunderstanding concept				
Errors related to wrong operation				
Errors related to faulty facts				
Errors look like random responses				
Errors reflect faulty algorithm/procedure (involving extra zeroes, order of operations, etc.)				
Errors related to copying or transposing numbers				
Errors related to misuse of calculator, chart, or other supports				

Sample Analysis Charts Toolbox

Analysis of Problem Solving Across Different Level/Types of Problems				
	Format 1:Read problem embedded in single question	**Format 2: Listen to a single-step problem presented with illustrations**	**Format 3: Read a single step problem with illustrations**	**Format 4: Read a multistep problem with illustrations**
	$(+, -, \times, /)$	$(+, -, \times, /)$	$(+, -, \times, /)$	$(+, -, \times, /)$
Describe what the student does, the thinking he or she shares, and the qualities of responses				
Restate problem, telling action and identifying operation(s) to use				
Translate information into an equation				
Calculate equation				
Label answer				
Check answer to determine if it makes sense				

Sample Analysis Chart: Participant in the Learning Environment/Member of the Classroom Community

Observations/Behavior in Contexts

Analysis of Single Observation, Representing Chain of Events			
Setting Events (setting/context description of learning environment: materials, place, topic, etc.)	**Antecedents** (event, behavior that preceded/precipitated behavior)	**Behaviors** (objective description of actions, dialogues, nonverbal gestures exhibited by the student)	**Consequences** (responses and events that occur directly following the behavior or performance)

Analysis of Sets of Observations, Identifying the Contexts in which Behaviors Occur				
	IDENTIFY APPROPRIATE BEHAVIORS AND MISBEHAVIORS OBSERVED			
	Compliance with expectations	**Responsiveness to corrections**	**Ways seeks help or initiates conversation**	**Ways shows frustration, anger, strong emotion**
Large group instruction				
Small group instruction				
Morning or classroom meetings				
Independent work time				
Choice time				
Cooperative learning groups				
Recess activities				
Lunch activities				

The Interaction Formula for Analyzing Individual Tools and/or Cross-Referencing Assessments Toolbox

Interaction Formula Elements:	Descriptive statements gleaned from each tool:
What to Teach: What skills per cluster are problematic for the student in the tasks/activities?	
What to Teach: What skills per cluster does the student use effectively in the tasks/activities?	
What to Teach: How do skill errors and competence compare with academic standards and behavior expectations in general education?	
How to Teach: In what ways does the student struggle with the tasks/activities?	
How to Teach: How does the student respond to the task/activity approaches/formats?	
How to Teach: How does the student respond to the types and/or levels of task/activity/materials?	
How to Approach: How does the student work through the tasks/activities?	
How to Approach: In what ways does the student prepare for, engage in, and self-monitor while completing tasks/activities?	

The Interaction Formula for Analyzing Individual Tools and/or Cross-Referencing Assessments Toolbox

Interaction Formula Elements:	Descriptive statements gleaned from each tool:
How to Approach: What thinking strategies does the student use in his or her attempts to problem-solve during the tasks/activities?	
Under What Conditions: How does the student make use of time on task?	
Under What Conditions: How does the student handle the amount of work required by the tasks/activities?	
Under What Conditions: How does the testing situation (instructional arrangements, space, time of day, setting) impact how he or she attends, engages, and performs the tasks/activities?	
Why Teach: What is the student's understanding of the purpose of the tasks/activities?	
Why Teach: How does the student state and/or appear to feel about his or her performance on the tasks/activities?	
Why Teach: How does the student respond to expectations, feedback, and incentives?	
Why Teach: What is the student's sense of self in the area(s) of concern?	

Stage IV

Engage in the Individualized Education Program Meeting

As you read through this chapter, *think about:*

- What the team does to make the IEP process collaborative

- What cooperative steps the team takes to integrate assessment data to profile the student and define present levels of performance

- How the team collectively constructs the education plan and program based on the synthesis of authentic assessment data

- How the team determines eligibility based on substantiated student needs and the demands of general education

- How the team ensures that the education plan and program reflect the needs of the student in the area(s) of concern, tailoring learning opportunities and behavioral interventions in and out of the general educational curriculum

Overview of Stage IV

In stage IV, the team convenes to pool assessment data and develop a composite picture of the learner, figure out where instruction begins, and determine what support options are needed by the student and/or teacher. Members collaborate to merge their evaluation findings and multiple perspectives to build a comprehensive description of the student that responds to referral concerns and assessment questions (**K**now-**W**ant-**H**ow chart). The integration of evaluation data reveals insights about patterns of errors/misbehaviors, accounts for factors that impede and/or enhance learning, discerns student needs, explores eligibility, and leads to group decisions around planning and programming. It is during this stage that team members:

- Participate in the IEP meeting, prepared to share their evaluation data, analyses, hypotheses, conclusions, and recommendations
- Engage in a cooperative process and through effective communication integrate assessment findings
- Synthesize and summarize the collective data to account for factors that impact student performance, products, and engagement and conclude with what areas of need will be addressed
- Use the composite picture of the learner to justify and design the elements essential to individualized education interventions, planning, and programming

The team's vision for a constructive educational program depends on the collective understanding of the student as a learner. Members present documentation of student performance, sharing findings that describe successes and account for challenges. It is important for them to acknowledge how data supplement the referral description, respond to parent/caregiver concerns, answer questions raised during assessment planning, and contribute to the collaborative picture of the student. When members create a common and clear image of what competencies the student has and the challenges he or she faces, they have the basis to articulate and coordinate the elements of a sound educational plan and program (Drasgow et al., 2001; Dettmer, Dyck, & Thurston, 1996).

Developing a cohesive profile of the student in the area(s) of concern leads to making informed educational decisions to address needs and promote growth. The more instructionally relevant the picture of the student, the more direction is given to the development of a constructive educational program proposal. Members use the composite description to brainstorm ideas for designing individualized instructional plans that focus on constructive outcomes for the student (Cramer, 1998; Reeve & Hallahan, 1994). By identifying learner needs and corresponding educational plans, they establish the foundation for objectively determining eligibility and proposing and justifying program components and service delivery (Drasgow et al., 2001).

The purpose and structure of the evaluation/planning meeting guide team members in collaborating to cross-reference and synthesize assessment data to describe the learner and design an informative education plan. The development of a useful IEP rests heavily on members' adeptness to sort through and organize assessment data and their competence to match student needs with a well-defined education program. Team members thus make decisions about curricula priorities based on their combined grasp of student academic and/or social competence and expectations for achievement. They agree on instructional approaches that address needs, learning experiences and settings that prompt student engagement, and accountability measures that monitor progress. They determine appropriate services and program delivery to afford opportunities in general education and/or alternative settings that align with student needs (Forest & Pearpoint, 1992; Mount & Zwernik, 1988). The actual IEP is written following the meeting, derived from the collated information and ideas. Creating the plan together before writing the document invites members to contribute to substantive discussions and encourages shared ownership of the resulting program. The recommended agenda (see Figure 5.1 on p. 161) guide the team through a productive meeting.

Step 1: Build a Composite Picture of the Learner Collaboratively

The first segment of the IEP meeting was never meant to be a round-robin reading of assessment reports but rather a cooperative pooling and consolidation of information (Smith & Brownell, 1995; Ysseldyke, 2001; Ysseldyke et al., 1983). Blending the assessment data requires the team to cross-reference their findings systematically. The charge is to piece together the evidence to detail student performance in the area(s) of concern, identify how struggles influence progress in the general education curriculum, and formulate reasons to account for roadblocks the student encounters. The emphasis on collaboration underscores the importance of combining member input about learner strengths and struggles with reference to standards for effective performance and teacher expectations (Menlove, Hudson, & Suter, 2001; Reeve & Hallahan, 1994).

During the initial part of the meeting, team members actively participate by sharing and listening to information and viewpoints. Being prepared to engage in dialogue facilitates building a cooperative description of the student (Bradley, King-Sears, & Switlick, 1997). This involves each member getting ready by reviewing data gathered, analyses conducted, reports written, hypotheses developed, and conclusions reached about the learner during stage III. To present what they learned and weave their findings, members identify descriptive statements that capture what the student does successfully, discerning what, when, where, and how. They note difficulties and patterns of errors and sort them in terms of the contexts and conditions under which they occur. They pinpoint particular skills and strategies the student knows, uses, or confuses as he or she works in the area(s) of concern. They isolate how student sense of purpose and self make a difference on his or her performance. They revisit possible ways to account for challenges and accomplishments and generate preliminary ideas for interventions/accommodations.

In preparation for the meeting, members develop and use their own organization systems to help them report their data. They may list summative statements to share or key questions to pose, highlight reports or analyze charts, color-code sticky notes on work samples to indicate error patterns, and/or draw diagrams to illustrate relationships among expectations, performance, evaluation standards, and situational factors. Regardless of the organizational strategy adopted, using the dimensions of the Interaction Formula as applied in stage III, helps team members prepare to combine information. Getting ready to convey findings succinctly and access supporting evidence readily helps assert and substantiate statements, interpretations, and reasoning. When members come together prepared, they are more fluent while sharing information and participating in collaborative discussions. This results in creating cohesive descriptions of the learner and developing collective hypotheses and conclusions that lead to corresponding academic/behavioral program decisions.

Just as preparation for the meeting sets the stage for cooperative and substantive discussion, the way the meeting is framed also influences team member interactions and how assessments are shared and integrated. Introductions, statements of purpose, and roles each member takes clarifies what is involved and how voices are heard. This is particularly important for the student, when appropriate, his or her parents/caregivers, and the classroom teacher less familiar with the process (Martin, VanDycke, & Christenson, 2006). As part of the formalities take place (welcome, introduction, roles), it is critical to establish the intent of the first part of the meeting, to integrate assessment data into a coherent description by posing the following questions:

- What is our understanding of the student as a learner and the struggles he or she faces?
- What have we learned about the student as a reader, writer, mathematician, participant in the learning environment, and/or member of the classroom community?

Beginning with these open-ended questions, members refer to their documented evidence to connect what they learned about student effectiveness and challenges in the area(s) of concern. The team develops a core set of statements, encapsulating what the student says, does, and produces with attempts to focus on one area of concern at a time. Team members share concrete and objective descriptions of student overall performance, when he or she is successful and challenged, using observable language with reference to authentic tasks and activities, curriculum standards and/or behavioral expectations, and instructional/social materials and settings (see Checklists to Guide Descriptions Toolbox at the end of the chapter).

The more closely the documentation of performance relates to general education demands, the more likely the data fit together to yield a usable, instructionally relevant picture of the student. The Interaction Formula elements listed here facilitate an in-depth, organized, and productive collaborative discussion. These considerations help team members to elaborate on core statements; ensure parent/caregiver, teacher, and student (when present at meeting) contributions; and cross-reference data by answering, "What additional information adds to our understanding of the student?" Team members compare, contrast, and blend their assessment results to profile the student by articulating:

- Skill repertoires per clusters, levels, and gaps (what to teach)
- Responsiveness to task formats, materials, and activities (how to teach)
- Strategies for thinking through tasks, finding answers, solving problems, and self-monitoring (how to approach)
- Interactions in relation to the demands of instructional/social setting and physical environments (under what conditions)
- Engagement and investment in learning and participation(why teach)

Whereas the elaborated core statements give direction for how to teach, how to approach, and under what conditions, the details regarding student use of skill clusters provide direction regarding what to teach. Identified skills per cluster pinpoint baselines of what the student does/knows and discerns the gaps in his or her skill repertoires. Each is defined with a sense of precision by identifying and naming which particular skills the student uses in a variety of situations. As the team continues the discussion about how the student functions academically and socially, the focus is directed toward:

- What specific skills and behaviors does the student have relative to each skill cluster in the area(s) of concern?
- What are the conditions under which he or she uses the skills and/or exhibits the behaviors?

The cross-referenced data present the basis for writing student profile/ learning style, impact of disability, and present levels of performance/student entry levels sections on IEP forms, addressed in Stage V. With the collated information, the team now summarizes: "What are the predominant obstacles the student experiences?" In the next step, the team draws from the definitions of concerns and supporting evidence to articulate error patterns and formulate data-based hypotheses to account for what contributes to student challenges and successes.

Step 2: Summarize, Draw Conclusions, and Hypothesize

Once the team has a description of what the student says, does, produces, and what the struggles look and sound like, the focus shifts to generating hypotheses as the basis for individualized education planning. Hypotheses represent making connections among patterns of error to unravel the factors that account for student challenges. Members use their common understanding of student status (profile and present levels of performance statements), agree to what contributes to his or her struggles, and designate areas that warrant attention. They work together to respond to these questions:

- How do we use the data to offer possible explanations about identified challenges noted in the area(s) of concern? How do we account for typical patterns of errors/misbehaviors?
- How do we take into account student competencies/strengths to understand the area(s) of concern?

To answer these questions, team members pull back to analyze what the data are saying about when and under what conditions the student succeeds or struggles, his or her difficulties meeting grade-level standards, the types of tasks that prompt or deter performance, the levels of materials that are suitable or undermine effectiveness, the qualities of physical and instructional environments that support or dissuade participation, and consequences or feedback that encourage or discourage involvement. The team considers the following:

What to Teach (skill clusters)

- What skill competencies does the student demonstrate? How do skill repertoires indicate where to begin instruction?
- In what way do skill gaps or challenges account for difficulties, quality of overall performance or product, and error patterns?
- What challenges does he or she demonstrate with reference to grade-level expectations?

How to Teach (formats for performance):

- With which types of tasks, activities, assignments, and materials does the student demonstrate competence?
- With which types of tasks, activities, assignments, and materials does the student show evidence of challenge?

How to Approach (strategic thinking):

- How does the student's use, misuse, or nonuse of thinking strategies and problem solving affect execution of tasks, performance, and/or self-monitoring?
- How does student attention to pre-during-post strategies affect performance and/or product?

Under What Conditions (context for participation):

- How does the student respond to different instructional arrangements?
- In what contexts does the student engage, perform effectively, and produce work?
- In what contexts does the student experience challenges that impact the quality of performance and product?
- What does student participation and/or behavior say about the structures of the classroom or the qualities of learning situations?

Why Teach (investment):

- What does the student do or say to convey a sense of purpose and self with regard to the area(s) of concern?
- How does the student handle challenges or frustrations as he or she works on the different tasks?
- How does misbehavior and errors reflect student understanding of the purpose of expectations, tasks, assignments, situations? What is the function of the misbehavior or errors? What does the student want to gain/access or avoid/escape?

Transforming the hypotheses into statements of prioritized needs is the first step to bridge student description to individualized education planning. To establish areas of need and make the transition to planning, team members answer these questions:

- What do hypotheses indicate about student needs in relation to the focuses for academic and social program planning?
- What would we like to see the student doing that he or she is not doing now?
- What does the student need to enhance performance, participation, progress with reference to the area(s) of concern? What would help this student to be more effective in the area(s) of concern?
- What do the parents/caregivers want addressed in the plans to enhance the student's educational experiences?

Preliminary Eligibility Decisions

When the whole team concurs with the description of student strengths and needs, feels that key points are included, is comfortable with how challenges are accounted for, and defines priorities to address, the meeting shifts focus to first determining eligibility and then outlining the education plan. Team members agree to reach an initial decision about eligibility as required by IDEA 2004. They weigh how student challenges impact how he or she functions in school as a reader, writer, mathematician, and/or participant/member in the learning community. They wrestle with whether identified instructional needs and priorities may be addressed informally, require modifications to general education curriculum and classroom, or demand specially designed instruction (Fuchs, Fuchs, & Speece, 2002; Fuchs et al., 2003; Marston et al., 2003; Reschly et al., 2003; Vaughn et al., 2003).

The general education teacher(s) is an important voice in explaining grade-level standards, instructional materials and experiences, and academic and behavior expectations of which the student is to be a part. It is this input, along with student profile and present levels of performance, that help the team justify how to access the general education curriculum with modifications and/or create specially designed instruction and services to support student performance, participation, and progress in the area(s) of concern. Regardless of the determination, a plan should be designed to support the student and his or her teacher(s) in the least restrictive educational setting. The plan may be formal according to IDEA criteria, or informal, similar to prereferral intervention plans (Menlove, Hudson, & Suter, 2001; Weishaar, 1997).

Step 3: Develop Content of the Individualized Education Program

Whereas the first part of the meeting defines the student as a learner, the second part focuses on articulating individualized plans and corresponding program needs before placement decisions are made (Katsiyannis, Yell, & Bradley, 2001). The team focuses on the essential questions:

- What academic/social skills per cluster are priorities for instruction?
- What instructional approaches and materials, problem-solving strategies, learning experiences, and environments will promote student competence, participation, and progress?

Members commit to designing a differentiated program that centers on what will enhance student competence and learning experiences. The program is built on the student's current status to identify targets for instruction, coordinate suitable methods and materials, match optimal environments, and incorporate interests and sense of purpose. The team approaches this segment of the meeting systematically to:

- Design individualized curriculum, identifying priorities and sequences for instruction and strategies to document and monitor progress
- Plan instruction, determining modifications and supplemental aids to provide access to general education, teaching approaches and materials suited for specially designed explicit instruction, and adjustments to performance assessments to accommodate the student
- Identify program components, figuring out the most effective environments and service delivery to support the student and teacher

The intent of this part of the meeting is for the team to construct a proposed education plan and program tailored to serve the student (Eber, 2003). The planning consists of brainstorming what constitutes individualizing instruction in the area(s) of concern and designing what delivery of that instruction looks like. Team members work together (Friend & Cooke, 2000; Walther-Thomas, Korinek, McLauglin, & Toler Williams, 2000) to establish clear focuses for instruction that prioritize what the student needs, consult the general education curriculum as a point of reference, determine the progression of skills that will optimize student progress, create guidelines for teaching approaches and materials, identify characteristics of environments or conditions for learning, and examine instructional situations that specifically match or are modifiable to serve the student (Tracy & Maroney, 2000; Weishaar & Konya, 2001). The team is involved in thinking through what gets included in the written document as components of the educational plan, consisting of goals, objectives, instructional experiences, learning environments, performance assessments and monitoring strategies, and service delivery plans.

Involvement in this part of the meeting is a matter of drawing from the team's development of student profile and present levels of educational performance to determine systematically what constitutes a corresponding individualized education program and what defines and documents evidence of progress (Weishaar & Konya, 2001). It is important for members to set expectations for a substantive plan that reflect student and parent/caregiver dreams and concerns, be creative to envision the types of learning experiences that support growth, and be open to the ideas of others (Forest & Pearpoint, 1992).

Design Individualized Curriculum

Designing individualized curriculum involves establishing priorities and sequence for *what to teach* the student in the area(s) of concern. The team refers to the description of the student, drawing from present levels of performance, hypotheses, and needs as points of reference to figure out instructional outcomes. They ask:

- What skills per and across clusters do we want the student to attain, use, and apply?
- What do we want the student to do as a result of instruction that will increase effectiveness in the area(s) of concern?

These questions ask the team to examine entry-level skills per cluster to project where the student will be within a year's time. (Presently, some states are experimenting with three-year IEPs, projecting student growth further into the future.) As they examine what he or she needs to learn to become effective in the area(s) of concern, they generate a list of targeted areas for instruction that defines relevant skill clusters as pertinent outcomes for the student and focuses for instruction. The team compares student curricular priorities with state standards/school frameworks to decide whether they align with the general education content and achievement standards (NCLB) or fall outside, requiring alternative curriculum. The ideas brainstormed are the basis for writing IEP goals.

Once the team establishes direction for writing the goals, they turn their attention to defining the progression of intermediate steps that move from entry-level skills to the desired outcomes. These steps are described in terms of skills the student will acquire along the way to achieve the goals and how he or she demonstrates those gains. As the team outlines what they want the student to achieve, they use observable, meaningful, and measurable terms. Discussion is thus extended to identify tasks, activities, situations, and conditions under which the student is expected to perform. They also identify criteria/standards as markers to set the *bar* for evaluating and monitoring student accomplishments that are documented through authentic assessment tasks. The ideas recommended are the source for writing objectives and monitoring strategies on the IEP. (At this time, some states are piloting IEPs that do not include objectives.)

The following questions help the team conceptualize and outline the goals, objectives, and monitoring strategies. Members draw on the student's present levels of performance. See the Checklists to Guide Descriptions Toolbox at the end of this chapter and/or listings of scope and sequences or state and district curriculum frameworks as resources to figure out *what* to teach to promote student effectiveness as a reader, writer, mathematician, and participant in the learning environment/member of the classroom community.

Brainstorm the focuses for goals:
- Where is instruction for this student headed? What are the next "giant steps" per skill cluster (Bateman & Linden, 1998) in the area(s) of concern the student will work to achieve?
- How do proposed instructional outcomes fit with general education and/or require alternative curriculum?

Add detail by framing objectives:
- Given each skill cluster that warrants attention in the area(s) of concern, what set(s) of specific skills is targeted for instruction? What is the order of skills/"baby steps" per cluster that will advance student progress?
- What skills within and across clusters make sense to be taught concurrently?

Identify the criteria for monitoring progress and performance:
- What standards/markers will be used as indicators of student understanding and mastery of skills?
- What types of assignments/instructional activities/conditions will yield evidence of meeting objectives and evaluating student performance in the area(s) of concern?

Plan Instruction

Instructional planning involves the team in figuring out whether and how to access general education experiences and/or adopt specially designed instruction to address proposed goals in the area(s) of concern (Giangreco, Dennis, Edelman, & Cloninger, 1994; King-Sears, 1997; Switlick, 1997). The intention is to connect the *what to teach* with the *how to teach, how to approach, under what conditions,* and *why teach* to ensure that instruction is differentiated and matches student profile and needs. Team members generate ideas around activities, materials, and learning experiences that address the set of proposed goals and objectives, which constitute direct and explicit instruction to develop student competence in the area(s) of concern and participation in the least restrictive learning environment. Members identify activities and materials to teach skills that enhance proficiency and confidence in the area(s) of concern.

Planning instruction involves plotting out approaches, materials, methods, thinking strategies, environments, and purposes that relate directly to the identified skill clusters. To make the determinations, the team addresses the following questions:

- How do proposed *what to teach* goals and objectives for the student correspond with existing, modified, and/or alternative grade-level curriculum standards? What skill focuses for instruction can be addressed through access to the general education curriculum and/or warrant specially designed content?
- What *how to teach* formats for instruction (introduce, practice, and show mastery) and *how to approach* strategies (pre, during, and post) will guide the design of learning experiences? What levels of materials, types of lessons, assignments, activities, and problem solving will be used to promote student growth in the area(s) of concern?
- How and *under what conditions* will the physical and instructional environment be arranged to promote student engagement? How will the pace, length of lessons, structure of tasks and activities, use of groupings, and use of physical space be designed to involve the student in planned instruction?
- In what ways does *why teach* recognize the intent of instruction, student achievement, and engagement in the area(s) of concern? What types of feedback, incentives, and interests will be used to encourage the student's sense of purpose and self?

Efforts are made to consider how goals and objectives may be addressed in the context of general education with or without alternative focuses, approaches, materials, and experiences. The team's primary emphasis is on working with the general education curriculum. Members figure out whether and/or how existing teaching and learning content and experiences allow the student to gain from classroom instruction and achieve desired outcomes. When the defined goals and objectives require adjustments to the general education curriculum, the necessary in-class modifications are outlined. When such adjustments do not meet student needs, the team discusses what alternative curriculum, methods, materials, strategies, and/or learning environments are warranted. They concentrate on establishing a match between how the student learns and what specific activities and resources individualize and balance instruction to address needs.

The team also explores how to support student participation and learning across content areas in a variety of general education settings. They address ways to adjust existing behavior expectations and curriculum standards, assignments, and instructional activities, materials, and settings. The intent of these modifications is to ensure benefits of inclusive experiences for the student by determining appropriate demands of subject matter, ways to participate in instruction, and genuine involvement with peers (Schumm, Vaughn, & Leavell, 1994). The team asks, given the needs of the student,

- When does it make sense to use grade-level materials/methods/ approaches to address the goals and objectives directly?
- How much direct instruction of the skills targeted by the goals and objectives can be addressed in the classroom through the general education curriculum with adjustments to materials, assignments, criteria for evaluation, or delivery?
- When does it make sense to replace grade-level materials/methods/ approaches with alternatives or specially designed instruction? Why? What comprises the alternatives?
- What types of modifications will give the student access to learning experiences across the general education content areas? What types of adjustments allow the student to use the same materials and facilitate interactions with peers? When is the use of comparable materials at different levels and shifts in expectations warranted? What are these?
- What considerations for adapting the learning environment, instructional, and physical settings will foster active student involvement during instruction?

Determine Eligibility

Team members make the decisions about student eligibility required by IDEA 2004 by weighing the impact of presenting challenges on how the student functions in school as a reader, writer, mathematician, and/or participant/member in the learning community. They examine how difficulties persist and significantly affect performance, participation, and progress in general education to justify the need for specially designed instruction and services. Making the eligibility determination therefore requires objective evaluation of assessment data and the resulting proposals for academic and social outcomes, accessibility to general education curriculum and learning experiences, and options for alternative direct instruction in the area(s) of concern. Cast in this light, eligibility reflects student status and required programming to address identified needs rather than relying on broad federal or state disability categories and definitions (Fuchs et al., 2002; Fuchs et al., 2003; Marston et al., 2003; Reschly et al., 2003; Vaughn et al., 2003).

Participate in Performance Assessments

The alignment of IDEA 2004 with NCLB requires student participation in statewide assessments and achievement tests with or without modifications or alternative testing. The purpose is to measure school and student achievement levels with reference to state content standards and district curriculum frameworks (Stetson, Jewett, & Mitchell, 2000; Turnbull, 2005). Students found eligible for special education participate in modified or alternative state and district testing when stipulated and justified in the IEP. As team members develop recommendations for performance assessments in and out of the general education classroom, they stipulate how the student will participate in various instructional testing situations, what adjustments are required, and/or what will be appropriate alternative demonstrations of growth. Based on the proposed recommendations, student involvement in state and district testing requires adjusting test content to align with state curriculum or with alternative standards. Adaptations of test formats to reflect student needs may include varying answer forms, time adjustments, locations for testing, time of day considerations, reading test items to the student, alternative tests or portfolios, and so on. (Edgemon, Jablonski, & Lloyd, 2006). The team considers these questions:

- What are the alternative expectations for student participation in classroom assessments, and how are the modifications described in the IEP?
- What frustrations and/or challenges are placed on the student as a result of participation in statewide testing (e.g., handle the area(s) of instruction addressed through the instrument—levels of materials, formats of tasks and response requirements, testing situations—place, timed tasks, number of items per section and number of different sections given in a period, etc.)?
- What types of adjustments are needed for test administration and task completion, taking into account skills/concepts/levels evaluated and formats used to give the student an opportunity to demonstrate competence?

Engage in Transition Planning

For the student identified in need of special education who is sixteen years old or older (some schools work with students earlier), the team creates a transition plan to support him or her systematically in improving academic and functional achievement. This involves establishing goals, examining postsecondary options, making course selections, and/or accessing vocational opportunities relevant to stated aspirations, strengths, and needs. Transition plans are designed to help the student develop independence, targeting self-awareness, goal setting, self-determination and advocacy, and self-monitoring skills. In addition, the plan supports the student gaining comfort with available community services and agencies, learning ways to work with others in jobs and higher education settings (Mandalwitz, 2006). To approach transition planning in this way requires additional assessments that leads to making action plans (MAPs) (Forest & Pearpoint, 1992). This consists of engaging the student and families in interviews, observations, site visits, vocational inventories, and more.

Identify Program Components

Identifying program components involves the team in configuring where, who, and when the individualized plans (goals, objectives, monitoring techniques, teaching approaches, suggested modifications to general education curriculum, and alternative instruction) are delivered. The team determines what delivery options look like, identifying which IEP outcomes will be addressed where and for what duration of time, who will design and implement instruction, and what additional services the student will receive (Bateman, 1994; Yell, Katsiyannis, Drasgow, & Herbst, 2003). Once the program is established, they develop a corresponding matrix to schedule service delivery. To guide the discussion, team members consider:

- What are optimal instructional settings that support student learning needs and progress?
- Where will proposed learning experiences take place?
- Who will assume responsibilities for case management and design and implementation of the plan and program?

Note Taking

Throughout the meeting, note taking serves the team as a written record of discussions, assessment data shared, points made, ideas brainstormed, and plans defined. Making notes public and organized supports the flow of the meeting, keeps the focus on the agenda, ensures that voices are heard, and captures team data and ideas. Visible notes promote collaboration by serving to affirm messages are understood, avert repetition, and minimize off-task discussion (Doyle & Straus, 1976; Kroeger et al., 1999). With notes in view, members can consider what is said, ask clarification questions, offer relevant views, address contradictions, and connect related perspectives together.

The notes help the team gather and collate information and summarize input at key points of the meeting. Notes are intended to give the team clarity and produce a constructive integrated summative description of the learner. During the sharing of assessment data, the note taker helps ensure the cross-referencing process by recording core statements, placing complementary evidence, assertions, or views nearby and arranging pertinent Interaction Formula evidence to add clarity to the description of the student. Displaying the notes and information helps the team reach a common understanding of student status, agree to what factors contribute to his or her struggles, and designate areas that warrant attention. Once members feel key points have been discussed and assessment data are presented, the note taker or another person volunteers to summarize the synthesis of data and description of the student.

Summarizing the discussion and notes at this point in the meeting allows for bridging to instructional planning. When recorded notes that describe the learner remain in view throughout the meeting, it is more likely the information will be used to generate constructive ideas to address learner needs and constitute a comprehensive instructional program. When the team brainstorms curricular priorities, instructional strategies, modifications, and interventions, the displayed notes stimulate idea building around what to do with the student.

Notes provide the basis for writing the IEP document, drawing on the ideas generated and agreements reached during the collaboration. They give IEP authors tangible information, so they may put pen to paper or fingers to keyboard. Graphic organizers may help capture relevant information collected during the meeting that is then used to write the IEP document.

Agenda for IEP Development

The process of integrating assessment data is captured during the first half of the agenda. During the first part of the meeting, the team pulls together the description of the learner. The focus is on building a common in-depth understanding of the "concern(s)." As they follow the Agenda for IEP Development in Figure 5.1, it is important to continue to cultivate working relationships as well as attend to the content of the meeting (Friend & Cook, 2000; Johnson & Johnson, 2000). Working together to blend information meaningfully requires participants to be actively involved, listen constructively, and use language that all members understand. In the second part of the meeting, the focus is on individualized curriculum development, instructional planning, and decisions around the program proposal.

Time (minutes)	Topic	Who	Process	Expected Outcome
	Agenda Part I: Integrate Assessment Data			

10	Welcome
	• Introductions of team members
	  • Roles and responsibilities—overview of team members' tasks
	  • Review—Who are you in relation to the student?
	• Agenda overview—structure of meeting
	• Procedure for integrating data
	• Expected outcomes
		Facilitator
		
		Team
			• Agenda handout
			• Whip share (rapid, successive brainstorming)
				• To clarify intent of meeting
				• To continue team building
				• To explain the importance of integrating assessment information as the basis for decision making

15	1) Summarize referral concern
	2) Review the description of the KWH meeting
	3) Build a common database:
	  • What is our understanding of the student? What have we learned about the student with regard to the area(s) of concern?
	  • Profile—competencies: Start with describing student strengths. What evidence of effectiveness of student performance is there in the area(s) of concern?
	  • Profile—challenges: Describe student struggles. What evidence of challenges is documented?
		Person with referral
		Notetaker/ Facilitator
		Team
			Review
			
			Jigsaw share (complementary responses to an agenda item)
				• To create an in-depth description of the learner
				• To share information with concrete examples

10	4) Generate hypotheses: • Given the data, what might you conclude about student challenges as a reader . . .?	Facilitator Full team	Quick-write and then brainstorm	• To directly address the qualities of challenges and ways evidence addresses them

(continued)

FIGURE 5.1 Agenda for IEP Development

10	• How do errors, misbehaviors, and patterns help account for those challenges?
	5) Present levels of performance:
	  • What do we know about student use of skills per cluster?
	  • How are skills used and applied in isolation and context?
		Facilitator
		Team
			Jigsaw
			share
				• To pinpoint where to begin instruction
				• To share information about skills per cluster with concrete examples

15	6) Summarize findings:
	  • Describe the student to include challenges and successes with regard to area(s) of concern.
	  • Check for agreement.
	  • How well have we addressed referral concerns?
	7) Reexamine hypotheses and state needs.
	  • How do the skill details substantiate or refute our initial conclusions?
	  • Given our conclusions, what does this student need to support his or her growth in the area of concern?
		Recorder
		Team
			Present
			Q and A for
			revisions
				• To ensure the group sees student description as complete
				• To draw conclusions regarding what is contributing to student challenges
				• To ensure agreement about what areas to address

	Agenda Part II: Program Development			

15	8) Initial eligibility decisions—shift focus to planning:
	Given identified student needs . . . .
	  • How well can they be met in general education?
	  • Is specially designed instruction warranted?
	  • In what ways will specific planning justify eligibility?
		Team	Whip share	• To make a preliminary decision regarding eligibility
				• To generate a draft of ideas for goals and objectives in the area of concern
				• To identify ideas for documenting performance and progress

FIGURE 5.1 *Continued*

9) Design curriculum—given the current status of the student in the area of concern:
   • What are our dreams and hopes for her or him as a reader . . .?
   • What do we want the student to learn in the area(s) of concern?
   • What learning sequence makes sense from entry level to goals?
   • What criteria will determine progress?
   • What evidence will be used to document and monitor progress?
	Team
	
	Classroom Teacher, Parent/ Caregiver/ Student
		Brainstorm
		Q and A	

25	10) Plan instruction—determine learning experiences through access to general education and/or specially designed instruction.
	  a) Access to General Education:
	   • How are skill needs consistent with what is taught in the general education curriculum?
	   • What types of adjustments to the curriculum, instructional approaches, tasks, and/or materials will directly address stated goals and objectives?
	   • How do discrepancies between student's status and general education curriculum impact participation in testing?
	   • What are the potential benefits for this student participating in general education?
	   • What adjustments are necessary to facilitate that participation?
		Facilitator
		Team
		Recorder
			Quick-write
			Brainstorm
			Present
			Review
				• To generate a list of ideas for modifications of instructional approaches, tasks, and materials that address the identified area(s) of concern in general education
				• To design a plan and teaching strategies for explicit instruction in and out of general education curriculum
				• To articulate modified testing procedures and how they apply to district and statewide testing

FIGURE 5.1 *Continued*

	b) Specially designed instruction: • How do skill needs warrant development of alternative curriculum and instruction? • What are the potential drawbacks for this student participating in general education? • What explicit instruction and alternative learning experiences will promote progress? • What alternative testing does the student need? • What transition plans are needed and when?			
10	11) Propose program components—decide how the student's program pieces together. • How is determination of eligibility confirmed or rejected based on proposed learning experiences? • What are optimal experiences for delivering instruction? • What services does the student require, and where will they take place? • How will services be coordinated to provide the student with a cohesive program?	Facilitator Full team	Quick-write Whip share	• To reach conclusions about eligibility determination • To establish a matrix of learning experiences that identifies who, when, and how • To distribute responsibilities for planning, delivering, and monitoring instruction • To clarify who does what when
5	Review decisions made: • Recap the meeting. • Revise, if necessary. • Set timeline for consideration of formal document.	Facilitator Full team	Whip share	• To schedule follow-up

FIGURE 5.1 *Continued*

Chapter Review: Focus and Decisions

Stage IV: Engage in the IEP Meeting

❏ Enter the educational planning meeting prepared, having conducted and analyzed assigned assessments. Share perspectives based on information gathered to develop a picture of the student that includes factors contributing to or interfering with participation and progress.

- What have we learned to enhance our understanding of the student in the area(s) of concern? How does the information each of us gathered add to our understanding of student status and the challenges he or she faces?

❏ Participate in the discussion to summarize understanding who the learner is with regard to the area(s) of concern.

- How does the information fit together to create a comprehensive picture? How informative is the profile description and articulation of the present levels of performance?

❏ Determine whether there is sufficient descriptive data to develop a comprehensive picture of the student, understand the challenges he or she experiences, target instructional and/or behavioral needs, and determine eligibility.

❏ Agree on the focuses for instruction; select instructional sequences and approaches to accommodate the student and promote success.

- How does the information help us pinpoint starting points for instruction, approaches and formats for learning experiences, and design of learning environments to support student growth and development in the area(s) of concern?

❏ Brainstorm ways to address learner needs with explicit instruction (access the general education curriculum and/or specially designed instruction services), instructional approaches, modifications, interventions, and learning environments to promote participation and progress.

❏ Choose the ways in which instructional experiences will be delivered and progress monitored.

❏ Verify whether assessment data and corresponding educational plans address initial referral concerns and propose ways to optimize learning experiences.

❏ Discuss and decide where, when, who, how services will be most effectively accomplished, using access to general education curriculum as the ideal circumstance.

- Given student needs and proposed instructional plans, what are effective approach(es) for delivering the qualities of instruction identified? How will modifications, adaptations, or other uses of the general education be made to maximize meaningful student involvement? Who will be responsible for what?

❑ Discuss the ways in which student progress will be documented and how that information will be used to maintain or revise course of action.

- What kinds of ongoing assessment data/documentation will be collected to help make the determination whether approaches to instruction, uses of modifications, and types of service delivery are effective in promoting student progress, participation, and self-concept? What are the criteria for making judgments about student progress and program effectiveness?

❑ Plan informally to bring the team of implementers together to decide the details for implementation of the IEP.

- How will implementers work together to make the IEP a reality?

Stage IV: Apply and Learn

1. In a reflection paper, discuss your understanding of the purpose of Stage IV: Engage in the IEP Meeting. Think about how the IEP meeting promotes collaborative efforts and includes parents/caregivers and classroom teachers in the process. Consider how a formal agenda supports attention to the steps. Include justifications and examples of what it means to:
   - Step 1: Build a composite picture of the learner collaboratively
   - Step 2: Summarize, draw conclusions, and hypothesize
   - Step 3: Develop content of the IEP

2. How do you ensure the involvement of the classroom teacher and parents/caregivers in sharing assessment data and developing the IEP? What steps can be taken to ensure their participation and understanding of what transpires?

3. One of the issues of IEP meetings is the tendency for the team to read their reports in a round-robin fashion. Use your understanding of stage IV to write a proposal to convince members of your team to share assessment findings and develop the IEP in a more collaborative way.

Checklist to Guide Description of Student: Reader

What to Teach/Skill Clusters

Being a strategic reader depends on student mastery of skills so he or she has access when in challenging situations. Distinguish evidence of awareness, mastery, or difficulty with specific skills. Determine whether the student does or does not use the skill when it is presented in *isolation* versus in *context* of a reading passage.

Fluency

_____ Reads fluently
   _____ reads text haltingly, at a conversation pace, or using rapid speech
   _____ clusters words by phrases consistent with that of talk
   _____ moves through text at a rate of _____ words per minute
   _____ reads _____ level book or _____ type book with fluency
   _____ reads word by word when _____ level book or _____ type book

_____ Reads with expression
   _____ reads in an animated or monotone voice
   _____ observes punctuation by pausing at commas and ends of sentences
   _____ modulates voice in response to punctuation
   _____ intonations are in accord with syntactical patterns and meaning
   _____ changes volume, tone, and modulation of voice to convey mood
   _____ changes voice tone, volume, or intonation to represent characters
   _____ shifts between narrative and dialogue
   _____ responds to the story with facial expressions and gestures
   _____ seems to have an internal dialogue about the story and can forecast what is about to happen
   _____ seems to be aware of role of different characters
   _____ seems to extract the mood and tone of the story

Word Recognition

_____ Applies sight vocabulary
   _____ recognizes sight words (phonetically irregular words)
   _____ uses small word to determine unfamiliar word
   _____ confuses word with one that looks similar in shape, sequence of most letters

Word Solving

_____ Applies phonics skills in isolation
   _____ applies phonics rules to decode one-, two-, multisyllabic words (mastery of phonics rules: e.g., CVC, CVCe, CVVC, CCVC, CCVC, CVCle, CVrC)
      _____ analyzes written words into component letters or letter clusters; associates with sounds and blends to make a word
      _____ blends sounds of letters to make a word

_____ uses rhyming or word families to figure unknown word
_____ uses rules of syllabication to determine vowel sounds
_____ reads prefixes and suffixes and applies to root words

_____ **Applies context cues**
_____ refers to the picture when comes to unfamiliar word and guesses word that makes sense in the sentence
_____ refers to the picture when comes to unfamiliar word; inserts one that connects to story line but not necessarily the sentence
_____ uses words/ phrases/ sentences surrounding unfamiliar word to determine what makes sense
_____ uses meaning to fill in unknown word (blank in cloze)
_____ uses part of speech to fill in unknown word (blank in cloze)
_____ reads suffixes to indicate plural and tense consistent with text
_____ uses a combination of context and first letter to "guess" word
_____ rereads sentence to insert word or self-correct when word does not make sense
_____ predicts oncoming words or phrases, sometimes getting ahead of self
_____ returns to the beginning of the sentence for further attempt when stumped
_____ pauses if and when word read is not consistent with expected meaning

_____ **Commits miscues/errors as reads aloud (offer examples) important to:**
• evaluate whether patterns exist when skills are in isolation or context *and* with what level of materials
• examine how miscues reflect student language skills and style
• determine the ways in which miscues impact understanding of text
_____ mispronounces words as reads, relying on phonetic applications
_____ mispronounces same or similar words and sounds when speaking
_____ omits small words as reads (infinitives, prepositions, articles) that are usually minor alterations to text
_____ omits unfamiliar words
_____ inserts words into text
_____ substitutes words that are graphically similar (look similarly)
_____ substitutes words that are semantically similar (have similar meaning)
_____ substitutes words that are syntactically correct (hold similar grammatical purpose in sentence)
_____ substitutes words that are unrelated to the story or text appearance
_____ repeats words and phrases as reads-aloud
_____ rereads words and settles on mispronounced word
_____ rereads words and self-corrects
_____ rereads segments or sentences before proceeding further

_____ starts to decode word and gives up
_____ transposes letter order in word
_____ inverts word order in sentence or phrase

Comprehension

_____ **Understands what reads/ attributes meaning to pictures and/or stories** (indicate how remains constant or changes when student reads aloud, reads silently, or is read to)
_____ retells the story unaided
_____ retells story or expository piece with a sense of coherence
  _____ summarizes key events or information by stating gist of story or general topic
  _____ relates main ideas to supporting details
  _____ recalls facts as appeared in text and connects to what happened
  _____ identifies events presented in sequential order
  _____ represents story in terms of beginning, middle, and ending
  _____ conveys a sense of story structure, connecting problem to solution
  _____ identifies main characters (by name, refers to by pronoun)
  _____ describes qualities of characters (physical appearance, attitudes, feelings, behaviors, relationship to other characters, personality, morals)
  _____ identifies supporting characters (by name, role, relationship to main character)
  _____ identifies setting (time, place) and impact on the action and mood of the story
  _____ identifies problem (refers to main character's goal or challenge), theme supporting details
  _____ identifies solution (refers to main character's achievement)
_____ responds to questions to convey understanding of what read
  _____ answers *who?* questions, telling the characters of the story
  _____ answers *when?* questions to indicate setting information and support how time of day, use of temporal descriptions serve as foreshadowing, cues of sequence
  _____ answers *where?* questions to indicate setting information and support how place sets the mood, serves as context for events
  _____ answers *what?* questions, telling key events, sequence, beginning-middle-end of the story
  _____ completes web or set of questions to represent story elements, demonstrating understanding of each
  _____ uses web or set of questions to retell story, indicating an understanding of the function of story elements in a story
_____ **Uses strategies to help understand what is happening**
  _____ locates responses to specific questions in text
  _____ rereads text to remember key information

_____ paraphrases sections as reads through story

_____ distinguishes important, trivial, redundant information

_____ generates questions and reexamines reading material

_____ **Commits miscues/errors related to understanding what reads important to:**
- evaluate whether patterns exist when reading materials at different levels or when prompted by questions
- examine how miscues reflect student sense of stories
- determine how misunderstanding of text reflects word miscues

_____ **has difficulty summarizing what has read**

_____ misinterprets key messages or events (misses connections between setting and mood, dialogue and character attitude, problem and subsequent events, etc.)

_____ misses the plot of the story and provides a series of details

_____ **has difficulty drawing information from story to construct an understanding of story elements** (setting, character, problem to solution sequence)

_____ omits supporting detail critical to character description, problem identification, story outcome

_____ has difficulty recalling details that add depth of understanding of the story

_____ recalls events or details out of sequence

_____ has problem linking cause and effect and in turn has difficulty accounting for why events/situations occur in the story

_____ initial predictions do not reflect cues presented in the title, picture, or information known

_____ predictions during reading do not reflect information provided, understanding of the problem the character faces

_____ has difficulty distinguishing fact from fiction or opinion

_____ has difficulty locating information in text

_____ constructs meaning if is stopped to review content, and think about event or exchange among characters or the introduction of a symbol or twist in the story line

_____ has trouble evaluating what thinks about . . . when new information is presented

_____ analyzes what would happen if . . . , given what is presented about character, setting, events

How to Teach/Formats for Performance

Level of Materials

_____ maintains story line in spite of struggles with a number of words

_____ loses sight of story when required to read materials containing unfamiliar words

_____ understands stories with single story line, when most words familiar

_____ understands stories with tangled story lines, when most words familiar

_____ loses track of interwoven story lines, even when most words are familiar

_____ sorts out interwoven story lines, character relationships, symbolism when reads aloud, silently, or hears

Silent Reading

_____ subvocalizes while reading materials silently

_____ pace of reading is faster or slower when reads silently

_____ reads with book close to face or reads with book at arm's-length distance

_____ uses finger to keep place

_____ comprehends material read as evidenced by . . . (describe retell, response to questions)

_____ comprehension differs or is constant when reads silently as evidenced by . . .

Listening to Story (proficient reader, tape, computer reads text)

_____ follows along while other is reading, looking at text, pictures, and/or reader

_____ follows along in own copy of text, using eyes and/or finger and/or tachistiscope

_____ engages reader in conversation, asking questions, sharing own related experience, discussing events, talking about pictures, and/or making predictions

_____ moves self close to the reader and/or book

_____ comprehends material read as evidenced by . . . (describe retell, response to questions)

_____ comprehension differs or is constant when reads, listens to story as evidenced by . . .

Picture Book vs. Text Only

_____ uses pictures to prepare for reading

_____ uses pictures to corroborate what reads

_____ refers to pictures when unsure of a word in text

_____ refers to pictures when unsure of what is happening in the story

_____ refers to pictures for cues of what is about to happen

_____ rereads sentences or passages when text only

_____ asks questions as reads (note how these change when pictures or text only)

_____ comprehension differs or is constant when reads text with pictures and text-only stories as evidenced by . . .

Impact of Topic, Genre

_____ active engagement in reading differs or is constant when topic
is . . .

_____ active engagement in reading differs or is constant when genre
is . . .

_____ comprehension differs or is constant when reads topic/genre . . .

How to Approach/Strategic Thinking

Prepares to Read

_____ reads story title

_____ previews illustrations on cover

_____ scans pictures in story or chapter titles

_____ makes predictions about the content based on the title or
pictures or table of contents

_____ turns to text and begins reading without stating title or thumbing
through pictures

_____ asks self or others questions about book prior to reading

_____ states information intends to find out from reading the book

_____ makes connections with own experience, understanding of the topic

Participates in the Reading Experience (During Reading)

_____ **Follows text**

_____ sustains left to right sequence

_____ sustains line-to-line sequence down the page

_____ uses finger to maintain place

_____ reads word by word

_____ reads phrase by phrase (identify number of words per phrase),
clustering connected words together

_____ reads narrative at a pace slower than conversation and/or consistent with the mood of the description

_____ reads dialogue at a pace consistent with typical conversation

_____ pronounces words correctly

_____ **Uses one or more word-solving strategies when confronted with
unfamiliar words**

_____ accesses word recognition skills systematically

_____ relies on a single word-solving technique to figure out unknown
words

_____ attempts to decipher words using phonics

_____ attempts to decipher words using context (i.e., rereads phrase
before unfamiliar word, scans ahead to get further understanding
of meaning)

_____ pauses or rereads if and when word read not consistent with
meaning

_____ attempts to decipher words using pictures (i.e., reads phrase, stops, examines picture, possibly discusses picture and resumes reading)

_____ uses the structure of the sentence/parts of speech to determine unknown word

_____ waits for listener to prompt (e.g., What word makes sense? What sounds do the letters make?)

_____ waits for listener to supply word when stumped

_____ **Reads for meaning**

_____ makes comments or conversation about what is happening in story

_____ makes connections with own life

_____ stops to check what is going on, asks questions and/or talks through events

_____ stops reading when content "feels" like it does not make sense; asks questions and/or rereads sections to figure out own confusion

_____ looks at pictures and relates to what is reading

_____ makes predictions, demonstrating an understanding of the problem, goal of main character, relationships among characters

_____ checks predictions against what reads, evaluate information, and revises accordingly

_____ summarizes what is happening

_____ benefits from periodic questions that encourage sorting out information presented and putting the pieces together

Processes What Reads (After Reading Story or Book)

_____ retells stories and includes:

_____ main idea

_____ beginning, middle, and end

_____ sequence of events

_____ connection between problem and resolution

_____ identification of the twists in plot

_____ connection of twists in plot to process of resolving problem/conflict

_____ relationship of setting to events

_____ character sketches, examination of how impacted outcome of story

_____ web of relationships among characters

_____ impact of events on characters

_____ responds to different types of questions

_____ tells facts about the story—who, what, when, where

_____ makes connections among events, characters, cause and effect—how? in what way?

_____ evaluates what likes and doesn't like about the story or information gathered

Under What Conditions/Context for Participation

Impact of Setting

_____ keeps focused on independent reading when room is quiet or student is separated from activity

_____ reads on own when someone is readily accessible to help with challenging words or content

_____ keeps place when reading with others in a group

_____ flips through pages, loses place, looks around when reading with others in a group

_____ listens, but does not necessarily maintain place in book while others read

_____ attends to story being read aloud when . . .

_____ prefers to read while sitting on floor, at desk

_____ volunteers to read aloud in (small, large) group when . . .

Why Teach/Investment

Intent

_____ **Reads with a sense of purpose**

_____ flips through pages

_____ asks questions about the book or topic

_____ shows interest in reading

    _____ selects _____ types of books

    _____ participates in DEAR (Drop Everything and Read) or SSR (Sustained Silent Reading) sessions

    _____ gets involved in book talks

_____ sees reading as leisure activity

_____ views reading as a means of finding out information

_____ seldom reads or chooses to read unassigned books or other materials

_____ makes excuses for not reading

Confidence

_____ **Views self as a reader**

_____ says enjoys reading (what types or titles?)

_____ states purpose and values for reading

_____ expresses confidence in reading

_____ discusses challenges reading presents

_____ has strategies for dealing with the frustrations reading presents

_____ shows frustrations with reading challenges by . . .

Checklist to Guide Description of Student: Writer

What to Teach/Skill Clusters

Expression of Ideas

Develops story:

_____ includes beginning/introduction

_____ develops middle/supporting details

_____ provides ending/conclusion

_____ organizes events of a story sequentially

_____ describes characters (names, physical features, personality characteristics, relationships to others)

_____ explains the setting of the story in terms of where (location, appearance, weather) and when (time of day, era)

_____ identifies the story problem or goal

_____ incorporates twists in the plot

_____ creates relationships among characters and events

_____ describes how the problem is solved or goal is met

_____ gives story a title

Develops theme:

_____ provides an overview of the topic and key points in an introductory paragraph

_____ presents arguments, supporting detail through treatment of subtopics

_____ introduces paragraph through a topic sentence

_____ supports topic sentence in a paragraph

_____ draws conclusion to presentation of ideas

Uses different types of writing

Journals, letters: qualities of expository writing that involves self

_____ shares personal information and experiences in coherent manner, offering a sequence of events

_____ writes about personal experience as a string of events

_____ includes emotional aspects of reporting on personal experiences

Reports on researched topics, persuasive papers,

_____ asserts thesis/argument

_____ develops ideas succinctly

_____ conveys a flow and coherence

Creative pieces

_____ develops the elements (e.g., setting, characters, problem/solution) that correspond with demands of type of writing

_____ develops own twist on ideas, use of facts

_____ uses metaphors, analogies to convey a picture, thought

_____ uses different forms of writing (poems, songs, stories) to share original ideas

Checklist to Guide Descriptions Toolbox

Grammar

_____ uses tense consistently
_____ keeps subject and verb agreements
_____ uses pronouns with proper referents
_____ uses variety of sentence structures
     _____ simple sentence
     _____ compound sentence
     _____ complex sentence
     _____ statements
     _____ interrogative
     _____ exclamation
     _____ run-on sentences
     _____ incomplete sentences or fragments
_____ uses descriptive words or phrases

Conventions of Print (capitalization and punctuation)

_____ capitalizes the first word of a sentence
_____ capitalizes proper nouns (person's name, geographical location, breed of animal, etc.)
_____ uses period at the end of a sentence
_____ uses period after abbreviations or initials
_____ uses a question mark for an interrogative sentence
_____ uses an exclamation mark at the end of an exclamatory word or statement
_____ uses an apostrophe in contractions
_____ uses an apostrophe to show possession
_____ uses a comma
     _____ between the day of the month and the year
     _____ between the city and state
     _____ to separate items in a series
     _____ to separate a direct quotation
     _____ before and after an appositive or parenthetical phrase
_____ uses quotation marks to designate a direct quote

Handwriting

_____ reads own writing
_____ has difficulty discerning what puts on paper
_____ copies own handwriting accurately/inaccurately
_____ copies words from board accurately/inaccurately

Proceeds from

_____ left to right consistently
_____ confuses left to right progression

176

Checklist to Guide Descriptions Toolbox

Forms letters
_____ based on top to bottom, counterclockwise circles, and lines left to right
_____ proceeds bottom to top, clockwise for circles, and right to left
_____ writes disjointed, unconnected letters
_____ makes letters very small
_____ uses much of the space with large letters
_____ mixes uppercase and lowercase letters
_____ crowds letters close together
_____ spacing between words difficult to distinguish
_____ scatters letters across the line
_____ letters tend to be on and off the line
_____ inconsistent size
_____ irregular spacing between letters in a word and words in a sentence

Grasps Pencil . . .
_____ too far from point
_____ with a fist
_____ with thumb and forefingers and remaining resting on pencil
_____ holds pencil loosely and lettering is very light
_____ holds pencil perpendicular to paper
_____ holds pencil tightly
_____ presses down hard onto paper (often makes smudges with pencil lead, holes in the paper)
_____ moves fingers only
_____ moves arm as writes rather than wrist and arm
_____ adjusts paper as writes on paper

Positions Body for Writing
_____ leans close to the paper
_____ slants paper away from body
_____ paper at a distance for student

Spelling
_____ spells sight words accurately
_____ tends to use inventive spelling
_____ spelling closely resembles sounds contained in word
_____ spelling closely resembles what the word looks like
_____ one letter omitted
_____ letters transposed
_____ vowel substituted
_____ spelling errors consistently contain
_____ vowel substitutions
_____ consonant substitutions
_____ erroneously applied phonics rules
_____ silent or double letters omitted

How to Teach/Formats for Performance

Type of Writing

Qualities of development, coherence, and use of language vary or are consistent across

_____ personal, expository writing that includes self (e.g., journals, letters)
_____ research reports
_____ opinion pieces
_____ reader responses
_____ "creative" work

Use of Supports and Prompts

Quality of idea development, coherence, and use of language vary or are consistent across opportunities to express self

_____ freewrite
_____ write with opportunity to preplan
_____ write with requirement for using a preplanning tool
_____ write in response to a sequence of pictures
_____ write in response to own illustrations
_____ write when given a story starter
_____ write when given a topic
_____ write when given the choice of a topic
_____ write when involves personal experience
_____ dictates or tape-records story to a scribe
_____ word-processes own writing
_____ responds to suggestion to "do best can" with regard to spelling
_____ has access to peer or adult to ask "how to spell" those words with which unsure, even when suggestion to "do best can"

Quantity of what writes is impacted by

_____ assigned minimum of sentences
_____ requirement to hand-write, use printing or cursive
_____ expectation to include certain information
_____ use of preplanning tools

How to Approach/Strategic Thinking

Prepares to Write

_____ selects topic about which to write
_____ analyzes stimulus question, problem, story starter before begins to plan or write
_____ considers audience/who will read or hear paper
_____ takes into account what wants to accomplish through the paper
_____ develops own prewriting structure based on assignment
_____ uses a prewriting structure to plan out what he or she writes

_____ maps out ideas prior to drafting a story using a web, outline, illustrations, trees

_____ uses story elements or related questions to generate ideas

_____ uses illustrations to sketch out story

_____ organizes note cards or uses color coding to arrange
information researched

_____ develops story/expository piece one element at a time

_____ develops story/expository piece by taking an idea and branching
from it

Drafting (Participates in the Writing Experience)

_____ uses prewriting tool as reference to draft story/essay

_____ begins writing without preplanning, letting ideas unfold

_____ drafts story/essay as a freewrite, putting ideas on paper to be
organized later

_____ focuses on content of writing, showing little regard for spelling,
conventions of print

Brings Closure to Writing

Revision

_____ rereads own work for sequence, idea development, flow of ideas,
coherence and cohesiveness

_____ rearranges sentences to enhance organization

_____ adds detail to enhance description, fill in gaps of sequence

_____ corrects sentences for completeness, coherence

_____ checks story/expository piece for parts, order, details, clarity, and
cohesiveness

_____ adds, eliminates, rewords, rearranges to enhance the flow and
quality of product

_____ rereads work aloud to self, peer, or teacher

_____ participates in a writing conference

_____ responds to feedback offered

Editing

_____ examines words for possible misspelling

_____ reviews sentences for use of capitalization, appropriate punctuation,
tense, agreements

_____ copies or word-processes to increase legibility

Under What Conditions/Context for Participation

_____ stays focused on independent writing when room is quiet or he or
she is separated from peers/activity

_____ writes on own when task is broken into specific substeps

_____ writes on own when someone is accessible to help with being stuck
with spelling, ideas, or feedback

_____ contributes ideas to group stories, reports

_____ shares own writing with large group

_____ shares own writing with peer or teacher in a one-to-one situation

Why Teach/Investment

Interest

_____ writes with a sense of purpose

_____ takes time to think through topic, develop ideas, revise and edit word

_____ sees writing as a leisure-time activity

_____ views writing as an opportunity to create

_____ views writing as a way to organize information learning

Confidence

Views self as a writer

_____ says enjoys writing (what types?)

_____ states purposes and values of writing

_____ expresses confidence in writing

_____ discusses challenges writing presents

_____ has strategies for dealing with frustrations writing presents

_____ shows frustrations with writing challenges by . . .

Checklist to Guide Describing the Student: Mathematician

What to Teach/Skill Clusters

Computation

Counting

_____ counts by 1's to _____
_____ demonstrates use of one-to-one correspondence by counting objects and pictures accurately
_____ recognizes numerals up to _____
_____ compares sets for greater than/less than
_____ writes the numeral to represent number of items in a set
_____ orders numerals and sets in sequence
_____ counts by 2's to _____
_____ counts by 5's to _____
_____ counts by 10's to _____
_____ counts by 3's to _____
_____ groups by 10's/100's
_____ renames 10's and 1's/100's, 10's, and 1's

Addition

_____ reads equations set up vertically and horizontally using vocabulary (e.g., and, plus, add)
_____ reads equations and represents addends and process with manipulatives, on a number line, with place value board when appropriate
_____ calculates addition facts (using fingers, objects, drawing, number line, in head); sums through _____
_____ states addition facts by rote; sums through _____
_____ adds two-digit or three-digit numbers without renaming
_____ adds two-digit numbers with renaming

Subtraction

_____ reads equations set up vertically and horizontally using vocabulary (e.g., take away, minus, from)
_____ reads equations and represents minuend and subtrahend and process with manipulatives, on a number line, with place value board when appropriate
_____ calculates subtraction facts (using fingers, objects, drawing, number line, in head); minuends through _____
_____ states subtraction facts by rote; minuends through _____
_____ subtracts two-digit or three-digit numbers without regrouping
_____ subtracts two-digit numbers using regrouping

Multiplication

_____ reads equations set up vertically and horizontally using vocabulary (e.g., times, multiplied by)
_____ reads equations and represents multipliers and multiplicands and process with manipulatives, on a number line, with place value board when appropriate
_____ calculates multiplication facts (using chart, fingers, pictures, in head) with products through _____
_____ states multiplication facts by rote; products through _____
_____ multiplies two-digit numbers by a single digit or two digits without renaming
_____ multiplies two- or three-digit numbers by a single digit or two digits with renaming

Division

_____ reads equations set up in formal bracket and horizontally using vocabulary (e.g., divided by, into, how many in)
_____ reads equations and represents divisor and dividend and process with manipulatives, on a number line, with place value board when appropriate
_____ calculates division facts (using chart, fingers, objects, pictures, in head) with divisors of or quotients of _____
_____ division facts by rote; divisors through _____ or quotients through _____
_____ computes division examples involving single-digit divisors with and without remainders
_____ computes division examples involving two-digit divisors with and without remainders

Fractions/Decimals

_____ reads isolated fractions as parts of whole and represents with a pictured object or number of objects as a subset of the whole

Checklist to Guide Descriptions Toolbox

_____ reads equations involving fractions that are written horizontally and vertically and represents with manipulatives

_____ recognizes fractions/decimals as representing parts

_____ matches fractions/decimals with figure

_____ adds and subtracts fractions/decimals with like denominators or according to column

_____ reduces fractions to lowest terms

_____ finds common denominators of fractions, using common multiples

_____ adds and subtracts fractions with different denominators

Money

_____ identifies coins

_____ compares amounts of coins

_____ counts money, including bills

_____ makes change

_____ adds and subtracts using $. in the example

Measurement

_____ uses a ruler to _____ inch, centimeter

_____ calculates perimeter of an object

_____ calculates area of an object

Time

_____ recognizes where numbers belong on a clock

_____ tells time on a clock to the hour/half hour/quarter hour/five-minute intervals/one-minute intervals

_____ translates digital time to analog time

_____ calculates time differences consistent with time zones

_____ sets up schedules for tasks to be done

_____ calculates time, rate, distance problems

Problem Solving

_____ reads story problem

_____ understands implications of vocabulary (in all, less than, etc.)

_____ selects operation to represent action(s) of problem

_____ writes a number sentence that represents the word problem

_____ applies computation algorithm to solve the problem

_____ attaches correct units to answer

_____ solves single-step problem when only necessary information is provided

_____ solves single-step problems when distracting information is included

_____ solves two-, three-step problems when only necessary information is provided

_____ solves two-, three-step problems when distracting information is included

How to Teach/Formats for Performance

_____ calculates single-digit examples

 _____ by rote

 _____ when manipulatives, number line are made available

 _____ when draws out figures to represent operation

_____ calculates single-digit equations

 _____ when written vertically

 _____ when written horizontally

_____ writes equations vertically and aligns numbers

 _____ when given open space

 _____ when given graph paper

How to Approach/Strategic Thinking

Prepares

_____ reads math equations as an incomplete sentence; estimating the sum, difference, product, or quotient to figure out what makes sense

_____ reads through an entire story problem before doing any work

_____ extracts key information and questions of a story problem before performing calculations
_____ talks aloud as reads equations, sets up to proceed, and moves through calculations

During Work
_____ relies on memory for math facts
_____ counts on fingers, uses manipulatives, refers to number line, or draws marks when calculating math facts
_____ calculates equations; applying the procedures required of the operation (e.g., starting in the ones column for addition, subtraction, and multiplication; regrouping when required)
_____ arranges manipulatives according to prescribed operation to calculate sum, difference, product, or quotient
_____ talks self through the calculations
_____ responds to timed activities by . . .
_____ sets up equations for story problems as reads through it
_____ uses graph paper to align placement of numbers in vertical computation examples

Post
_____ looks at answer to computation to determine whether it is reasonable and consistent with operation or questions of the word problem
_____ checks computations by using inverse operations (e.g., subtraction for addition, addition for subtraction, division for multiplication, and multiplication for division)
_____ checks computations by using a calculator
   _____ errors tend to involve mistakes copying numbers
   _____ tends to leave insufficient space in which to work out problems
   _____ errors tend to be due to using the wrong operation
   _____ computation errors indicative of working as if had rote memory of facts, but not mastered
   _____ errors tend to be due to not knowing how to proceed (faulty algorithms)
      _____ starts two-digit addition or subtraction with the column furthest to the right
      _____ subtracts smaller number from bigger number, regardless of where located
      _____ uses wrong number when regrouping

Under What Conditions/Context for Participation

_____ stays focused on independent tasks, using pencil and paper, manipulatives, drawing materials, and so on
_____ figures out situations on own using problem solving and computation
_____ explains own thinking in journal or aloud when asked specific questions by the teacher
_____ contributes ideas to group challenges
_____ responds to timed tasks with accuracy
_____ works in cooperative groups to solve problems, taking on a role
_____ responds to large-group, small-group instruction

Why Teach/Investment

Interest
_____ calculates, problem solves, uses tools with a sense of purpose
_____ takes time to think through how math concepts relate to daily life
_____ uses math to calculate time, distance, scores, and so on
_____ views math strategies as a way to organize time, space, objects

Confidence
Views self as a mathematician
_____ states enjoys working with math concepts and problems (what types?)
_____ states purposes and values of learning concepts
_____ expresses confidence in competence as a mathematician
_____ discusses challenges mathematics presents
_____ has strategies for dealing with frustrations mathematics presents
_____ shows frustrations with mathematics challenges by . . .

Checklist to Guide Description of Student: Participant in the Learning Environment/Member of the Classroom Community

What to Teach/Skill Clusters

What does the student do, say? How does the student approach, respond, react to different situations? Under what conditions does the student . . . ? What reminders, prompts support the student?

Is Aware of Self

Is attuned to own feelings. Has vocabulary to label and represent feelings and thoughts. Expresses emotions.

_____ picks up on own cues of feelings and evaluates what is going on for self

_____ identifies and labels own feelings

_____ expresses own feelings and values

_____ deals with strong personal emotions (e.g., frustrations, anger) by:

    _____ acting out what is going on

    _____ using words

    _____ taking time for self

    _____ finding an outlet

_____ identifies topics, activities that hold interest

_____ feels comfortable with sharing views

_____ times expression of emotion in rhythm with what is going on in situation

_____ blurts out expression of emotion to relieve self

_____ listens to the views, opinions, beliefs of others

_____ acknowledges the ambiguity of how to look at the world, allowing "free to be" (not needing to convince right and wrong)

_____ connects feelings-thoughts-behaviors

_____ acknowledges own feelings and appropriate ways to deal (process, express, self-monitor) with them

_____ shares information honestly

_____ says no

_____ deals with disappointment (when hears "no" or wants something that is inaccessible)

_____ **sees self as a participant in the learning environment**

_____ **sees self as a member of the classroom community**

Takes Control of Self and Behavior

Weighs options of what to do with feelings and thoughts, and engages in responsible decision making about own behaviors

    _____ assesses situation to understand feelings (e.g., boredom, anger, hurt) and figure out ways to address (e.g, ways to keep self engaged, express feelings, get out of situation "gracefully")

    _____ stops in the midst of "spiral" of emotions and evaluates own choices

_____ gathers information about what is happening in a social situation
_____ foresees consequences of own behaviors
_____ uses techniques to assert self-control (e.g., self-talk, finding ways to calm down or move out of a situation, etc.)
_____ accepts consequences for behaviors
_____ deals with accusations, difference of opinion, correction
_____ accepts responsibility for own behaviors
_____ makes choices about what to do in a situation
_____ avoids fights
_____ figures out strategies for responding to teasing
_____ addresses own embarrassments
_____ finds ways to handle being left out
_____ generates ways for dealing with complaints, accusations
_____ sets goals for behavior in different situations

Interacts with Peers and Adults in "Community" Situations

Participates in communications/conversations/discussions. Differentiates between the demands of cooperative ventures, parallel activities, and isolated tasks.

Gets Involved

_____ uses greeting behaviors to introduce self or signify hello
_____ initiates conversation
_____ appears to listen (eye contact, head shaking)
_____ shows making an effort to understand what is said
    _____ paraphrases
    _____ stays with the topic
    _____ checks with speaker to make sure ready to "move on"
    _____ uses the topic to shift the focus
    _____ responds to questions
    _____ asks questions to help clarify understanding
_____ takes turns (waits for speaker to complete thought or wait for pause before speak)
_____ acknowledges what others say
_____ builds on what others say
_____ encourages others to contribute ideas
_____ acknowledges the contributions of others
_____ uses active and reflective listening
_____ responds to verbal and nonverbal behavior of others
_____ draws closure to conversation

Shows Awareness of Others

_____ recognizes the feelings of another
_____ shows understanding of the feelings of others

_____ takes the perspective of someone else

_____ acknowledge other points of view

_____ expresses concern, anger, affection, fear, etc., in response to . . .

_____ verbalizes feelings, thoughts, ideas at acceptable times

Cooperates

_____ makes a suggestion

_____ suggests an activity

_____ distinguishes types of positive gestures (compliments, kindness)

_____ says thank you

_____ responds with "random acts of kindness"

_____ rewards self and others for accomplishments

_____ takes on roles to contribute to completion of joint activity

_____ completes task to which commits contribute to group project

_____ shares ideas, materials, tasks to work in complementary fashion

_____ offers and receives feedback

Tolerates and Appreciates Diversity

_____ gives and receives compliments

_____ negotiates/compromises

_____ shows appreciation

_____ recognizes the contributions of others

_____ accepts difference of opinions

_____ identifies the values of others' work, contributions

_____ takes on others' perspectives to attempt to see situation, opinion differently

Reads, Initiates, Engages, and Responds to Social Situations

_____ determines how and when to ask questions

_____ differentiates appropriateness of questions

_____ figures out when to begin and end a conversation

_____ brings closure to a conversation or activity

_____ gauges the timing of situations to determine when to:

    _____ ask to join an activity

    _____ ask a favor

    _____ ask for help

    _____ offer help

    _____ express concern

_____ uses wording and timing according to the demands of the social situation

Averts and Resolves Conflict

_____ examines the impact of one's own behavior or words to discern when or if to apologize

_____ avoids confrontation/ trouble/ fights

_____ assesses situation to determine own role/ responsibility or causes of the "problem"

_____ deals with group pressure, weighing personal values and wants against demands of peers

_____ discusses events objectively and enters into problem-solving process to resolve conflict

_____ listens to peer to hear views on situation

_____ brainstorms a mutually agreed-on approach to dealing with difficult situation with peer

_____ problem-solves situations when there are limited resources, finding ways to share

_____ problem-solves situations when peers see situations differently, identifying different viewpoints that get confusing

Works Within the Structures of the Classroom

_____ follows written or oral directions

_____ questions directions when they do not make sense

_____ stays with assigned task through to completion

_____ breaks up tasks into small increments

_____ takes breaks as needed

_____ asks for assistance after trying to complete task

_____ focuses on assignments (length of time, type)

_____ completes assigned tasks

_____ brings or accesses materials needed for task

_____ ignores distractions

_____ moves self to a place conducive for working

How to Approach/Strategic Thinking

_____ prepares self for entry into situation

_____ maintains attention

_____ is active in the learning experiences when left to own resources

_____ talks self through a situation as a means of rehearsing for demands

_____ uses steps to think through situations prior to entry

_____ weighs value, interest of choosing to participate in a learning experiences and consequences for not getting involved

_____ participates in "free time" activity as a loner, parallel player, relater, interdependent member

_____ is a part of the social network and fabric of the community as he or she contributes, establishes role, interacts, cooperates, collaborates

Preparation for an Event

_____ uses transition periods to shift gears from one activity to another

_____ uses transition periods as an opportunity to take time for self

_____ uses transition periods to shift gears when given warning signals to stop what doing, forewarnings of what to do in the interim, preparation regarding what is upcoming

_____ predicts how expectations for behavior change from one situation to the next by picking up on how the setting is arranged, the materials the teacher takes out, the information presented

_____ gets self prepared for situation when teacher restates rules, identifies purpose of activity, reminds students of expectations and choices

During Learning Experience

_____ maintains attention to activity
    _____ when teacher uses animated voice
    _____ when requirements for participation change
    _____ when work independently
    _____ when there is talk and/or motion around him or her
    _____ when work with peers
    _____ when task is designed at student instructional level
    _____ when doodles as listens
    _____ when given opportunities to talk with peers
    _____ when given opportunity to move self from possible contaminants

_____ picks up on the rhythm of discussion, adding input and listening to others

_____ uses rule of raising hand to access opportunity to talk during discussion

_____ tends to talk out and/or interrupt other speakers during discussion

_____ maintains physical space (sitting in chair, assigned place on floor) during independent and/or group work

_____ moves out of physical space during session after _____ minutes

_____ changes position when seated on the floor, moving into others' spaces

_____ keeps hands in motion during lesson
    _____ tapping fingers
    _____ doodling
    _____ flipping pages in book
    _____ touching people in close proximity
    _____ manipulating small toys, objects

_____ watches activity that surrounds him or her

_____ initiates activity by poking or talking with others after _____ minutes of working independently

_____ cuts out the extraneous activity in the setting while working

_____ removes self from situations in which misbehaviors are about to occur

_____ seeks help from adult or peer when situation is challenging

_____ uses "techniques" (e.g., counting to self, self-talk) to get through difficult situations

_____ misbehaves to gain attention, avoid failure, take control, get revenge, or other

_____ responds to different types of lesson or assignments with different misbehaviors

_____ responds to different types of lessons or assignments with consistent misbehaviors

_____ interacts with peers and adults

_____ in an awkward manner
_____ makes limited contacts, stays to self
_____ develops close ties with limited number of students
_____ develops teasing relationships with others
_____ engages in conversations with others
_____ works cooperatively with others
_____ works parallel to others
_____ seeks attention by
_____ asking for help, time
_____ misbehaving to attract attention, not distinguishing the quality of attention

Postsituation

_____ acknowledges responsibility for own appropriate and inappropriate behavior
_____ states the misbehavior commits
_____ identifies what wants as a result of the behavior (e.g., attention from teacher, "get back" at peer, "get out" of work)
_____ attributes misbehavior to an external "force" (e.g., blames peer, says ignored)
_____ examines the situation in which the misbehavior occurs and generates alternative ways of handling
_____ examines the situation in which the misbehavior occurs and indicates what others can do to make things better
_____ reflects on situations in which behaves appropriately and calls attention to what contributes to positive aspects

Under What Conditions/Context for Participation

_____ responds to established routines (entry into classroom, independent work time, morning meeting, group instruction) and engages in expected behaviors
_____ tends to get involved in "off-task" behavior when
_____ in a new situation
_____ routine of the day is altered
_____ activity exceeds _____ minutes
_____ routine of an activity is varied
_____ transitions between activities are open ended
_____ directions for transition periods are general or directed to the class as a whole
_____ has trouble entering a new situation
_____ tends to misbehave during transition times
_____ responds to situations in which expectations are explicit (directives are given prior to . . .)
_____ tends to make off-task contacts (tease, poke, talk) with peers during small group instruction

Why Teach/Investment

_____ denies being a part of misbehavior

_____ states unsure as to what wants to achieve through behavior

_____ identifies what does that is inappropriate, labels goal of misbehavior, and suggests alternative

_____ accepts responsibility for own behavior

_____ accepts consequences for own behavior

_____ tends to blame others for behavior

_____ often says "I can't" when asked to perform academic tasks independently and/or in small or large group

_____ questions the purpose of completing assignments, working with peers, sharing materials

_____ refuses to follow a directive, often responding with "I don't have to" or "You can't make me"

_____ responds to choice statements

Adapted from Goldstein, A. (1988). *The prepare curriculum.* Champaign, IL: Research Press.

C h a p t e r **6**

Stage V

Write the Individualized Education Program

As you read through this chapter, *think about:*

- The purpose of the IEP and how it documents student competence and struggles and serves as a blueprint for a comprehensive plan tailored to meet the student's needs

- The elements of the educational plan and the criteria for writing each

- How to ensure that what is written represents team efforts to integrate assessment data and apply that information to educational planning

- How the components of the IEP are linked by the Interaction Formula

IEPs According to Dr. Seuss

Author unknown

Do you like these IEPs?
I do not like these IEPs
I do not like them, Jeeze Louise
We test, we check, we plan, we meet
But nothing ever seems complete.
Would you, could you like the form?

I do not like the form I see
Not page 1, not 2, not 3
Another change
A brand-new box
I think we all
Have lost our rocks.
Could you all meet here or there?

We could not all meet here or there.
We cannot all fit anywhere.
Not in a room
Not in the hall
There seems to be no space at all.

Would you, could you meet again?
I cannot meet again next week
No lunch no prep
Please hear me speak.
No, not at dusk. No, not at dawn
At 4 pm I should be gone.

Could you hear while all speak out?
Would you write the words they spout?
I could not hear, I would not write
This does not need to be a fight.
Sign here, date there,
Mark this, check that
Beware the student's ad-vo-cat(e).

You do not like them
So you say
Try again! Try again!
And you may.

If you will let me be,
I will try again
You will see.

Say!
I almost like these IEPs
I think I'll write 6003.
And I will practice day and night
Until they say
"You got it right!"

Overview of Stage V

Stage V is about the process of writing the IEP. This chapter will help you write the document to capture the evaluation and planning results of the RSVP special education process. Composing the IEP requires organizing team ideas into sentences and narratives that document efforts to integrate assessment results, agree on instructional priorities and plans, and coordinate program components. The IEP document offers assurances about meeting student needs, justifies proposed services, and creates a resource for program implementers. The purposes for investing in writing a quality document are to (1) provide a record of the team's work, (2) present justifications for why decisions and proposals were made, (3) link elements of the IEP to a comprehensive program, and (4) serve as a working document to offer practical guidelines for program implementers (Bateman & Linden, 1998; Bauwens & Korinek, 1993; Dudley-Marling, 1985; Edelen-Smith, 1995; Huefner, 2000; Johns, Crowley, & Guetzloe, 2002; Lignugaris-Kraft, Martella, & Marchand-Martella, 2001; Smith, 1990b; Smith & Simpson, 1989; Yell et al., 2003).

A quality IEP is readable, understandable, credible, logical, and useful. Its content conveys the results of data-based decision making, articulates agreement among team members, and serves as a road map to working effectively with and for the student (Bateman & Linden, 1998; Burns, 2001; Edelen-Smith, 1995; Katsiyannis, Yell, & Bradley, 2001; Simpson, 1996; Sopko & Moherek, 2003). Thus the IEP provides its readers with an understanding of the student's status in the area(s) of concern and an action plan for addressing his or her needs (Bateman & Herr, 2006b; Drasgow et al., 2001). It is critical for you as the IEP author to recognize the importance of this undertaking and the significance of the purposes and qualities of the IEP document you produce. Thinking about the IEP as a logical document and developing a clear writing style helps make the task fluid and practical.

Approaching the IEP meaningfully requires representing the team's work to:

- Describe a comprehensive picture of the learner in the area(s) of concern (*Profile*)
- Identify skill repertoires per cluster (*Present levels of performance, or PLOP*)
- Prioritize focuses for instruction (*Goals*)
- Specify the progression of instruction, using the PLOP(s) as starting points (*Objectives*)
- Set criteria for judging student progress and identify strategies for documenting and monitoring it (*Monitoring progress*)
- Determine modifications (adjustments to curriculum, levels of materials, tasks, methods, and environments) to access general education and participate in classroom and state/district performance assessments
- Select specially designed explicit instruction to promote competence in the area(s) of concern (*Instructional and intervention approaches and strategies and transition plans*)
- Coordinate service delivery to indicate placement decisions (*Service matrix*)

In this chapter, these individual components of the IEP are treated separately to examine what concepts mean and offer guidelines for writing them in ways that complement one another. Write the content so readers recognize and understand the links among the components of the document (Huefner, 2000; Smith, 1990b; Smith & Simpson, 1989; Zickel & Arnold, 2001; Zigmond, 2003) and thus can implement the plan with confidence and fidelity.

In Stage IV the steps the team takes to develop the content of the education plan establish the interrelationships among the IEP components. The process lays the groundwork for you to write an internally consistent document that accounts for student challenges and coordinates them with plans and recommendations. The intent is to write the description of the student and substantiate the corresponding instructional priorities, which, in turn, justifies the content of and approaches to learning experiences and the configuration of services the student receives (Bateman & Herr, 2006b; Huefner, 2000; Johns et al., 2002; Smith, 1990b; Smith & Simpson, 1989; Zickel & Arnold, 2001; Zigmond, 2003). Internal consistency of the IEP document is achieved by making the following connections:

- Student's present levels of academic achievement and functional performance align with proposed goals
- Stated instructional priorities and sequences reflect student's individual needs per skill cluster and with reference to a comprehensive understanding of the academic and/or social content
- Learner description/profile justifies selected academic/social experiences and environments to promote student growth
- Ideas for documenting and monitoring student progress are direct outgrowths of program activities and plans
- Service delivery of program implementers is designed to complement one another and provide a coherent program (Johns et al., 2002; Thompson, Thurlow, Quenemoen, Esler, & Whetstone, 2001)

Authoring the IEP

Perhaps the greatest challenge in composing the IEP is to find a comfortable professional writing style, one that balances conciseness, detail, clarity, and objectivity in ways that communicate information constructively, represent the voices of team members, and fulfill the purposes of the document. Team members must understand the information presented in the document and its connections to the student and instruction to consider it purposeful and make effective use of it. This chapter provides writing guidelines for transferring the meeting notes and expanding ideas onto the IEP forms to make these connections.

Writing the IEP requires you as the designated author to draw on the notes recorded during the planning meeting(s) in stage IV. You are responsible for conveying team decisions in a comprehensible, coherent manner. You collate and put words to the information shared, ideas developed, and proposals designed by the team according to sections of the IEP. When you see your role as representing the team's cooperative work, the document projects the tone of shared ownership and responsibility (Weishaar, 2001).

When writing the IEP, carefully consider the audience of parents/caregivers, student, general education teachers, special educators, related service providers, and administrators. These readers are often the members of the team who contribute to IEP development and/or users who implement and monitor suggested instructional ideas and program structures. In this respect the actual writing of the IEP serves as the record of team assessment and planning and as the working document to guide implementation (Bateman & Linden, 1998; Dudley-Marling, 1985; Yell et al., 2003). As a record of team discussions, members read through the document to make sure it accurately represents the collective description of the student and cooperative decisions made. As a working document, program implementers evaluate the extent to which the plans are practical and give direction for how to work systematically to meet student needs (Lignugaris-Kraft et al., 2001).

The value of the IEP is ultimately judged for how it meaningfully serves as a reference for understanding the challenges the student faces, a resource for instructional ideas, a matrix to coordinate the work and time of service providers, and a commitment to accountability (Bateman, 1995; Drasgow et al., 2001). Readers each have their own filters as they read the IEP. The extent to which parents/caregivers see assurances, students find relevance, and practitioners have guidelines for understanding the student and justifying approaches as well as designing, implementing, and coordinating instruction impacts how well received it is (NICHCY, 1999; Wood, Karvonen, Test, Browder, & Algozzine, 2004; Yell et al., 2003). Members of the team should read through the document and find the content valuable (Bauwens & Korinek, 1993; Edelen-Smith, 1995; Lignugaris-Kraft et al., 2001; Smith, 1990a).

Word choice is an important part of communicating with the diverse audience to articulate the content of the IEP document clearly. The use of objective, concise wording, unencumbered by professional terminology (also known as jargon or technical language), is key to conveying understandable and practical descriptions of the student and guidelines for instruction. It requires organizing team ideas and decisions and putting them into phrases, sentences, and narratives that concretely describe the student, define instructional priorities, and/or specify learning opportunities. Finding the appropriate wording to communicate ideas and respond to formats and styles can be challenging, along with making connections with prescribed forms (Kamens, 2004). Practice means reflecting and reworking but not necessarily ascribing to one of the messages in the poem in the beginning of the chapter—"writing 6003 . . . [to get . . .] it right."

When writing the IEP, keep parents/caregivers and the student in mind. Both (depending on the student's age and/or developmental level) should be able to read through the document and understand it completely. They should also feel assured that the concerns they have raised and discussed with the team are being addressed. Further, they should get the message that professionals are committing time and energy to continue to get to know the student and promote his or her growth. The student, when appropriate, should read through the document and see that his or her goals and priorities are addressed and approaches feel both relevant and valuable (NICHCY, 1999; Wood et al., 2004).

The general education teacher(s) should also read the document to get a clear sense of what and how to teach the student to promote progress in the area(s) of concern, see connections with state standards, and support participation in the general education curriculum (Walsh, 2001; Yell et al., 2003). They should feel confident that colleagues intend to provide support and complement their work with the student. Special educators and related service providers should read through the document and have a clear understanding of who the student is, what is meant by supporting access to general education, and what constitutes direct instruction and coordinated service delivery. The IEP does not preclude ongoing conversations and collaborations among team members, but rather it serves as the springboard for discussing and providing complementary experiences for the student (Bauwens & Korinek, 1993; Edelen-Smith, 1995; Lignugaris-Kraft et al., 2001; Smith, 1990a).

Stage V guides you in a step-by-step approach to the thinking and writing involved in producing a comprehensive and usable IEP. The remainder of the chapter provides criteria for what to include in writing the IEP components so they are stated clearly and practically and link learner needs with program plans. Each section of the IEP is treated in this stage to align closely with legal mandates, be tied together by the elements of the Interaction Formula, and thus create plans and programs that are universal in design (see Figure 6.1). Adopting this thinking to write IEPs is preparation for completing the variety of forms used across the country. Explanations of components and corresponding word banks, examples, and writing criteria are presented to support IEP authors as they think through how to make use of the information generated at the planning meeting. These guidelines help you compose an IEP that represents team efforts, is internally consistent, communicates a comprehensible and thorough description of the learner, conveys a clear plan for instruction and programming, thus meeting the RSVP criteria for effective IEPs (see the Toolbox at the end of the chapter).

Step 1: Develop Profile and Present Levels of Academic Achievement and Functional Performance to Present a Comprehensive Picture of the Student

A coherent and comprehensive accounting of the student in the area(s) of concern is conveyed through two sections of the IEP that report the team's synthesis of assessment data. The section labeled *profile* or *learning style* or *impact of disability* asks for an overview of the student's status in the area(s) of concern with reference to learning experiences, environments, and instructional demands, indicating strengths and accounting for identified needs and patterns of difficulties. This description is reported in narrative form.

The Interaction Formula Approach to Universal Design

IEPs: **A WAY OF THINKING AND DOING**				
DESCRIPTION OF THE LEARNER		**DESIGN OF CURRICULUM, INSTRUCTION, AND PROGRAM**		
Present Levels of Performance	**What to Teach/** Skill Clusters	Goals Objectives	Monitoring and Evaluation Techniques	S E R V I C E
	How to Teach/ Formats for Performance			
Profile/Learning Styles/ Impact of Disability	**How to Approach/** Strategic Thinking and Problem Solving	**Access to General Education/Specially Designed Instruction:**		D E L I V E R Y
	Under What Conditions/ Environments— Context for Participation	Teaching approaches and methodology, modifications, adaptations alternative instruction		
	Why Teach/ Investment			

FIGURE 6.1   The IEP Document as a Blueprint for Student Outcomes

   The section *present levels of academic achievement and functional performance* (PLOP) defines the specific student competencies with regard to skill clusters in the area(s) of concern. These descriptions provide in-depth information that contributes to portraying student status. The information is organized by the specific skills per cluster the student has mastered in relation to the tasks the student is asked to do or the social situation in which he or she is asked to participate.
   The intent of capturing this comprehensive description of the learner in the IEP (profile and PLOP) is to merge the input of team members and share the understanding of the student with readers and implementers. The overview/profile of student status provides a rationale for the design of proposed individualized instruction, identifying teaching approaches and methodologies and organizing the time, spaces, and social structures of the learning environment. The description of student PLOPs provides justification for determining priorities and selecting instructional strategies and structures to optimize progress and participation in learning experiences. The profile and PLOPs are discussed separately in greater detail.

Profile/Learning Style/Impact of Disability

In the profile, a narrative describes student status in terms of what he or she says, does, and/or produces when engaging in the area(s) of concern. You capture what characterizes student performance as a reader, writer, mathematician, and/or participant/member of the classroom community. Describe the products the student creates under various circumstances, conveying qualitative evidence of competence and challenges. Present patterns of errors and/or behaviors that emerge in different situations and offer examples to represent student struggles in the area(s) of concern. The narrative connects the evidence of difficulties with the conclusions the team reached to account for problems. Relate how skills per cluster, task and performance demands, problem-solving requirements, settings, and investments make a difference in facilitating or impeding student progress, participation, and proficiency. The profile section of the IEP objectively depicts who the student is in the area(s) of concern by providing an overview of how he or she is:

- Responsive to task formats, materials, and activities (How to Teach)
- Strategic in thinking through tasks, finding answers, solving problems, and self-monitoring (How to Approach)
- Interactive in relation to the demands of the instructional/social setting and physical environments (Under What Conditions)
- Engaged and invested in learning and participation (Why Teach)

In preparing to write the profile, review the notes from the IEP meeting and figure out a strategy to help summarize findings and conclusions and include supporting details. Different highlighters may be used to identify competencies that describe the student and key patterns of errors/misbehaviors that account for challenges to code related information. Or you may choose to arrange notes by constructing a web or outline, using Interaction Formula components or other headers related to the area(s) of concern to guide writing the profile. Another way to organize information is to reread and respond to the _K_now-_W_ant-_H_ow (stage II) questions per area of concern as the basis for generating the profile narrative or the Guideline Questions Toolbox that appears in Chapter 3. Regardless of the approach used, it is important to extract meaningful descriptions and evidence of patterns, making use of assessment data collected and integrated to bring clarity to what is stated. Figure 6.2 offers questions that provide an organizational system and will help you write an instructionally relevant profile.

In the IEP writing process, examine the messages of descriptions so they convey a sense of realistic hope and do not intimidate or confuse readers. When you see your responsibility as reporting a picture of how the student engages in the area(s) of concern with reference to learning situations, you will look to find the _right_ words to recreate what is happening. Written descriptions that depict concretely what happens when the student works in the area(s) of concern are readily understandable and have credibility. Sometimes you may look at your writing and worry it does not sound professional enough. Sometimes authors of IEPs use professional language that readers and implementers do not understand. Sometimes the tone of the IEP meeting was such that more negative statements than positive emerge. In any event, these _sometimes_ may affect profile descriptions by choosing

Profile

- What characterizes student performance on survey-level tasks in the area(s) of concern?
- What does the student do when asked to respond to an authentic task (e.g., read continuous texts, solve word problems, summarize a chapter in a book, compose a story, participate in a cooperative group, engage in conversation with a peer)?
- What is indicative of challenges and evidence of competence? What examples offer perspective?
- How do successes and struggles the student experiences relate to the demands of learning experiences and environments, skills, and investment in the area(s) of concern?
- Under what conditions is success optimized?
- What deters effective performance and contributes to struggles?
- How does performance change across different levels and qualities of tasks and materials, conditions, environments, and contexts?

How to Teach

- How do the level of material, formats of task(s), types of activities, and corresponding expectations influence the quality of student performance? How do his or her performance and products change in response to different demands and formats?

How to Approach

- What strategies for organizing thinking through tasks, finding answers, solving problems, and self-monitoring does the student use? How do the strategies influence effectiveness?
- How does the student approach interacting with a book, a writing task, a math problem, a social situation? What pre, during, and post strategies does the student use to prepare for, engage in, and/or self-regulate performance? How does his or her approach impact the quality of performance?

Under What Conditions

- How do setting arrangements, structures, and features affect the way the student participates, interacts, attends, engages, responds, or produces?
- How does the student respond to demands of the learning environment and interactions with teachers and peers, including use of time/schedule, pace, rules/expectations, groupings, physical setting, and accessibility to and/or direction from adults?

Why Teach

- In what ways does student investment in various activities germane to the area(s) of concern impact performance and learning?
- How are student's sense of purpose, sense of self, and interests in related activities evident? What purposes does the student see for becoming proficient in the area of concern?
- How do difficulties with the area(s) of concern and ways the student handles challenges impact investment? What types of feedback encourage the student to respond? How do these help the student stay with the task, correct errors, and find alternative behaviors?

FIGURE 6.2 Guidelines for Writing the Profile Narrative

language to label rather than describe, focusing on what the student is not doing or how ineffective he or she is and judging what the student says or does. Objective, practical messages must be conveyed so readers feel competent, confident and, in turn, willing to work with the student (Huefner, 2000; Ysseldyke, 2001; Ysseldyke et al., 1983). As you reread and revise, refer to Figure 6.3 for helpful ways to shift from general to descriptive statements.

General Profile Statements	*Descriptive* Profile Statements
Mary's *poor auditory processing* accounts for her difficulty staying with and participating in story time.	When a story is read aloud, Mary shifts her body position and moves her location in the group several times within a 20-minute period. When asked what the story is about, she gives a summative statement that conveys the gist of the story. However, when prompted to describe factual information, she has difficulty recalling details such as character names and ages, specific actions, and qualities of places where events took place.
Noah's *memory deficits* interfere with his retaining math facts.	Noah uses his fingers to calculate arithmetic equations by touching his thumb to each finger and counting out loud as he adds. Repeated use of drill and practice worksheets has not helped him learn the facts by rote. In these situations, he often "guesses" answers, which are frequently off by one or two.
Denny's *limited visual memory* interferes with his acquiring a sight vocabulary.	Denny's sight word vocabulary consists of reading words from the first list of Dolch words in isolation and in context. When presented with words in isolation outside of this list, he responds, "I don't know" or he asks for a hint. When prodded, he offers a word that begins with the first same letter sound. When reading a Level 2 (Fountas & Pinnell, 1996) picture book, Denny tends to "read" the pictures, making up the story as he goes. However, when reminded to look at the picture first, make a prediction, and point to the words as he reads, he will recognize words and fill in others, based on first letter sound, context, and/or picture clues.
Lynn's *attention-seeking behaviors* interfere with her completing assigned work.	At the outset of independent writing time (report, narrative, or expository), Lynn raises her hand and requests to talk with the teacher. Most times, Lynn shares an unrelated personal story. Lynn will focus her attention and begin her assignment after the teacher reviews the task and provides prompts for getting started. When the teacher is unavailable, Lynn walks around the room, talks out to her peers, or doodles all over the assigned paper.

FIGURE 6.3   From General to Descriptive Profile Statements

Present Levels of Academic Achievement and Functional Performance (PLOP)

In contrast to the descriptive nature of the profile, the present levels of academic achievement and functional performance specify student skill competencies in the area(s) of concern. The PLOP section defines *what skills* the student uses in academic and social situations, indicating precise starting points for instruction and providing the baseline against which student progress is measured (Knowlton, 2007).

The PLOP is written to convey a comprehensive inventory of the specific skills per cluster that the student has mastered and those he or she is learning to use with consistency and with reference to curricular scope and sequences and instructional demands. In writing the PLOP, sort the skill information by the clusters that comprise the area of concern. Capture the team's working knowledge of the skill clusters per academic and/or social area(s) and student status relative to expectations set by general education curriculum standards and contexts (Yell & Shriner, 1997). Organize team findings systematically, gathered primarily from authentic survey and probe-level assessments to report which skills the student uses effectively and/or with difficulty, when, and how.

PLOP identifies those skills the student uses on his or her own automatically, those with which he or she is familiar and learning to use, and those that he or she uses sporadically or when prompted. Lists of skills alone are not sufficient because they risk isolating them without attending to task demands. The PLOP is only complete when there is reference to whether the student uses the skills in isolation and/or in context and how he or she accesses them relative to different materials and types of activities.

To construct a thorough PLOP, create a bulleted list or a combination of connected phrases or statements that bridge the identified skills per clusters to relevant authentic tasks in the area(s) of concern. The following questions offer guidelines for writing specific PLOP descriptions:

- What specific skills and behaviors per cluster does the student demonstrate on his or her own and/or with prompting relative to the area(s) of concern?
- What skills and behaviors per cluster does the student use solely in isolation?
- How does the student use the skills and behaviors to engage effectively across task demands and levels of materials in the area(s) of concern?

Defining student status in terms of profile and the breakdown of skill hierarchies in isolation and context, PLOP creates the argument for the next instructional steps in working with the student. When PLOP provides sufficient detail, it establishes where to begin instruction, which leads to and justifies instructional priorities (goals), the progression of learning outcomes, criteria for evaluating student performance (objectives), and tools for monitoring and documenting progress (Strickland & Turnbull, 1993). For more supportive criteria for constructing effective PLOP, focus on the guidelines presented in Figure 6.4.

Present Level of Performance Considerations

SKILL CLUSTERS

1. Identify the sets of skills per cluster that the student has mastered, distinguishing what the student knows automatically, with prompting, or with which he or she is confused (e.g., rules for punctuation, calculation of math facts, specific phonics rules)
2. Associate discrete skills with tasks, formats, and situations when they are used.
3. Answer:
   - What does the student do to demonstrate proficiency with regard to each skill cluster? When does the student demonstrate competence?
   - What skills does the student access and apply when performing in the area(s) of concern? How does student's consistent/inconsistent use of skills in isolation and in context contribute to effectiveness in the area(s) of concern?
   - How do errors reflect *missing skills*? How does student performance reflect evidence of gaps in skill development?
   - How do demands of level of materials and/or features of tasks impact student use of skills?

Present Levels of Performance—Three Elements to Include

Identify set of skills per cluster:	Distinguish between automatic and prompted learning or confusion:	Associate skills with tasks, formats, and situations the student uses:
• Sequence events from the story read aloud	• Darla identifies key events in the story, placing them in succession	• when the story is illustrated and she uses as reference as she retells • but confuses the order when she reads the story silently
• Rules for capitalization	• Paul capitalizes the first word of the sentence consistently	• when journal writing • does not apply capitalization rules for proper nouns with the exception of his own name
• Addition of single-digit numbers	• Rick calculates single-digit addition examples with sums to 10	• when he counts each number on his fingers or draws pictures or using manipulatives • responds to flashcards or timed addition facts with high rates of errors, giving answers that appear random/often equal to or greater than the larger number in the equation
• Expresses frustration	• Lucy asks for help when she starts a task	• having an adult repeat directions and guide her to a first item of a task, the beginning of a story • but when left on her own rips up her paper when she has difficulty completing an assigned task

FIGURE 6.4   Guidelines for Writing Present Levels of Performance

Step 2: Record the Design of the Individualized Curriculum

Each aspect of the proposed individualized curriculum is tailored to respond to the student's current status (profile and present levels of academic achievement and functional performance) and communicate the direction for *what to teach* and how to evaluate student progress. This curriculum is articulated through written sets of goals, objectives, evaluation criteria, and monitoring procedures designed to support the student becoming more competent in the area(s) of concern. These are stated as outcomes for the student, setting instructional priorities, sequences, standards, and strategies to document and appraise progress. The individualized curriculum serves as the basis for developing weekly plans, daily lessons, assignments, and ongoing assessment through general education or alternative instruction (Drasgow et al., 2001).

Goals and Objectives

The individualized curriculum structures what instruction will be targeted. This is proposed as a series of goal statements on the IEP document that constitute long-range plans that define academic and/or social skill outcomes per cluster to be gained over a designated period of time and incorporate content for instruction in terms of what the student will do (Price & Nelson, 2007). Short-term plans elaborate what specific skills the student will learn relative to each cluster to move from his or her present levels of academic achievement and functional performance to the identified goals (Lignugaris-Kraft et al., 2001). These are specified as objectives on the IEP, which are arranged as a progression of measurable instructional steps or milestones.

Well-defined goals and objectives craft instruction, based directly on student needs rather than fitting the student into what already exists (Hitchcock, Meyer, Rose, & Jackson, 2002; Johns et al., 2002). Establishing clear skill focuses and expectations for instruction set criteria for determining the suitability of general education curriculum and/or justifying specially-designed instruction. They are stated in observable terms that can be seen or heard, are relevant to promoting student progress in the area(s) of concern, and are assessable so performance and behavior can be documented and monitored. To address the identified area(s) of concern with specificity, keeping the focus on student individual needs, write:

- *Goals* that articulate measurable outcomes in terms of student academic and social gains per and across skill clusters to foster growth as a reader, writer, mathematician, participant/member of the classroom community
- *Objectives* that break down each goal statement into a progression of subskills/learner actions, setting conditions for performance and criteria/ markers as indicators of progress
- *Documentation of progress* that identifies what evidence (student products and performance) is collected and what tools are used to monitor and evaluate student achievement with regard to individual objectives, corresponding goals, and overall performance

Write Observable, Relevant, and Assessable Goals

Goal statements establish what the student is to accomplish to reach academic and/or social competence, effectiveness, and proficiency. These statements reflect what the student is likely to learn in a year, although the designated time period may possibly change for some states with reauthorization of IDEA 2004. Goal statements establish the next *giant* steps, setting realistic expectations and a purposeful framework for instructional planning. They provide the foundation for individualizing learning experiences by considering student needs in light of grade-level curriculum and competence in the area(s) of concern.

Articulate a *set* of goal statements per area(s) of concern, each one concentrating on an identified skill cluster based on what is flagged by the present levels of academic achievement and functional performance. The goals are the intended outcomes of instruction, stated in terms of what sets of skills or behaviors the student is expected to learn using objective vocabulary. Effective goal statements define what the student is expected to do as a consequence of instruction *and* the standards against which his or her performance will be assessed. When writing goal statements for the area(s) of concern, answer these four questions:

1. What skill clusters correspond with PLOP statements, establish academic and/or social outcomes in the area(s) of concern, and set the direction for what to teach?
2. What will the student *do* with each skill cluster (action) to demonstrate learning and progress in the area(s) of concern?
3. *With what* materials, tasks, and/or situations is the student expected to use or apply the identified set of skills?
4. What criteria will be used to measure *how or in what way* the student advances toward the desired academic and/or social outcome(s)?

Avoid the tendency to write an all-inclusive broad goal statement that covers an area of concern (e.g., to improve reading). Such a general statement gives no clear indication of what the student is expected to learn or how the instructor knows when the student has met expectations. Instead, formulate statements of where the student is headed by writing phrases that are observable, measurable, and meaningful. A format for writing focused goal statements includes: *The student will **do what** action that shows using or applying a set of skills in relation to **with what** materials, tasks, or situations according to established criteria for **how/in what way** performance or behavior meets expected competence and/or proficiency.*

The following prompts serve as helpful hints for writing specific goal statements per skill cluster. They . . .

1. **Set the direction** *for formulating goals* (what to teach): Identify the set of skills per cluster that encompasses what the student is expected to learn within a given time frame to address the area(s) of need. Target each academic/social skill cluster to narrow the focus for instruction (e.g., fluency, prediction skills, story writing, revision of writing, word problems, single digit addition and subtraction, work habits, managing anger, etc.), using the corresponding set of PLOP statements as reference points.

2. **Do what** (*Behaivor Phrase*): Articulate what the student is expected to do to demonstrate meaningful learning of the identified skills in the cluster as a result of instruction. Use observable, measurable words to describe what action (behavior phrase) the student will **do** *and* **what** materials he or she will use *or* **what** he or she will produce in response to tasks, as evidence of learning (e.g., apply prereading strategies to understand a picture book, write a persuasive essay, illustrate the sequence of the story read, solve a word problem by acting it out, take time away from cooperative group activity when frustrated with peers).

3. **How/In what way:** Identify **how** or **in what way** each goal will be accomplished by specifying what criteria you are expecting the student to demonstrate the targeted skill cluster. Define the standards in terms of level of quality and/or quantity to assess student performance, product, or behavior and evaluate instructional outcomes (e.g., what rate is appropriate, what accuracy is meaningful, what characteristics constitute what is acceptable/competent, etc., for that student at that time).

See Figure 6.5 for examples of goal statements that contain these identified elements. These are organized according to reader, writer, mathematician, and participant/member and represent several skill clusters per area of concern.

GOAL STATEMENTS		
1) **Set the direction** for instruction per skill cluster based on corresponding present levels of performance (PLOP) to determine what to teach.	2) The student will **do what** action using skill, **with what** materials, tasks, and/or situations (behavior phrase).	3) Specify **how/in what way** criteria will be used to assess the quality and/or quantity of student performance and products.

READER

- (pre-reading skills) Darla will preview a picture book referring to title, cover, and sequence of pictures to make connections with personal experiences and predict plausible story line.
- (sight words) Darla will increase sight word vocabulary from the Dolch reading lists levels one through three in isolation and continuous text by reading out loud at a rate of one per second with correct pronunciation.
- (word solving) Darla will read aloud and solve unknown words using the strategies of context, word analysis, and/or picture clues in levels E & F texts (Fountas & Pinnell) with accuracy in pronunciation and making sense in the text.
- (fluency) Darla will read a narrative story aloud written at level D & E (Fountas & Pinnell) with fluency, connecting phrase to phrase, pausing at punctuation, and using expression.
- (extract sequence/key information) Darla will read silently and retell a narrative story written at mid-first grade level, identifying the plot as sequenced and connected events.

(*continued*)

FIGURE 6.5   Examples of Goal Statements

WRITER

- (pre-writing) Paul will <u>preplan ideas for writing a story</u> <u>on a labeled web</u> describing key characters, problems confronting characters, events, and solution in phrases.
- (expository writing) Paul will <u>develop a topic for an essay, research it, and categorize information on index cards or in notebook</u> answering where, who, what, how, in what way.
- (persuasive writing) Paul will <u>take a stand on a topic stating personal opinions</u> <u>in essay form</u> conveying his ideas and opposing views in a substantiated and cohesive argument.
- (revision of own writing) Paul will <u>reread, critique, and revise content</u> <u>of his own written narrative</u> asking himself a series of questions that support his evaluation and changing development of ideas and organization of information.

MATHEMATICIAN

- (single digit addition and subtraction) Rick will <u>read, calculate and write answers</u> <u>to single digit addition and subtraction equations</u> using manipulatives and number lines to represent the processes.
- (work habits/self-monitoring) Rick will <u>check his own written calculations</u> <u>of one digit addition and subtraction examples</u> asking self if the answer seems reasonable and using inverse operation to verify his answers.
- (word problems) Rick will <u>read, translate, and calculate responses</u> <u>to single step word problems,</u> reading through the "story," extracting action and critical information and vocabulary, assigning appropriate operation, and labeling answers.

PARTICIPANT/MEMBER OF CLASSROOM COMMUNITY

- (work independently) Lucy will <u>increase attention to task by focusing and working on</u> (eyes on paper, pencil in hand, etc.) <u>independent written assignments at her desk</u> asking for help as needed, taking appropriate break time, and completing tasks.
- (express emotions) Lucy will <u>make appropriate choices</u> (use inside voice and eye contact, write a note, etc.) <u>in challenging situations</u> (argument with friend, reprimand from teacher, etc.) conveying how she is feeling when confronted with issues, sharing personal frustration, using words of emotion, or taking self out of a situation.
- (resolve conflicts) Lucy will <u>suggest solutions</u> for <u>interpersonal conflicts with peers</u> taking time to get in touch with her own feelings, listening to the perspective of other(s) involved, and participating in brainstorming a plan to address the issue(s).

Key:

(   ) **Set the direction/skill cluster**

_____ **Do what**

_____ **With what**

.... **How/In what way**

FIGURE 6.5 *Continued*

Write Observable, Relevant, and Assessable Objectives

Objectives provide the intermediate steps that link student present levels of academic achievement and functional performance to the identified goals, establishing the sequence of instruction. They add detail to the curriculum plan, offering program implementers a breakdown of *what and how to teach* that customizes general education or alternative benchmarks to meet individual needs. Objectives state the set of skills (*what to teach*) to be acquired, the conditions under which they are to be used or applied (*how to teach*), and the criteria for determining mastery and readiness to proceed to the next step. They provide the focus for weekly and daily instructional plans and/or behavioral interventions.

Objectives are written similarly to annual goals, although the skills, tasks, and standards for judging performance are articulated more precisely. They are arranged to build on one another until mastery is attained. The number of objectives identified is contingent on creating an explicit set of steps for progressing from where the student is currently operating (present levels of academic achievement and functional performance) to moving through mastery of each stated goal. IDEA 2004 suggests eliminating objectives when goals are related to and measured by general education standards but requires them when goals serve as the bases for alternative assessments (Council for Exceptional Children, 1998; Salend, 2005). However, RSVP contends that the specificity the objectives offer is significant in guiding implementers to focus, plan, balance, and manage instruction and evaluate student progress. When writing objective statements for the area(s) of concern, answer these four questions (Gronlund, 2004; Hyatt, 2007; Knowlton, 2007; Mager, 2001; Price & Nelson, 2007):

1. What set of subskills comprises the targeted skill cluster/goal for the student?
2. What is the student expected to *do* with each subskill to demonstrate his or her proficiency and progress toward reaching each goal?
3. With what types of materials, tasks, and/or situations is the student expected to use or apply each subskill?
4. What are the indicators used to measure student performance, behavior, and product to meet individual objectives?

These questions direct the thinking involved in writing clear and concise objectives. They help you set the direction for instruction and articulate the required components; *Given* **with what** (*conditions: types of materials, tasks, and/or social situations*), **who** (*the student*) *will* **do what** (*behavior phrase: action using skills to show learning*), **how/in what way** (*criteria: standards used to assess the quality and/or quantity of performance and products*). The format for structuring and wording the objective is provided to guide authors in making sure all components are included.

The following prompts serve as helpful hints for writing the progression of specific objectives. They . . .

1. **Set the direction** *for formulating the objectives:* Identify the sequence of subskill(s) that moves the student from each entry level (PLOP) to the corresponding designated goal. Reference state/district curriculum standards, scope and sequence outlines, and/or RSVP checklists (see Checklist Toolboxes, Chapter 5).

2. **With what** (Conditions): Write a phrase that indicates the *Given* **task demands** to which the student responds. Address the level and type of material, task format, nature of question, kind of problem, time constraints, social situation, or so on. Identify conditions for performance, for example, given an illustrated story, a picture, an equation, a role play of entering a situation.

3. **Who** (the Learner): Include the name of the student.

4. **Do what** (Behavior Phrase): Articulate what the student is expected to do to demonstrate meaningful learning of the targeted skill being addressed. Use observable, measurable action words to describe what the student will *do*, say, or produce in response to the *with what* (conditions) as evidence of learning. Write an observable action/behavior phrase, for example, describe a character, write a story or sentence, read a paragraph, calculate a sum using regrouping, use a greeting.

5. **How/In what way** (Criteria): Present the *how/in what way* phrase to define the indicators against which student performance, product, or behavior is evaluated. Designate *how* or *in what way* each student objective will be considered accomplished by specifying criteria that define expectations in observable and measurable terms. Attainment of the identified skill in the behavior phrase (*do what*) is measured by qualitative or quantitative criteria that indicate competence.

Qualitative criteria provide descriptive characteristics of what constitutes effective performance or behavior. When setting qualitative criteria, use observable attributes or behaviors to establish expectations of what you are looking or listening for as the student performs the skill [e.g., write essay (behavior phrase) containing an interesting lead to hook readers, descriptive language, and voice that appeals to audience; expresses anger (behavior phrase) using *inside* voice, eye contact, and an I-message].

Quantitative criteria clarify how frequently you expect the student to perform the skill and/or the level of accuracy that is acceptable. Establish numerical expectations against which performance is to be judged, for exanple, the number of repeated trials, rate of response, and/or number of appropriate answers. Consider the ramifications for assigning numerical criteria: What are acceptable numbers or true indicators of mastery? Ask yourself if counting student actions or recording percentage or rate is feasible, ensures all of what you want the student to learn, and represents mastery of skills that generalize to authentic tasks related to curriculum or alternative standards germane to the area(s) of concern. Quantitative criteria make most sense when used in conjunction with qualitative criteria. [e.g., summarize and retell stories (behavior phrase), including problem to solution for four illustrated books; read sight words (behavior phrase) pronouncing each at a rate of one per second and defining it; write paragraph (behavior phrase) including topic, supporting, and clincher statements for 3 consecutive assignments; greet teacher or peer (behavior phrase), making eye contact and using person's name 5 mornings in a row]. Whether using qualitative and/or quantitative criteria, you are evaluating student performance or behaviors for competence and consistency within and across academic tasks and/or social situations. Be vigilant about the type and specificity of the criteria assigned. Remember that regardless of what is used, these criteria should set the gauge for monitoring student progress and determining when the student is ready to move on to the next skill.

Figure 6.6 offers a word and phrase bank that provides prompts to help you write objectives. Figure 6.7 has examples of objective statements that contain the identified elements. These are organized according to reader, writer, mathematician, and participant/member and represent several skill clusters per area of concern.

CONDITIONS PHRASE BANK

- given a set of flashcards . . .
- given a list of twenty words . . .
- given a series of sentences/poem/story/comic book/newspaper column/ magazine article (about . . . with readability/length) to read . . .
- given a five-page short story with readability of . . .
- given a story map
- given a set of pictures
- given a set of story element terms
- given a set of questions (who, what, when, etc.)
- when presented with a poster/bulletin board/film/set of pictures/demonstration to observe . . .
- after listening to a(n) lecture/audiotape/dramatic reading/recording about . . .
- during independent study time, large or small group instruction, recess, learning center activities . . .
- given a worksheet with fill-in the blanks/multiple choice/short answer questions
- when presented with a worksheet containing 10 examples of
- given an independent study time of 35 minutes
- upon entering the classroom
- during the 15-minute large group time

ACTION-WORD WORD BANK

accept	add	agree	answer
apply	arrange	ask	blend
brainstorm	calculate	capitalize	categorize
classify	compare–contrast	compile	compliment
compute	connect	contribute	convert
count	create	critique	debate
defend	describe	develop	diagram
disagree	discuss	display	edit
examine	expand	explain	express

(continued)

FIGURE 6.6 Guidelines for Writing Objectives

extend	extract	figure out	find
formulate	give examples	give feedback	graph
identify	illustrate ideas	indent	infer
inform	label	lend	link information
listen	locate	look at	modify
name	nod	offer	order
outline	participate	plot	pose
predict	preplan	propose	punctuate
read	rearrange	recognize	record
reorganize	rephrase	report	represent
reread	restate	retell	revise
say	sequence	share	simplify
solve	sort	sound out	state
suggest	summarize	synthesize	tabulate
tally	tell	wait	

BEHAVIOR PHRASE BANK

- act out the process
- define vocabulary
- diagram process of . . .

- draw a cartoon, satirical picture
- graph/chart observations, relationships of . . .
- illustrate a poster, mural, picture of . . .
- manipulate objects, cubes

- participate in/contribute to debate, panel, group discussion
- select correct choice (title, sentence, word)
- specify the theme
- summarize the plot
- write full sentence/phrase responses

- construct collage, map, diorama of . . .
- describe the character's intentions
- dramatize/perform play, interpretive dance
- draw slash marks, pictures
- identify main idea

- illustrate, draw, color, map, diagram
- match synonyms, definitions, pictures and captions
- point to a picture that indicates . . .

- select/recite/quote poem, story that goes with theme
- state the sequence of events
- write equation
- write/arrange ideas in an outline, chart an editorial, position paper

CRITERIA

Rote tells the extent to which skills/facts are memorized and/or automatic
- reciting the poem without looking at the book
- enumerating the multiples at a rate of one per second
- listing the rules for . . .

Use of prompts
- using the multiplication chart to check her work
- asking herself the questions related to COPS

FIGURE 6.6 *Continued*

Use of skills in a specific context
- blending sounds together to pronounce the word as a whole
- describing the mood conveyed by the setting description
- proofreading and editing unpunctuated sentences
- translating into a number a sentence

Attributes of what to include in product or performance (qualitative standards)
- report includes title page, summary of . . . , bibliography
- story contains at least three complete statements of noun-verb-object that identify an event and character
- retell includes the sequence of problem to solution
- character analysis includes struggles and emotions experienced, way perceived problem, interactions with others, and attempts to reach solution
- spelling of words includes sounds heard and application of CVC and CVCe patterns in one-syllable words
- explanation of finding the sum includes related vocabulary (e.g., combine, add, and, all together, in all) and corresponding illustration

---

Level of proficiency indicates the acceptable number of items correct and/or expected percentage of items correct
- number acceptable—all "x," at least 8 correct
- percentage correct or proportion—75%, 5 out of 7

Level of difficulty of material (defined by publisher or the rating system)
- using book written at a third-grade level as a reference
- reading set of words from a fourth-grade sight word list
- answering challenge problems from a sixth-grade math text

Rate focuses on the speed of performance, frequency of desired behavior, or pace/ tempo of response, within a specified time period.
- reading at a rate of twenty words in isolation per minute
- completing fifteen multiplication facts accurately in a minute
- completing five items in a ten-minute independent period
- staying in seat for seven of eight minutes
- exhibiting the behavior over four consecutive days

FIGURE 6.6   *Continued*

Documentation of Progress: Identify Monitoring and Evaluation Strategies

Identifying the *monitoring and evaluation strategies* represents a commitment to accountability through ongoing assessment and documentation of student progress (Clark, 1999; Heward, 2003; Marston & Diment, 1992). Ongoing assessment means collecting data systematically to substantiate what the student is learning, the effectiveness of materials and methods being used during instruction, and the efficacy of the IEP.

Conditions: *Given with what task demands?*	The student: *Who?*	Behavior Phrase: *Will do what?*	Criteria: *How?/ In What Way?*

READER

- Given a simple sentence (noun-verb-object) comprised of Dolch 1 & 2 vocabulary, on individual sentence strips, Darla will recognize and read the set of words in a single breath, pronouncing each correctly.
- When assigned a dialogue part of a story comprised of Dolch 1 & 2 vocabulary, Darla will read and express the feelings of the character using her voice to convey the emotions and enthusiasm.
- Given a set of CVCe words containing different vowels and written on flashcards, Darla will apply the rule and *blend* the sounds pronouncing each one correctly.
- Given an illustrated sentence with one word omitted, Darla will use context and picture clues, providing a word that coincides with the meaning and what is depicted.

WRITER

- Given a blank web, Paul will brainstorm and arrange the ideas to write a story outlining the who is in the story, what problem(s) is faced, and what events will lead to resolution.
- Given a topic that he researched, one that asks him to take a side or state a preference, Paul will stake a claim and connect key points in a paragraph using a topic sentence, supporting evidence, and a "clincher."
- Given Daily Oral Language unpunctuated sentences on individual sentence strips, Paul will capitalize and punctuate each, applying rules for beginning sentences, proper nouns, and periods to end sentences and abbreviations.

MATHEMATICIAN

- Given an equation written on an index card, Rick will compute and write sum or difference for single digit addition and subtraction using manipulatives to represent and check his thinking.
- Given data from surveys completed by peers, Rick will tally, sort, categorize and diagram the information representing and interpreting the distribution of results on bar graphs.

PARTICIPANT/MEMBER

- Given large group instruction in which attending to directions is not met, Lucy will respond to reminders or behavior corrections by making eye contact with the teacher, stating the expectation, and telling what she will do next time.
- Given time when she feels confused or frustrated by independent work, Lucy will ask a question about what she is doing using a calm, inquisitive tone of voice.

Key:

(   ) Set the direction/skill cluster

_____ Do what

_____ With what

.... How/In what way

FIGURE 6.7   Examples for Writing Objective Statements

The elements of the goals and objectives suggest tasks for assessing student performance and provide standards for judging growth. They do not indicate how data will be collected and analyzed, records kept, and IEP effectiveness determined. Instead, the documentation of progress section of the IEP augments the goal and objective statements by indicating how student performance/behaviors are measured and evaluated and the frequency with which the data are gathered. Consider the following questions when describing monitoring and evaluation strategies:

- What evidence provides a record of the student working toward and meeting individual objectives and stated goals?
- What tools generate the evidence that documents and monitors student achievement?
- In what ways do the tools generate evidence that correlates with the targeted skill(s)/cluster to evaluate student performance and report his or her progress?
- How often will data be collected and progress reported?

Writing the monitoring and evaluation strategies section of the IEP involves defining which assessment tools document student performance, mastery of individual objectives, and progress toward each goal. The proposal to collect, record, and evaluate performance and behavior requires indicating how the student will be assessed regularly (daily, weekly, bi-weekly). Specify authentic tasks, approaches, and procedures that generate desired evidence and document how the student does acquiring and applying specific skills. Making anecdotal records of observations, charting evidence of responses to specific tasks, and/or collecting and analyzing student work samples/performance are all legitimate techniques for evaluating progress.

Assign specific tool(s) per objective or set of related objectives to measure student gains authentically as a reader, writer, mathematician, and/ or participant/member of the classroom community. The annotated list of documentation/assessment strategies and record keeping devices in Figure 6.8 provides a resource of options that can be shaped to evaluate the effectiveness of stated IEP goals and objectives. Refer to Stage II *Assessment Idea Toolbox* at the end of Chapter 3 as it contains evaluation strategies per area of concern that may also be used for documenting progress. The thinking involved in identifying documentation strategies is similar to that used to choose tools for the *How* column in *Know-Want-How* assessment planning. Regardless of the approach designed for recording performance or behaviors, make sure that documentation tracks student responsiveness to intervention, readiness to proceed to next objective(s) in the identifed sequence, and meeting stated goals. Data generated and collected as a result of these ongoing assessment approaches substantiate effectiveness of the education plan and decisions for moving to the next least restrictive environment, using school curriculum or alternative standards and benchmarks as points of reference.

Observation is generated from student participation in daily instructional experiences to note how often behavior/performance occurs, impact of instructional context, effect of the type of task, to count or tally the frequency of behaviors, rate of performance.

TYPES OF DOCUMENTATON/ASSESSMENT STRATEGIES	RECORD-KEEPING DEVICES
• anecdotal records of in-class performance • running record of in-class performance, participation in lesson, group work • frequency counts	• teacher logs, journals, notebooks • charts, graphs

Focused observation is set up to examine progress through defined task(s) to analyze student performance in terms of identifying evidence of specific skills, error patterns, accuracy, rate of response, impact of task formats, indicators of level of mastery and/or to gain perspective on how student goes about performing task.

TYPES OF DOCUMENTATION/ASSESSMENT STRATEGIES	RECORD-KEEPING DEVICES
• running records of assigned passage reading • interviews with student regarding books read/retelling approach taken to problem solving • writing conferences • examiner's copy and charts of miscues	• teacher logs, journals, notebooks • charts, graphs • tape recordings • checklists

Work Samples to analyze student performance on tasks in terms of identifying qualities, evidence of specific skills, error patterns, accuracy, rate of response, impact of task formats, indicators of level of mastery, to determine progress over a period of time.

TYPES OF DOCUMENTATION/ASSESSMENT STRATEGIES	RECORD-KEEPING DEVICES
• responses to open-ended questions • literature response logs • learning reflection logs • journals • completed projects, reports, assignments, research, graphs, charts, illustrations • writing samples (drafts vs. published pieces, stories, plays, poems, letters) • reading records of books read • responses through visual arts • prewriting-drafts-revisions-published copy	• checklists • charts to enter date and make notes regarding qualities of work • portfolios • folders of selected or all work • copies of work (selected or all) • completed rubrics

Informal Assessments to examine identified skills under specified conditions to determine levels of mastery, conditions under which performance is enhanced, and comparison of different scores (number of items, percentage) over time.

FIGURE 6.8   Guidelines for Writing Monitoring and Evaluation Techniques

TYPES OF DOCUMENTATION/ASSESSMENT STRATEGIES	RECORD-KEEPING DEVICES
• flashcard tasks	• checklists
• cloze exercises	• completed rubrics
• proofreading tasks	• folders of completed tasks
• reading or writing or calculation or story problem assessments	• copies of completed tasks
• taped readings, retellings, descriptions of problem solving over time	

FIGURE 6.8 *Continued*

Step 3: Write the Plan for Instruction

To focus on the individual student, IDEA 2004 requires defining explicit instruction independent of and prior to determining the place(s) or type(s) of service delivery. IEP forms ask authors to present instructional plans that address the sets of individualized goals and objectives directly through access to the general education curriculum and/or specially designed instruction. You outline teaching approaches, types of materials, and instructional arrangements to support how the student will acquire skills and build competence and proficiency in the area(s) of concern. Although IEP documents may vary, there are sections in which to frame direct instruction, to provide implementers with clear guidelines.

Explicit/Direct Instruction

Explicit instruction focuses on materials, approaches, and instructional arrangements that match the student's entry-level skills and profile to foster attainment of the IEP goals and objectives. Depending on the decisions made by the team, the approaches to direct instruction are recorded under *access to the general education curriculum* with or without modifications and/or *specially designed or alternative instruction*. The design of instructional experiences, interactions, and environments that directly address the goal priorities and objective sequences is critical. Based on the team's decisions, the writer composes the appropriate section(s) on explicit instruction to include brief guidelines for approaches, materials, and arrangements to introduce isolated skills and strategies, teach them in authentic context(s), and coordinate them with related skill clusters simultaneously. The descriptions of teaching approaches and materials for direct instruction, based on the learner's individualized goals and objectives answer these questions:

- How will skills/concepts be presented, reinforced, and evaluated?
- How will instructional experiences be designed to promote student learning with reference to proposed outcomes? What instructional

methods, materials, strategies, and setting arrangements in and out of the general education curriculum will be used?

- What levels and qualities of approaches, materials, activities, and tasks will support student independence and confidence?

The intention of designing a framework for direct instruction is to describe what will be done to support the student becoming a more effective reader, writer, mathematician, and/or participant/member of the classroom community. Given that the team meets and determines instructional and service delivery plans before the IEP is written, you will have a clear understanding of what recommended learning experiences will be delivered through the general education curriculum and warrant modifications and which ones fall under the auspices of special education services and programming.

Access to the General Education Curriculum

IEP forms have a section that asks how the student will access the general education curriculum. There are two ways the general education curriculum is accessed. First, general education curriculum and instruction may be used with or without modifications to directly address the goals and objectives of the IEP. Second, general education curriculum and instruction may be used with or without modifications to involve the student in other curricular areas or engage him or her in a variety of social experiences, taking into account his or her challenges in the area(s) of concern. It is helpful to develop details around each of the two ways the student will participate in the general education curriculum so clear modifications are designed systematically, and student involvement and corresponding expectations are defined.

Constructive involvement in the general education curriculum requires explanation of how to (1) concentrate on IEP goals and objectives through in-class instruction, materials, and focuses in relation to the grade-level expectations and curriculum standards, (2) offer learning and social experiences in other grade-level instruction, taking the area(s) of concern into consideration, and/or (3) make these learning and social opportunities productive for the student and feasible for program implementers. As the description of adjustments is read, it should be apparent what the benefits of access to the general education curriculum are and what adjustments are necessary to optimize experiences and support the student feeling comfortable, successful, and competent.

Adapting classroom instruction to meet the skill repertoires and learning profile of the struggling student is consistent with the concepts of universal design and differentiated instruction (Gregory, 2003; Tomlinson, 1999, 2006). In this section you present pertinent information regarding how to address goals/objectives in the context of the general education curriculum, providing guidelines for adjustments and setting outcomes for participation, using materials, establishing arrangements, and evaluating performance. It is a process of matching the skills the student has and how the student learns best with existing approaches, materials, tasks, and learning environments that will support his or her success (Brimijoin, Marquissee, & Tomlinson, 2003; Schumm et al., 1994; Tomlinson, 1999, 2006). These proposed adjustments are also suitable for describing and justifying how statewide and district testing may be altered to accommodate student needs. You respond to these questions:

- How will the student participate in general education curriculum and activities meaningfully?
- What adapted curriculum standards and adjustments to methods, materials, tasks, and learning environments will be used to support the student in classroom experiences?

Referring to the Interaction Formula components helps you think and write about the opportunities afforded through the general education curriculum and how modifications or adaptations of classroom curriculum standards/benchmarks and teaching strategies and arrangements will address student needs constructively. Adjustments to facilitate access to the general education curriculum may come in the form of modified expectations for performance (what to teach/skills); adapted instructional formats, alternative methods and materials, amended assignments (how to teach and approach/formats for performance and strategic thinking); varied arrangements of settings (under what conditions/contexts for participation); and ways to make instruction relevant for the student (why teach/investment) as needed across the curriculum. See Figure 6.9 for specific applications of the Interaction Formula for making modifications.

Modifications Based on Interaction Formula Considerations

Consider how skills and concepts will make sense to the student (*what to teach*)

- Break a concept/skill down into discrete, incremental, and sequential steps and teach step by step.
- Use webs or similar diagrams to show the relationship among ideas and organize them.
- Teach target skill through modeling, demonstration (directly perform the skill for the students), explanation, illustration, showing student how to perform a task—working side by side, asking him or her to imitate and/or providing frequent response, using a set of examples and nonexamples, and/or demonstrating how to think about planning and executing use of the skills/concepts.
- Set up opportunity for discovery, using an open-ended question, problem, and/or goal/outcome statements along with manipulatives to figure out responses.
- Show the skills in multiple ways to present information to student (illustrations, verbal description, listening to presentation or song, manipulating objects that represent skill/concept).
- Make frequent checks through direct questions, quick writes, think-pair-share, or other tasks to make sure student understands material covered.
- Guide student to memorize facts (introduce flashcards, gradual fading of manipulatives, mnemonics).

(continued)

FIGURE 6.9   Guidelines for Writing About Explicit Instruction: Access to the General Education Curriculum and Specially Designed Instruction

Figure out formats of instruction that indicate how direct instruction and accessing the general education curriculum can be structured and the types of materials to be used to help the student develop targeted skills and strategies (*how to teach*).

Introduction

How to involve student in thinking about related personal experiences and how to present the student with "new" skills, concepts, strategies, or rules—use of *guided exploration, demonstration, modeling, thinking-aloud.* Introductory tasks ask the student to:
- draw on personal experiences
- manipulate tangible objects
- examine illustrations
- view a film
- observe
- read
- listen to "mini" lecture or tapes
- discuss
- dictate

Practice

How to design activities to reinforce student understanding, increase familiarity, support skill acquisition, and/or facilitate memorization. Types of error correction that support student. Use of *teacher-directed, guided or independent tasks focusing skills/strategies in isolation and in context—uses of worksheets, explorations, repeated exposures (drills)and/or authentic materials.* Rehearsal of use of skills/strategies ask the student to:
- label, diagram, illustrate, plot
- respond to oral or written questions
- drill facts with flashcards
- do repeated recitations
- select responses to multiple choice, sentence completions
- simulate
- complete worksheets
- use game formats
- drill and practice activities (e.g., flashcards, timed worksheets, computer-assisted instruction, games)
- programmed instruction, self-correcting tasks

Competence/mastery

How to design activities that provide students opportunities to use and apply skills mastered—use of *authentic tasks, problem-solving activities across the curriculum.* Tasks to demonstrate level of proficiency ask the student to:
- take test of specified format (e.g., respond aloud to a series of factual questions; respond to a set of multiple choice items, fill-ins, essays; match related items)
- develop a written report/outline/summary
- illustrate a poster/chart/comic strip
- construct a diorama/model
- arrange pictures in a collage to represent . . .
- state/discuss/debate ideas about . . .
- dramatize a play/role play of an event
- read, report, write, calculate, solve problem

FIGURE 6.9 *Continued*

Alter instructional materials and formats

- increase following directions (state or write short notes, limit number of directions, write/say/illustrate presentation of directions)
- alternatives for writing (e.g., dictating responses, cooperative story writing, taping responses, use of computer)
- alternatives for reading text on own (e.g., books on topic written at instructional/independent levels, partner reading, read-alouds, taped books)
- alternatives for calculating (e.g., calculator, write out procedure, use of charts)
- alternative ways to get information—taping lectures as presented, partner reading of text, illustrations corresponding to a lecture/text material
- different ways to introduce, practice or show mastery of skills/concepts
  Consider:
  - *looking at, observing, watching, viewing:* pictures, photographs, illustrations, posters, post-cards, magazines, comic strips, cartoons, caricatures, diagrams, graphs, illustrated webs, scrapbooks, slide presentations, models, television, videos/movies
  - *reading:* words, signs, captions, webs/mapping, outline, poems, limericks, sentence strips, telegrams, directories, newspapers, magazines, or literature
  - *performing actions:* mime, play, demonstration, being in a video
  - *listening to:* lecture, interview, record, tape, CD, dramatic readings, storytelling, speeches, music
  - *manipulating, touching, tactually exploring:* manipulatives, model, facsimile, artifacts, games, play with miniatures/objects representing concept
  - *tracing, coloring, creating, designing:* collage, diorama, puzzle, scrapbook, computer simulation, timelines, graphs, models, puppets, mobile, sculpture, postcard, map, weaving, mural, diagram, chart, coloring book
  - *talking, discussing:* discussion, debate, dialogue, simulation, role play, interpretive reading, dramatization, panel, question-answer
  - *listing, labeling, describing, writing, summarizing, critiquing:* outline, text, fact file bulletin board display, song, rap, play, puppet show, story, tests

Adapt testing procedures and formats

- Adjust time frame: extend amount of time, eliminate time limits, give breaks in response to student or after designated period, cut test into increments and spread over days
- Adjust presentation of test items: use a tachistiscope to frame one section at a time, enlarge print, limit number of items per page, limit number of items in sections
- Provide assistance: identify what adult may do (reread or restate directions, read sections, reword directions, paraphrase questions, highlight key words in questions or text, available to answer questions, help with unknown words either giving prompts or reading them, allow use of calculators or spell checkers
- Change the format of the test items—read the test to the student, record it on tape/CD, scribe student responses or allow for recording answers, choose appropriate response modes (multiple choice, matching, true-false, open-ended)
- Find alternative methods for the student to demonstrate the skills and concepts—portfolios, posters, etc.

Provide enhancements to support student strategic thinking and work (*how to approach*)

- Allow for prompts that facilitate accessing answers (e.g., charts for arithmetic facts, calculators, spelling notebook, handheld spell check, computer-based web for prewriting, taped or computer books)

FIGURE 6.9 *Continued*

- Provide guideline questions, encourage illustrations first, give a web for structure to support prewriting and thinking
- Use advanced organizers (preteaching vocabulary, presenting a skeletal outline of materials to be covered, prepared glossary of terms/concepts, study questions) to facilitate access to information
- enhance legibility of written work (use of graph paper, pencil grip, darkened lines, etc.)
- help the student organize to complete independent work (time and task managers)—notebooks, folders, schedule, to-do list, etc.
- give the student cues for staying on task (verbal directions, nonverbal signals, coded rules to which will respond)
- give the student skeletal outline of lecture or web to facilitate note taking
- Reading process (e.g., KWL, SQ3R, reciprocal questions, etc.)
- Writing process (e.g., TOWER, COPS, etc.)
- Participating—self-talk, FAST

Vary arrangements of physical/instructional context (*under what conditions*)

In what way do structures support the student navigating through instruction, participating in activity, and meeting expectations? *Optimal situations for learning for student.*
- provide opportunities to work in isolation—study carrel, secluded floor space
- give option of when to do assignment within day

Instructional settings/situations/arrangements: structures to enhance quality of interaction with peers and adults and learning experiences
- *Teacher-directed groups:* one-to-one situation with the teacher, small group (10 students or less), large group (15 or more students)
- *Teacher guided:* use of question/answer, types of feedback (immediate vs. delayed), contracts, scheduled "check-ins"
- *Peer activities:* cooperative learning activities, partner tasks, group projects, skill reinforcement games
- *Independent seat work*
- *Time management:* support student use and management of independent time through a personalized schedule for the day/week, to-do list, project timeline, serves as timekeeper for group activity, teacher/peer check-in
- *Pacing:* response to the pace of a lesson—fast tempo of flashcards, timed worksheets, computer games *vs.* reflective tempo of puzzlers, problem solving, and "think time" incorporated into activity
- *Task management:* response to procedure for completing an assignment; setting time limits, given cues regarding priorities and expectations

Introduce ways to enhance investment (*why teach*)
- Provide encouragement and feedback through written and verbal comments, positive attention time, and home-school communications, etc.
- Incentives (internal vs. external)
- Incorporate student interests through instruction
- Design contracts and reinforcements to recognize appropriate student performance/behaviors
- Develop self-monitoring checklists to guide behaviors, portfolio collections, etc.

FIGURE 6.9 *Continued*

Special Education Services/Specially Designed Instruction
In and Out of the General Education Classroom

When participation in the general education curriculum with or without modifications is not conducive for meeting student needs, attention is paid to reporting the alternative curriculum, methods, and materials the team has deemed suitable to promote progress toward IEP goals and objectives. The information to include in the IEP is what will be done when there is significant disparity between student needs and the general education grade-level standards/benchmarks/curriculum. Based on the decision to implement specially designed instruction to address present levels of academic achievement and functional performance and profile, you outline alternative curriculum (goals and objectives), instructional approaches, materials, interactions, and environments outside general education expectations and opportunities. This does not suggest plugging a student into a prescribed or scripted specialized program but rather it suggests the importance of drawing from a combination of instructional experiences and interventions that are directly responsive and tailored to the individual student to be implemented in or out of the classroom.

The Interaction Formula also supports reporting specially designed instruction alternatives to what is available through general education. Outlining individualized learning experiences that address the IEP goals and objectives is accomplished by detailing how to use the alternative curricular expectations for performance (what to teach/skills) to select specific instructional methods, materials, and assignments (how to teach and approach/ formats for performance and strategic thinking); tailor arrangements for delivering instruction (under what conditions/contexts for participation); and define ways to make specialized instruction relevant for the student (why teach/investment). Figure 6.10 offers a sampling of introduction, practice, and mastery ideas per area of concern, complementing the ideas found in Figure 6.9. Paul has been presented as a case study at different points in the book. Excerpts from his IEP illustrate each of the elements of the document and the connections among them.

Step 4: Identify Service Delivery
Plan/Program Components

The IEP document includes the logistics for carrying out the proposed plans for instruction, support, and ongoing assessment. The service delivery plan is written to orchestrate the student's access to general education curriculum and/or specially designed instruction. It designates *where* the student will receive instruction defined by the IEP, *who* will provide that instruction, and the *amount of time* that will be devoted to that instruction on a daily or weekly basis. Responsibilities are generally described around developing materials, direct contact with the student, scheduling learning experiences, and maintaining records of performance. To the extent possible, each statement, schedule, and/or matrix

FORMATS OF INSTRUCTION	Introduction	Practice	Competence/ mastery
READER	Choral reading, teacher read-aloud, read along, guided reading, parrot reading. Word building, word wall construction. Picture and table of contents, book walks.	Repeated readings, choral reading, books on tape, literature circles, computer-assisted instruction, phonics and word games (e.g., letter tiles, picture-word matches, cloze activities), flashcards.	Tape student readings, book talks, literature circles, story maps and other graphic organizers, reading journals.
WRITER	Prewriting (e.g., webs, tapes, response to structured questions), use of literature as example of different aspects of writing, structured intro of spelling rules and word making.	Guides for moving from webs to free writing, tasks to help develop editing skills (e.g., punctuation songs, DOL), picture writing, writing center, rewriting a story's ending or setting.	Letter, journal, story, etc. writing. Editing prescribed or own paragraph. Correcting misspelled words, building words. Copying draft.
MATHEMATICIAN	Use manipulatives, number lines to guide students to discover or follow a concept. Use literature about math to make connections. Talk through concept or procedures.	Repetitive drills— programmed instruction, mad minutes, computer-assisted instruction, flashcards, timed activities for repeated exposures. Problems to solve with manipulatives, actions.	Response to flashcards, journal explanations for concept, word problems.
PARTICIPANT/ MEMBER	Structured format to labeling social skills, using a social script or prescribed simulation to examine what they look and sound like, reading literature that corresponds with desired behavior/ social responses.	Open-ended simulations/ problem solving, group activities related to identified skills, journal writing about a situation, processing challenges in relation to the identified skills.	Oral or written responses to *problems* involving skills, engagement in simulations, proposals of how to resolve social issues presented in children's literature.

FIGURE 6.10 Examples for Writing About Explicit/Direct Instruction In and Out of the Classroom: Introduction, Practice, and Mastery

describes how each component will be integrated into a cohesive program, answering these questions:

- Who, where, and for how long will instruction be delivered?
- What types of supports are beneficial for this student in and out of the classroom?
- Who will have what responsibilities?
- How will efforts be coordinated?
- What materials are available to support the student?
- When is it best for the student to be where?

The proposal for the overall program resembles a matrix of times, places, and people. Identify the context in which instruction will be delivered and those responsible for planning, developing materials, and delivering each aspect of the program. Commitments to collaborative planning are implicit in this section. Depending on student needs and program opportunities, direct instruction may be delivered by special educators or designated tutors/paraprofessionals and/or the classroom teacher in or out of the classroom setting. The service delivery plan may be presented on the IEP in chart form or as a formal schedule that shows *where* the student will receive direct instruction—a self-contained setting, resource room, or classroom; *who* will deliver services—a special educator, classroom teacher, related service provider, tutor or paraprofessional, two teachers teaming, classroom teacher with the support of the resource teacher/consultant; and the *way* the schedule will be structured—amount of time (increments of 15-, 30-minute blocks etc., or number of periods per day or week).

As you work to develop your understanding and writing of documents, you may find the checklist in the Criteria for Writing Effective IEPs Toolbox and the set of Think Abouts for Writing Education Plan Toolbox as helpful frameworks to apply what is discussed in this chapter. They guide articulation of each element of the document and help determine whether information is included and treated comprehensively. Often there is a limited amount of space allotted on the IEP for each of the elements. However, it is critical to include what is necessary to meet the criteria for writing an effective IEP as outlined, using attachments as needed.

Chapter Review: Focus and Decisions

Stage V: Write the Individualized Education Program

❏ Figure out how to convey the team's collective description of student status and struggles in the area(s) of concern

- How do I represent the team's collective data about the student as a reader, writer, mathematician, participant in the learning environment, and/or member of the classroom community?

❏ Determine how to communicate the substance of the individualized education program to facilitate access to general education and/or provide specially designed instruction

❏ Take the notes generated during the assessment integration part of the meeting to articulate IEP document components that convey:

- Profile of challenges the student faces with regard to the area(s) of concern, taking into account evidence of competence, levels and formats of materials, strategic thinking and approaches the student takes, patterns of errors he or she makes, impact of learning context on performance and products, and influence of his or her investment
- Description of the student's present levels of academic achievement and functional performance: entry-level skills/starting points for instruction

❏ Use notes from the planning part of the IEP meeting:

- How do I communicate the priorities, sequence, approaches to instruction, and documentation of student progress with regard to the area(s) of concern?
- How do I ensure that these sections serve as a guide to the teacher(s) responsible for instruction, as well as give the student and parents/caregivers a clear set of expectations of instruction that will transpire?

❏ Articulate statements and brief descriptions that communicate:

- The focuses and sequence of instruction in the area(s) of concern (goals and objectives)
- Criteria against which progress is judged and how evidence is documented
- The formats and materials for explicit instruction; ways in which the general education curriculum is accessed and/or specially designed instruction is outlined (teaching approaches and modifications)
- Delegation of cooperative responsibilities to team members to ensure proposed plans are implemented and documented (service delivery plan)

❏ Establish a plan for service delivery that is built on collaborative cooperation among the student, parents/caregivers, classroom teacher(s), special educator, and/or related service providers

- How do I represent the commitments that team members are making to implement the IEP? How do program components represent a collective effort to support student growth, participation, and progress in specially designed instruction and/or the general education classroom?

❑ Enter information into the corresponding sections of the school district's IEP form, checking for internal consistency across content.

- How does the content of the document fulfill requirements of internal consistency? How does the content of the document invite program implementers to use it as an ongoing reference?
- How does content of the document invite team members to conduct ongoing monitoring, report student progress, and amend what is needed?

Stage V: Apply and Learn

1. How do you ensure that the IEP reflects the data collected, has relevance to instruction in the area(s) of concern, and is internally consistent? How do you use the integrated data, the profile, and present levels of academic achievement and functional performance to construct the goals and objectives? What will you do to ensure connections between data collected and instructional planning?

2. As you go about preparing an IEP, how will the Criteria for Writing Effective IEPs in the chapter toolbox help support your thinking and remind you of what to include and address in the document?

3. Access an existing IEP. Make sure to preserve confidentiality. Critique each section of the document, using the Criteria for Writing Effective IEPs in the chapter toolbox. Identify ways to expand and clarify the content:
   a. Make suggestions about the student profile. Your task is evaluate the extent to which a comprehensive picture of the student in the area(s) of concern with respect to his or her educational setting is developed.
   b. Look back on student present levels of academic achievement and functional performance for each skill cluster to determine how well you understand where to begin instruction.
   c. Focus on how clearly the design of curriculum (goals, objectives, tools to monitor progress) provides a framework for instruction/intervention that reflects the present levels of academic achievement and functional performance and student needs and is related to grade-level curriculum/standards.
   d. Evaluate how the stated list of teaching strategies and modifications support student acquisition of skills and strategies identified by the goals and objectives.
   e. Given the set of present levels of performance (PLOP), yearly goals, and corresponding behavioral objectives, confirm the internal consistency among these proposed IEP elements.
   f. Evaluate the justifications for the service delivery plan.

Paul as a Writer

Profile

When given an open-ended assignment to write a story, Paul typically responds that he has nothing to write about. He stares into space, gets up to sharpen his pencil, and often shreds paper during writing time. These writing assignments are frequently not handed in. When given a prewriting web and some clear direction (story starter, outline of what to include, or set of general questions to be addressed in assignment), he illustrates ideas with stick figures and sketches, putting one to two words next to the pictures. After completing the prewriting tasks, he often asks the teacher or a peer to spell a word or offer an idea to help him get started or keep him going. Once he does get started, Paul writes a story that consists of a sentence per picture on the web, which basically informs the reader of who is in the story, where it takes place, and what happens. The sentences are short, simple ones of three to five words consisting of single-syllable words and limited description. Paul struggles to make connections among discrete ideas for a cohesive story or essay, often stringing the sentences together, using *and*, *then*, or *that*.

In contrast, when Paul dictates his story or essay to a scribe, the sentences are complex, vocabulary consists of multisyllabic words, and characters, setting, and events are better developed (use of description, action). The dictated stories still tend to be a series of actions that are related but not connected by a theme or threaded together by problem to solution. When Paul has an opportunity to talk about his ideas prior to writing, he includes more detail.

The amount Paul writes is, in part, influenced by the effort it takes for him to print and the challenges he experiences with spelling. Paul's own written work is full of erasures, retracing letters, and misspelled words. When he prints, he grips the pencil tightly close to the point and leans close to the paper. He forms letters by drawing and connecting shapes rather than making fluid motions. At times, Paul states that his hand is too tired to do any more writing. Paul uses a phonetic approach to spelling, and the words he writes closely resemble the intended word or are at least discernible. According to Paul, he tries to use words in his stories that he thinks he can spell or can get close to what he wants. He said he only uses his "talking words" when someone writes for him.

Present Levels of Performance

Idea Development for Story Writing

Paul preplans a story to include a limited number ideas for setting, characters, and events when given a blank web or story map that prompts him with questions where, when, who, and what happens. He sketches ideas for characters, setting, and events, jotting down one to two words per category. When he transfers information from his web, he tends to write a sentence per idea without creating connections among story elements.

Idea Development for Nonfiction

When writing nonfiction reports, essays, or journals, Paul strings basic ideas together in an order, connecting them with the word *then*. Ideas are listed in simple sentence, all related to the topic . . .

Spelling

When writing an essay or story, Paul analyzes words into their component sounds and applies VC, VCe, and some VVC (ai, ea, oa) patterns to single-syllable words, confusing er and ir. When Paul does attempt to spell multisyllabic words in isolation or text, he breaks them down by sounds rather than chunks omitting some of the sounds and missing some of the silent letters governed by rules.

Paul does spell some basic sight words accurately but again primarily single-syllable ones and those that appear on lists for grades 1 and 2 (seen when he does complete quick writes and drafts in class).

Conventions of Print

Paul capitalizes the first word of the sentence consistently when writing stories, journals, and essays. He applies rules for proper nouns when it is a person's name.

Paul uses a period, question mark, and exclamation point to mark the end of each thought/sentence during structured DOL writing tasks. He recognizes commas, quotation marks, and apostrophes in text when he is reading and states how they are used. However, he does not apply these marks in his writing of individual sentences or those in paragraphs.

Handwriting

Paul forms printed letters correctly, using a counterclockwise motion for circle letters, going top to bottom for line letters, and crossing letters with a left to right stroke. Letters tend to get clumped together or trail across the page, making it difficult for him and others to discern all that is written when writing a story or answering end-of-chapter questions from a text.

Goal 1: Idea Development for Story Writing (Use of Graphic Organizers)

Paul will develop skills in brainstorming story elements, writing phrases to describe the setting (where, when, mood) and character (what looks like, how acts, how deals with issues and others).

Objectives

Given a picture of a scene, Paul will brainstorm words and phrases that describe features of the setting (sky, terrain, landscape, shadows), representing time of day, place, climate, and mood.

Given a set of pictures representing a character involved in a situation, Paul will complete a character map, generating phrases that describe physical features, problems faced, emotions experienced, and actions taken.

Given a setting description, Paul will brainstorm a dilemma a character may face, indicating what brought the character to the place, how he or she handles the place, and the emotions he or she experiences.

Given a story, Paul will make a reverse web, identifying key elements that the author would include/stating how the main character handles the problem and reaches solution, the set of events that may have occurred, his or her dialogue or interactions with others, and changes in setting.

Given a character map and a stimulus picture, Paul will create a main character for a story, using sets of phrases to describe what he or she looks like, situations to address, dialogue he or she might use, and emotions he or she experiences.

Given a character map, Paul will create a main character for a story, writing sets of phrases to describe what he or she looks like, situations to address, emotions he or she experiences, and relations to others.

Goal 2: Idea Development for Story Writing (Use of Graphic Organizers)

Paul will develop skills for outlining a story by identifying a story beginning (introduction of problem), middle (sequence of events in which main character deals with roadblocks), and end (in which character finds a solution).

Objectives

Given the beginning and middle of a story, Paul will brainstorm solutions to end the story, identifying how the main character reaches solution, stating the set of events that may occur, his or her dialogue or interactions with others, and changes in setting.

Given the beginning and ending of a story, Paul will brainstorm ways for the main character to resolve problem, stating the set of events that may occur, his or her dialogue or interactions with others, and changes in setting.

Given a web of story ideas, Paul will state how he will develop ideas, coding the order in which he will use them and indicating how he will expand and connect them.

Given a completed story web, Paul will ask himself how to use the information to convey a cohesive story, focusing on ties between the setting as background for actions, relationships among characters, and connections from problem to solution.

Documentation of Progress/Monitoring and Evaluation Strategies

- Collect graphic organizers and chart quality of content against a rubric.
- Compare content of graphic organizer with story or reader response produced.
- Gather Paul's self-monitoring checklist of what he included on the graphic organizer and in the subsequent story.

Explicit Individualized Instruction for Goals 1 and 2

- Use picture books as models for setting, character development, examination of situations, connecting language used with key questions to guide thinking. Use same questions to prompt student's brainstorming and use of web. Structure the teaching experiences to start with student verbally brainstorming and moving to writing or using the Inspiration program to enter ideas.
- Introduce a variety of graphic organizers with key questions to engage the student in developing ideas.
- Use grade-level literature and have Paul extract elements of the story, predicting upcoming events. Have him use his set of predictions to write an alternate next chapter or ending or an alternate setting, character, etc.

Modifications for General Education for Goals 1 and 2

- For reader response activities, present entry questions that are related to the aspect of idea development he is addressing through explicit instruction, giving him opportunity to web or freewrite ideas.
- Provide Paul with an annotated web, using key questions to provide him with direction for his brainstorming.

Goal 3: Idea and Paragraph Development/Expository Writing

Paul will generate a written paragraph with a distinct topic of interest, identifying the focus and providing related supporting facts and details, and a connected clincher.

Objectives

Given a paragraph, Paul will identify what makes it cohesive and connected, explaining how the topic sentence establishes a focus and point of view, how supporting sentences present related and descriptive elaboration, and how the clincher brings the points made together.

Given a paragraph containing choppy/simple (short and to the point) sentences, Paul will explain what types of descriptions and connectors are missing, critiquing with reference to how the topic sentence establishes a focus and point of view, how supporting sentences present related and descriptive elaboration, and how the clincher brings the points made together.

Given a set of five sentence cards, Paul will arrange them to create a cohesive paragraph, explaining how the topic sentence establishes a focus and point of view, how supporting sentences presents related and descriptive elaboration, and how the clincher brings the points made together.

Given a paragraph written on separate cards and containing choppy sentences, Paul will rewrite and arrange sentences, creating a cohesive and flowing paragraph that ties topic sentence/focus and point of view with how supporting sentences presents related and descriptive elaboration, and how the clincher brings the points made together concisely.

Given webbed information on a topic, Paul will generate a cohesive paragraph, using an introductory sentence that establishes a focus or point of view, supporting sentences to elaborate on related details, and a clincher that ties the key points together.

Documentation of Progress/Monitoring and Evaluation Strategies

- Make anecdotal notes regarding Paul's response to practice activities.
- Collect samples of Paul's focused paragraph writing.
- Gather Paul's self-monitoring checklist of how he saw his paragraph writing.

Explicit Individualized Instruction for Goal 3

- Use nonfiction and fiction picture books that convey concise information in paragraphs as models and resources from which to draw. As move to Paul writing his own paragraphs, give him the opportunity to mimic those in literature and/or do a quick research related to topic.
- Use formula poems (cinquain, haiku, etc.) as prewriting for paragraphs to get the description and flow of ideas down as the bases for building.

Modifications for General Education for Goal 3

- Use journal writing as response to enhance topic-based writing, using the self-monitoring questions developed during explicit instruction.
- Give Paul the option to use formula poems to respond to essay-type assignments.

Goal 4: Sentence Structure

Paul will build and revise sentences to combine ideas, using compound subjects or predicates to convey descriptions and create pictures of objects, actions, and purposes.

Objectives

Given a set of pictures depicting actions and a common character, Paul will write a single sentence, incorporating the series of actions with parallel structures.

Given a set of pictures depicting actions and a common character, Paul will write a single sentence, conveying the relationships among the series of actions, using connectors (e.g., *but also, however, resulting in*).

Given a set of pictures with characters involved in common activities, Paul will generate a single sentence, capturing the themes across the illustrations, a collective noun or series of subjects to represent who is involved, and descriptors to convey shared emotions.

Given a set of the same picture with progressively more detail, Paul will build a sentence to incorporate the information, using adjectives, connecting words to combine the independent thoughts.

Given two simple sentences, Paul will write a single sentence, critiquing the choppiness of the ones presented and explaining how to use common subject and actions and determine relationships to combine them.

Given a simple sentence, Paul will expand the content while retaining sentence structure, adding descriptors and words to convey relationships among subjects or actions.

Documentation of Progress/Monitoring and Evaluation Strategies

- Make anecdotal notes regarding Paul's response to practice activities.
- Collect samples of Paul's writing to evaluate his application of sentence structure and fluency to assignments.
- Gather Paul's self-monitoring checklist of how he saw his development of sentences in his writing.

Explicit Individualized Instruction for Goal 4

- Use pictures and picture books to examine simple, *bare-bones* sentences and raise questions about readability, flow, and way to create picture. Provide opportunities to manipulate word cards to generate ways to expand simple sentences. Teach key questions to guide thinking about combining and expanding sentences. Use same questions to prompt student's brainstorming ideas for sentences and monitoring own writing.
- Use picture books and grade-level literature as examples of combined and expanded pictures. Select predictable books that illustrate building ideas into a single sentence.

Modifications for General Education for Goal 4

- During freewrites and revision stage of the writing process, prompt Paul with a set of questions to guide his looking at the quality of his sentences, applying the focus(es) of his direct instruction.
- Give Paul an opportunity to conference with partners, using prompts about sentence fluency as the focus.

Goal 5: Spelling Multisyllable Words

Paul will spell two- and three-syllable words segmenting root words from affixes and applying vowel patterns (e.g., ai, ui, ea, ou, etc.) on lists and in writing samples.

Objectives

Given a picture of an object/multisyllabic word, Paul will state the word, analyze it into component parts, separating affixes from root word, and write it, representing sound clusters and applying the double-vowel rule.

Given a sentence with a missing word, Paul will state and write the word, analyze it into component parts, separating affixes from root word, and write it, representing sound clusters and applying the affix and vowel rule.

Given a sentence containing multisyllabic words, Paul will read it aloud, asking himself whether the words look correct, represent sounds, and check by breaking them down by affixes and root words to figure out if they are spelled correctly.

Documentation of Progress/Monitoring and Evaluation Strategies

- Make anecdotal notes regarding Paul's response to practice activities.
- Chart Paul's performance spelling words from prepared lists.
- Evaluate Paul's spelling in writing samples, comparing use with words (or similar ones) from lists.

Explicit Individualized Instruction for Goal 5

- Use letter tiles containing root words and affixes, modeling how to chunk, think about vowel patterns, and looking at the way the word looks.
- Provide opportunities to use spelling words in journal writing, brainstorming their relationship to topics and connections among those targeted.
- Create a dictionary for rules and spelling of multisyllabic words.

Modifications for General Education for Goal 5

- Provide access to a handheld spell checker to support writing.
- Provide word banks or brainstorm key words as a class or with a peer for topic-generated writing.
- Remind Paul to use the dictionary he creates.

I. **Does the PROFILE/LEARNING STYLE** section provide an overview of who the student is as reader, writer, mathematician, participant in the learning environment, and/or member of the classroom community? How does the narrative describe the quality of the student's performance as a response to different learning conditions? How does the narrative . . .

❑ characterize how the student approaches books, the writing process, problem solving, and/or participation in related activities?

❑ describe how the student performs when demands change (e.g., dictate vs. write story, read silently vs. orally vs. read to, calculate equations by rote vs. using counters vs. in head)?

❑ indicate the strategies the student uses when challenged (e.g., ways asks for help or relies on teacher prompts, deciphers unfamiliar words, uses prewriting or editing tools, figures out problems or equations)?

❑ present both the challenges and successes the student has with participating in related reading, math, written language, content area instruction, and independent and group activities?

❑ elaborate the impact of instructional materials, learning environment, teacher input, and/or incentives on student performance as a reader, writer, mathematician, participant?

❑ identify how language and personal experiences (background knowledge) affect performance and progress?

❑ convey how student attitude or self-perception relate to performance as a reader, writer, mathematician?

II. **Do the PRESENT LEVELS OF ACADEMIC ACHIEVEMENT AND FUNCTIONAL PERFORMANCE** identify student's repertoires of skills? How are competencies described? In what way are these descriptions . . .

❑ organized according to categories/skill clusters that collectively define what the student does as a reader (e.g., fluency, word recognition, retell), writer (e.g., prewriting, drafting, spelling), mathematician (e.g., addition of single digits, word problems)?

❑ an articulation of specific skills mastered and the corresponding conditions/ task demands (e.g., in isolation vs. context, when prompted) under which these are evidenced?

❑ clarifications of how well the student is familiar with the skills, is at an independent level, and/or applies them to authentic situations (e.g., reading a book, writing a story or report, solving a math problem)?

❑ indications of starting point(s) for instruction?

❑ connected with grade level equivalents *only* when referenced with specific instructional materials and demands?

III. Do ACADEMIC AND FUNCTIONAL GOAL STATEMENTS . . .

❑ directly address the present levels of academic achievement and functional performance?

❑ convey priorities in the student's program?

❑ set direction(s)/parameters for instruction?

❑ state the general outcomes of instruction by indicating skill clusters to be addressed or general targets of instruction?

❑ include an expected level of mastery?

IV. Do SPECIFIC OBJECTIVES/ BENCHMARKS . . .

❑ begin at the "next step" that comes after the present levels of academic achievement and functional performance?

❑ establish skill sequences that progress toward each of the academic and functional goals?

❑ articulate the skills and actions the student will demonstrate?

❑ identify the conditions (tasks or activities) under which the student will perform/behave?

❑ define criteria for reaching mastery of the specific skills?

V. Do DOCUMENTATION OF PROGRESS/MONITORING AND EVALUATION STRATEGIES . . .

❑ reflect the criteria for mastery set in the specific objectives/benchmarks?

❑ specify the types of evaluative strategies to be used?

❑ identify the frequency of measurement?

❑ directly reflect instruction provided?

❑ document descriptive accounts of performance, error patterns, behaviors?

❑ count number of correct items or appropriate behaviors?

❑ provide substantial data to judge the effectiveness of the educational plan (specific components or overall program)?

VI. Do the DIRECT INSTRUCTION/ALTERNATIVE TEACHING APPROACHES and METHODOLOGIES . . .

❑ designate types of instructional materials?

❑ address direct instruction of the identified academic and functional goals and objectives?

❑ correspond with the descriptions provided in the profile/assessment report?

❑ prepare the student to participate in the next least restrictive environment (LRE)?

VII. Does the section, which asks about ACCESS TO GENERAL EDUCATION CURRICULUM, INCLUSION, and MODIFICATIONS to enhance classroom participation describe:

A. Ways to modify or adapt instructional strategies and materials so the student may participate in classroom activities even though specific reading, writing, or math skills are not sufficient to
- ❏ gain introductory information from lecture, text, activity?
- ❏ practice skills or information through assigned readings, writing tasks, calculations?
- ❏ show what learned through essays, reflections, oral presentations?

B. Types of supportive conditions that help the student to . . .
- ❏ organize and manage time (scheduling)?
- ❏ attend to the pace of lessons?
- ❏ tolerate frustration?
- ❏ maintain on-task behavior (support task completion)?
- ❏ respond to teacher direction?
- ❏ enhance or engage in peer interaction?
- ❏ be independent in daily activity?
- ❏ be an active part of group activities?
- ❏ find learning spaces in which to work productively?
- ❏ seek systematic feedback and incentives?
- ❏ see ties with own interests in the learning context?

VIII. Do efforts for **ACCESS TO GENERAL EDUCATION CURRICULUM/ MAINSTREAMING/INCLUSION** include . . .

- ❏ alternatives to/or modification strategies for classroom materials approaches and environmental arrangements?
- ❏ suggestions for cuing devices, time and task management techniques, study and cognitive strategies that would enhance student performance?
- ❏ positive behavior supports and strategies for classroom?
- ❏ design of groupings for instruction that incorporate skills needed?

IX. Does **SPECIAL EDUCATION SERVICE DELIVERY PLAN/CHART:**

- ❏ relate nature of service (remedial, supportive, integrated, consultative)?
- ❏ address academic and functional goals with respect to the concept of LRE?
- ❏ specify logistics of service delivery (location, hours, frequency and personnel)?
- ❏ indicate student code or program prototype?
- ❏ identify consultation activities between classroom and special education teacher to ensure continuity of program, ongoing evaluation of progress, and continued mutual support?

Think-Abouts for Writing Educational Plan—Reader
Areas to prompt what to include in . . .

IEP GOALS: *Think about which skill clusters will support the student become a more effective reader, interacting with literature, written messages, and expository text. Define do what, with what, how/in what way.*

- Word recognition (e.g., sight word vocabulary, word families) and solving
- Use of word analysis skills (e.g., prefixes, suffixes, phonics rules for multisyllabic words)
- Use of pictures as cues
- Use of context as cues (e.g. using words/sentences/information before and after)
- Development of fluency (rate, expression, phrasing)
- Development of self-monitoring strategies (e.g., self-questioning: Does word make sense? Does story make sense?)
- Prediction topic, possible events, solution (e.g., use pictures/problems, and character actions)
- Summarize or retell story, highlighting problem to solution sequence, highlighting message, gaining meaning conveyed
- Sense of story by identifying and connecting story elements, drawing on beginning-middle-end
- Understand each story element and impact on meaning (character development, setting-mood, problem to solution/cause and effect, sequence)
- Identify literal/factual information stated in text (e.g., identifies character by name, physical features, actions; states where and when story takes place)
- Extract inferential information (e.g., implied relationships based on dialogue, meanings of symbols in story, events that impact outcomes, conclusions not stated in text)

IEP OBJECTIVES: *Think about progression of skills that bridge student present levels of performance to goals. Articulate the successive skills that define what the student will do under specified conditions.*

- Acquisition of sight vocabulary, phonics rules and applications, strategies for discerning multisyllabic words
- Fluency with regard to phrases, sentences, passages, stories
- Attribution of meaning to words, pictures, sentences, stories
- Definition of story elements (setting, problem, solution, characters, events), relationship of story elements to questions (who, what, when, where, why, in what way) to ask self, recognition of narratives as integration of story elements, connection of parts to whole story
- Extraction of information with reference to story elements, set of questions (who, what, when, where, why, in what way)

CRITERIA: *Think about the standards against which to measure student progress, setting clear guidelines that coincide with the skills targeted by each objective.*

- Pronouncing words correctly and as written
- Segmenting words into sound chunks and blending together to state the word
- Reading phrase by phrase, pausing at punctuation marks, and raising or lowering voice in response to type of end mark
- Using synonyms to restate information read
- Making predictions of upcoming events based on dilemmas described
- Extracting the mood of the setting and characters
- Depicting the sequence of key events as a chain reaction

DOCUMENTATION: *Think about what evidence is collectible and demonstrates student growth over time and relation to student learning experiences.*

- Running records of meaningful stories with corresponding retell
- Analysis of student reading journal or reader response or other such activities
- Retell of stories read
- Timed reading of word lists, passages

TEACHING APPROACHES: *Think about what learning experiences enable and teach the student the skills and strategies to be an effective reader.*

- Ways to introduce skills, offer opportunities to practice
- Types of literature, levels of books used to apply skills taught
- Types of error correction, prompts used to support
- Materials used to address and highlight the skills (e.g., reading materials, cooperative group situations)

MODIFICATIONS/ADAPTATIONS: *Think about how to support the student as he or she works to use new skills in different situations and engage in the general education.*

- Ways to cue the student
- Strategies to access reading materials above level
- Opportunities to learn about topic using appropriate-level materials
- Alternatives to learn about story, topic that does not require direct reading of materials
- Environmental preparation: situations in which student has opportunity to comfortably practice reading fluency and comprehension

Think-Abouts for Writing Educational Plan—Writer
Areas to prompt what to include in . . .

IEP GOALS: *Think about which skill clusters will support the student become a more effective writer, communicating through writing. Define do what, with what, how/in what way.*

- Analyze topic or idea to consider possible areas for writing
- Convey a sense of story (elements, flow, development)
- Use structure of expository writing
- Use prewriting strategies and planning to organize thoughts (e.g., checklist of story element questions, mnemonic device, web)
- Compose freewrite (e.g., with story starter, topic list, picture)
- Develop composition/complete paragraph (e.g., centering on a topic, genre, story element)
- Use revision strategies to enhance quality, development of ideas, connections within writing piece
- Use editing strategies to enhance readability, accuracy of statements
- Listen to the quality of sentences and paragraphs for communicating clearly
- Develop spelling sense (e.g., types of words/compound, sight or use of specific rules)
- Edit written work for mechanics/conventions of print (e.g., type of punctuation, proper nouns)
- Develop handwriting to communicate legibly

IEP OBJECTIVES: *Think about* progression *of skills that bridge student present levels of performance to goals. Articulate the successive skills that define* what *the student will* do *under specified conditions.*

- Rules of capitalization, distinction of proper vs. common nouns, when to use, how to determine use
- Development of character (examination of appearance, relationships, dialogue reflecting attitudes, emotions, response to problem, involvement in solution)
- Analysis of topic, use of details, generation of thesis statements, construction of essay
- State rules, recognize use, use in isolation, application to editing
- Development and use of specific strategies (TOWER, TREE, COPS)
- Hearing how sentences sounds
- Recognizing the way words look, sounds represented, analysis of words into component sounds, rules of sounds

CRITERIA: *Think about the standards against which to measure student progress, setting clear guidelines that coincide with the skills targeted by each objective.*

- Formulating questions consistent with intent of the assignment (e.g., describe: asking self what does it look like, sound like, feel like, and do; journal: who is involved; what happened first, second, etc.; what was the experience like)

- Including connected parts (e.g., use setting to convey mood, describe events in sequence that connects problem to solution)
- Presenting an argument that involves acknowledgment of disagreement and supporting evidence for one or two sides
- Organizing thinking around story elements
- Applying rules of grammar
- Analyzing words into component sounds and applying phonics rules, judging the way the word looks
- Applying rules governing capitalization of . . .
- Using preferred format of cursive or print, following lines and spaces of the paper and spacing between words

DOCUMENTATION: *Think about what evidence is collectible and demonstrates student growth over time and relation to his learning experiences.*

- Analysis of writing samples for targeted skills
- Analysis of prewriting formats and comparison with writing samples
- Performance on spelling tasks and comparison with qualities of spelling and errors on writing samples
- Performance on application of rules (DOL, or daily oral language), examination and analysis of drafts and discussion when editing writing

TEACHING APPROACHES: *Think about how to support the student as he or she works to use new skills in different situations and engage in the general education.*

- Types of opportunities to write: assignments
- Materials used to address and highlight the skills (e.g., reading materials, cooperative group situations)

MODIFICATIONS/ADAPTATIONS: *Think about how to support the student as he or she works to use new skills in different situations and engage in the general education.*

- Ways to cue the student
- Structures for prewriting per specific types of assignments
- Types of questions that engage the student in rethinking what is written and encouraging revision and/or editing
- Opportunities to circumvent actual writing (dictate, word-process)
- Opportunities to address spelling (handheld spell checker, own dictionary, buddy)

Think-Abouts for Writing Educational Plan—Mathematician
Areas to prompt what to include in . . .

IEP GOALS: *Think about which skill clusters will support the student become a more effective mathematician, solving problems through quantitative thinking and operations. Define do what, with what, how/in what way.*

- Sense of number and numeration/counting
- Develop understanding of specific operation addition, subtraction, multiplication, **or** division facts to . . . (e.g., read equations and represent with manipulatives, recall facts)
- Compute two-digit addition with regrouping (e.g., isolated examples/paper and pencil, in word problems)
- Approach to solving word problems (e.g., number of steps involved, way stated—in a sentence or single question format, with and without extraneous information)
- Use of life skills (e.g., use ruler to measure and calculate the area and perimeter of a rectangle, objects, picture figures)

IEP OBJECTIVES: *Think about progression of skills that bridge student present levels of performance to goals. Articulate the successive skills that define what the student will do under specified conditions.*

- Recognize, order, sequence numbers
- Recognize symbols, read equations, represent equation with action, calculate, rote
- Use a sequence of read or listen, identify question, extract key numbers, generate equation, calculate, answer questions
- Measure, use ruler, keep checkbook

CRITERIA: *Think about the standards against which to measure student progress, setting clear guidelines that coincide with the skills targeted by each objective.*

- Checking computations by using subtraction for addition, addition for subtraction, division for multiplication, and multiplication for division
- Checking computations by using a calculator
- Copying numbers accurately, in proper alignment, with sufficient space in which to work out problems using the operation that leads to solving the problem
- Proceeding from right to left
- Applying regrouping
- Sorting through pertinent and extraneous information presented in the problem
- Understanding implications of vocabulary (in all, less than, etc.) in questions to select the operation and represent action(s) of problem
- Writing a number sentence that represents the word problem
- Attaching correct units to answer

DOCUMENTATION: *Think about what evidence is collectible and demonstrates student growth over time and relation to his or her learning experiences.*

- Types and frequency of observations of student approaches to calculations, solving
- Analysis of student journal to determine how thinks through processes
- Notes regarding student participation in, response to different situations
- Notes regarding shared thinking as to how goes about calculations, solving

TEACHING APPROACHES: *Think about how to support the student as he or she works to use new skills in different situations and engage in the general education.*

- Ways to introduce skills, offer opportunities to practice—sequence of manipulatives, finger counting, number lines, objects to support understanding of processes, acquisition of vocabulary
- Materials used to address and highlight the skills (e.g., reading materials, cooperative group situations)

MODIFICATIONS/ADAPTATIONS: *Think about how to support the student as he or she works to use new skills in different situations and engage in general education.*

- Ways to cue the student to use supports for calculating, key into strategies for problem solving
- Introduction of charts, calculators to support accuracy in situations requiring fast pace responses or those that are challenging
- Types of questions that engage the student in seeing the ideas and relationships to math skills has and is developing

Think-Abouts for Writing Educational Plan—Participant in the Learning Environment/Member of the Classroom Community (Behavioral Issues) Areas to prompt what to include in . . .

IEP GOALS: *Think about which skill clusters will support the student become a more effective member of the classroom community and participant in the learning environment, responding to expectations and interacting socially. Define do what, with what, how/ in what way.*

* Attention
* Self-control
* Compliance
* Cooperation
* Acceptance by peers
* Self-esteem
* Use self-talk to support waiting for attention/help from adult (e.g., asking questions, telling statements)
* Volunteer responses in group discussions (e.g., raise hand, wait turn, take turn when go around group)
* Complete independent tasks (e.g., daily, homework, free reading, worksheets, journal)

IEP OBJECTIVES: *Think about progression of skills that bridge student present levels of performance to goals. Articulate the successive skills that define what the student will do under specified conditions.*

* Getting attuned with feelings
* Acquiring language to label feelings, thoughts
* Learning how to handle emotions
* Weighing options of what to do
* Responding to situations
* Engage in exchange/conversations about . . .
* Attend to . . .

CRITERIA: *Think about the standards against which to measure student progress, setting clear guidelines that coincide with the skills targeted by each objective.*

* Recognizing own body cues (grimace, smirk, lip biting)
* Using an I-message to share
* Using an inside voice
* Taking time away from peers to use deep breathing and calm down
* Stating the advantages and disadvantages of possible response to a situation
* Talking about own intentions of misbehavior.
* Accepting the stated consequence by following teacher directions

DOCUMENTATION: *Think about what evidence is collectible and demonstrates student growth over time and relation to his or her learning experiences.*

- Types and frequency of observations
- Analysis of student journal or response to "situation questions"
- Notes regarding student participation in different situations
- Notes on response to literature with comparable issues

TEACHING APPROACHES: *Think about how to support the student as he or she works to use new skills in different situations and engage in general education.*

- Ways to introduce skills, offer opportunities to practice
- Materials used to address and highlight the skills (e.g., reading materials, cooperative group situations)

MODIFICATION/ADAPTATIONS: *Identify how to support the student as he or she works to use "new" skills in difficult situations.*

- Ways to cue the student (responding to cues—e.g., stop think measures)
- Environmental preparation (cutting down on contaminants)
- Ways to respond to the student that deter *and* encourage
- Types of questions that engage the student in rethinking and reenvisioning

Stage VI

Implement the Individualized Education Program and Monitor Progress

As you read through this chapter, think about how implementers:

- Reach a collective understanding of the proposed plans defined by the IEP in order for the team of implementers to design a coherent, cohesive program for the student

- Draw from the content of the IEP to create specific instructional plans, develop learning experiences, and incorporate interventions designed to meet student needs in and out of general education

- Coordinate service delivery options to reflect the action plans derived from the student's IEP

- Work together to carry out the IEP and monitor student progress and program effectiveness, according to established criteria

- Suggest amendments to the IEP based on ongoing documentation of student responsiveness to program plans

Flowers Are Not in Your I.E.P., Young Man

Dr. Gary J. Makuch

Teacher, the young man said, I found this flower over the weekend and I
    want to know what made it grow.
Look, young man, you're in special education. You must have an IEP, it's the
    law you see.
And flowers are not in your IEP, young man!

You have short-term objectives in math and reading, young man.
You have long-range goals in self-help and getting along with others.
But flowers are not in your IEP, young man!

But, teacher, the young man said, I really want to know what makes the
    flowers grow.
Look, young man, your mother and father and the principal and I wrote your
    IEP and then we signed it, that's the law you see. And flowers are not in
    your IEP, young man!
Your IEP has an evaluation component, young man, it's the law, you see.
    And we want you to reach your objectives and attain your goals.
There's no time for anything else, and besides . . . flowers are not in your IEP,
    young man!

Please, teacher, the young man said, I'd rather learn about flowers than math
    or reading.
OK, young man, if you insist, but this will be a significant change in your IEP
    and your parents will have to agree, it's the law you see.
A month has passed, a conference was held, the IEP was revised, procedural
    safeguards were observed and all the necessary paperwork completed, it's
    the law you see.
And flowers are now in your IEP, young man.

But, teacher, the young man said, my flower is dead and I found a frog over
    the weekend and now want to know what made it grow.
Look, young man, your mother and father and the principal and I revised
    your IEP and we signed it, that's the law, you see.
And flowers are now in your IEP.

You have short-term objectives in math, reading, and flowers, young man.
You have long-range goals in self-help and getting along with others.
But frogs are not in your IEP, young man!

Source: Used with permission of the author.

Overview of Stage VI

Implementing the IEP means using the information contained in the document
to construct specific plans of action (Bateman & Linden, 1998; Dudley-Marling,
1985; Yell et al., 2003). The IEP sets the priorities for instruction, proposes
sequences of skill development, suggests guidelines for instructional approaches,
guides ways to make the general education curriculum accessible and constructive,

and outlines avenues for direct instruction (Bauwens & Korinek, 1993; Huefner, 2000). The document offers direction, but it does not stipulate the explicit content and logistics of daily activities.

Action planning is required to transform the IEP from a document into practice. The focus of action planning is to meet the individual student's needs through a coherent program in which specific adjustments to existing instructional experiences are designed, optimal individualized learning opportunities are created, student performance and participation are continuously monitored, and IEP implementers' activities are aligned. The plans of action require professionals to collaborate to determine and coordinate cooperatively the appropriate instructional practices for the area(s) of concern in and out of general education. Team members are jointly responsible for reviewing student performance and participation to determine progress that may result in making program changes (Clark, 2000; Yell & Shriner, 1997).

Action plans are derived from the IEP through an open and ongoing dialogue among the IEP implementers (Lytle & Bordin, 2001). Clarity around how each person works with the student and what he or she is expected to do breeds shared ownership for the demands of the education plan, commitment to student success, and investment in delivering a cohesive program (Reeve & Hallahan, 1994). Collaboration leads to a common understanding of the plans, coordinated efforts that are complementary and/or supplementary, distributed tasks and responsibilities, and mutual support. The team of implementers agrees to make regularly scheduled contacts to establish and/or coordinate learning experiences for the student, set expectations for his or her performance and participation; and make assigned responsibilities explicit with regard to planning, delivery of instruction, documentation, and review of student performance.

Implementation of the IEP requires practitioners to:

- Translate goals and objectives into lesson objectives and academic and social learning experiences, adding details to the teaching approaches, modifications, and interventions outlined in the IEP
- Identify when and how student performance/behavior is observed and data are collected
- Define, set in motion, and evaluate ongoing collaborative activities (co-planning, co-teaching, co-assessment) that support the program plans
- Create systems for documentation of student progress, collecting data as the program is implemented

Collaboration and cooperation among program implementers are critical to giving the IEP form, function, and life. Implementers work together to use the IEP as the resource for determining how to infuse curriculum content to address student needs and make learning meaningful in the context of daily instruction and activity. The cohesiveness of the student's program rests on implementers' collective understanding of identified priorities, shared endeavors to thread connections among curriculum and different types of learning experiences, and interventions to create combined commitment for communicating about the student's successes and continuing challenges (Dearmen & Alber, 2005). Ongoing communication among program implementers is interwoven throughout this step as they collectively:

- Prepare for implementation, figuring out the details of content for instruction, behavioral expectations, corresponding teaching approaches and materials, and forms of service delivery
- Deliver the program, following agreed-on uses of resources, strategies for learning experiences, and approaches to documenting student progress
- Monitor student growth, collecting evidence of student performance and participation in learning activities to determine whether progress is being made or program adjustments are warranted
- Revisit the IEP and make revisions as needed, evaluating the effectiveness of the contents of the IEP, based on data collected

Step 1: Prepare for Implementation

Preparing to implement the IEP involves continuing to engage in teamwork. During this step, the team membership is comprised of general education teacher(s), special educator(s), paraprofessional(s), and/or related service provider(s). The team's charge is to figure out ways to work together to plan instructional activities, set expectations for behavior and performance, synchronize responsibilities, configure service delivery formats and schedules, and report regularly to each other and parent(s)/caregiver(s). The IEP Implementer To-Do List Toolbox outlines steps for moving through a collaborative action plan for implementing and evaluating the IEP.

Initial conversations among program implementers center on the directions the IEP sets and the recommendations it proposes to determine what instruction looks like, who takes the lead for what areas, who facilitates student participation in what situations, how people work together or separately to instruct the student, who designs tasks for the paraprofessional(s) to use, and who collects authentic data for review. Subsequent meetings hone in on instructional planning, design of interventions, distribution of assignments, engagement with the student, development of co-teaching models when appropriate, examination of student progress and the effectiveness of different strategies, conferencing with parent(s)/caregiver(s), and/or revisiting the IEP to revise it as necessary. For meeting discussions to lead to constructive outcomes, it is important for the team members to:

1. Craft agendas that define what needs to be accomplished together in the times allotted effectively and efficiently
2. Reach a shared understanding of how the intent of the meeting(s) reflects what is targeted by the IEP
3. Brainstorm ideas relative to the focus of what the instruction looks like for the student

4. Develop a clear plan of action, building on decision making during the meeting
5. Delegate responsibilities for followthrough and follow-up

As the team of implementers works together to translate the IEP from a document into practice, it shifts the focus of discussions from gaining clarity on expectations for and about the student, to planning curriculum and instructional experiences, to designing systems for accessing the general education curriculum and alternative specially designed instruction, to determining how instruction is delivered, to articulating the ways teachers and paraprofessionals take on teaching responsibilities and make use of instructional space. When implementers come together to use the IEP to guide their work, they have the basis on which to examine and enhance what about instructional practices works for the student, augment current approaches with ideas from brainstorming sessions, alter materials or access additional ones, adjust instructional arrangements, and coordinate the overall program with each other. The substance of this planning involves making in-depth comparisons and connections among the IEP, the general education curriculum, and alternative plans to:

- Develop the content of instruction for the individual student
- Determine how to differentiate instruction in the general education classroom, making adjustments to accommodate his or her needs
- Establish consistent behavior expectations, proactive approaches to support appropriate choices, and strategies for responding to misbehaviors and delivering logical consequences
- Figure out what types of alternative instruction and materials are warranted
- Examine what types of service delivery are compatible with approved instruction or interventions
- Identify how student responses to assignments and activities help track performance in the area(s) of concern

When implementers talk and co-plan, they target objectives and develop instructional procedures that lead the student toward mastering the identified goal(s). This requires examining the opportunities afforded by the general education curriculum as well as considering specially designed alternatives. When looking within the general education curriculum, questions about how to augment teaching through modified, supplementary, or complementary instructional experiences are discussed to determine whether these are sufficient opportunities to address the IEP objectives.

Determining the substance of explicit instruction means figuring out what skills can be taught concurrently, which corresponding teaching approaches and materials are appropriate, and where or how these opportunities will be made available to the student. Access to the general education curriculum needs to meet specific skill cluster expectations for the student, include suitable approaches and materials for his or her successful performance, offer appropriate avenues for developing strategic thinking, use compatible contexts for participation, and provide incentives for learning. If it is difficult to use the general education curriculum as a vehicle for addressing student needs in the area(s) of concern, then it is important to create alternative instructional experiences that directly address targeted skill clusters/content areas, align materials and methodology, and/or vary the structure of the environment to match his or her style of learning and interests. The Interaction Formula Co-Planning Toolbox at the end of this chapter provides a structure for designing action plans and subsequent lessons to implement the IEP. It applies the Interaction Formula to support a comprehensive team approach to co-planning and lesson development.

The planning of instructional requirements leads to spelling out the details of the service delivery system for the student. It involves considering the independent work required of professionals, where alternative instruction takes place (in or out of the general education classroom), the possibilities available through co-teaching options, and potential paraprofessional duties. Coordinating and scheduling the delivery of plans rests on translating the IEP and putting it into operation through open communication and shared responsibilities.

Through collaborative discussions, programs implementers think about the different ways general education and alternative instruction address the focuses and provide opportunities for the student. As the general education teacher and special educator review the IEP, they banter back and forth, generating questions and ideas for addressing the goals and objectives. Translating IEP goals and objectives into lesson plans is a process of blending opportunities available through the general education curriculum with the need for complementary, supplementary, and/or specially designed lessons and activities. As the classroom teacher and special educator sit down to figure out what is appropriate, they use the IEP and general education curriculum as starting points to ensure the student gets what he or she needs (Weishaar, 2001).

Plan Collaboratively

Collaboratively planning how daily instruction addresses the IEP goals and objectives and facilitates access to the general education curriculum and/or specially designed instruction is essential to bridging learning experiences and ensuring a coherent program for the student. Close examination of the general education experience in conjunction with the demands of the IEP helps differentiate how planned existing, supplementary, and/or alternative instruction is to be carried out systematically so the student gains what he or she needs. Working side by side, the general education teacher and special educator come to an agreement as to what takes place as part of the general education classroom and how additional supports facilitate, complement, and/or replace in-class work.

Co-planning helps organize thinking about how to implement differentiated instruction for the student, explicitly taking into account what is being taught, how to approach instruction, how to involve him or her in thinking strategically, and how to arrange the setting for implementing units of study, lessons, daily assignments, and activities in conjunction with behavior intervention plans as needed. Making decisions about appropriate learning experiences and the necessary modifications requires close examination of the IEP relative to classroom behavioral expectations and structures, content focuses, teaching methods, materials, and assignments, and instructional settings. Such planning offers the general education teacher and special educator ways to incorporate grade-level standards and benchmarks, address behaviors, configure alternative instruction, and direct their role(s) and activities as well as those of paraprofessionals to reflect the IEP.

Co-planning applies IEP information to design:

- *Learning outcomes:*   What the student is expected to accomplish and demonstrate with reference to specific skills per cluster and levels of understanding, examining the match between where to begin instruction for the student and what are considered acceptable gains for participation in the general education curriculum (Schumm et al., 1994)
- *Explicit instruction:*   Teaching approaches to activate prior knowledge and introduce skills/concepts through explanations, illustrations, and/or modeling
- *Practice and evaluation activities:*   Types of tasks, use of materials, levels of questions, and qualities of problems posed to engage the student; active learning and exploration, guided and independent practice, and response to authentic assessments
- *Environmental context or structures:*   The expectations, rules, procedures for participation, instructional arrangements (groupings of students, independent work, qualities of teacher direction), and classroom layout
- *Monitoring strategies:*   Analysis and recording of student performance; making use of charts, graphs, file folder systems that document student responsiveness to instruction

Step 2: Deliver the Individualized Education Program

An essential part of general and special education teachers' co-planning to address student needs in and out of the classroom is to outline ways in which they will continue to work together. The delivery of the IEP is contingent on establishing a web of support for the student and among the practitioners involved. This requires committing cooperatively to ongoing collaboration; articulating roles, responsibilities, and ways to share information and handle issues that arise. Coordinating implementation efforts is important in building a coherent set of experiences for the student, ones that share common and consistent expectations for behavior and performance, provide meaningful activities, establish accountability for engagement and assignments, promote participation and independent learning, and foster membership in the classroom community. Working together ensures communication to coordinate services, create complementary schedules, select suitable places for instruction, and facilitate and document student progress.

Develop Co-Teaching Models and Paraprofessional Responsibilities

Co-Teaching

It is during this step that ideas for co-teaching options and involvement of para-professionals are determined. Teachers negotiate which co-teaching strategies make sense given student needs, the situation(s), and the potential benefits for peers. Exploring *co-teaching options* (Bauwens & Horcade, 1995; Bauwens, Hourcade, & Friend, 1989; Friend & Cook, 1992; Friend, Reising, & Cook, 1993; Pugach & Johnson, 2002) based on the design of instructional plans driven by the IEP gives the classroom teacher and special educator a range of implementation strategies to individualize learning opportunities. There are many combinations of co-teaching options from which to choose, where practitioners decide what and how to teach and the various roles and responsibilities they will assume. Different models of co-teaching include the following:

- *Coach and Trainer:* One teacher provides direct instruction while the other circulates to help students participate.
- *Dance Team:* One teacher provides the instruction and the other provides the follow-up activities for additional practice with content or study skills
- *Mirror Image:* Teachers split up the group into two and teach the same basic concepts with the same material
- *Sculptors:* Teachers split up the group and work on the same concept but use different materials and approaches to teach it
- *Tag Team:* Each teacher does a segment of the lesson
- *Speaker and Interpreter:* One teacher has the primary role of presenting information while another teacher paraphrases, interprets, asks clarifying questions, or offers examples or illustrations
- *Shadow Boxers:* One teacher has the primary role of presenting information while another teacher writes notes, models, outlines charts and key points, and/or illustrates ideas on the overhead or board
- *Player and Commentator:* One teacher has the primary role of demonstrating what to do while another teacher describes how to go about each of the steps
- *Duet:* Both teachers present segments and build off each other's ideas and information, presenting a dialogue in front of students and feeding off each other

The Role of the Paraprofessional

Paraprofessionals take on a number of roles as they support the implementation of IEPs. They are often a part of the service delivery plan to provide assistance to students to access general education and/or specially designed instruction. Whether supporting the student in the general education classroom or alternative settings, they may be called on to facilitate small groups or one-to-one situation(s) to provide explanations, reinforce what is taught, pick up on student confusions, and/or reteach as needed. They may also assist in keeping the pace of instruction moving, supporting transitions between tasks, and maintaining student attention. When fulfilling responsibilities, paraprofessionals must understand classroom structures and expectations for when and how to shadow, supplement, and support in ways that are consistent with and complement the lead teacher.

Paraprofessionals require the tools to manage the different situations in which they are found. Regardless of what the situation presents, they need to have an understanding of the student's IEP and subsequent planning to be clear about how to work with the student, the performance and behavior expected, techniques for offering help and error correction, ways to respond to frustrations and/or misbehaviors, ways to provide the student feedback, and strategies to instruct and/or modify task demands on the spot.

Drawing distinctions between the roles of certified teachers and those of the paraprofessional is key to ensuring that quality services are provided to identified students. Rather than expect paraprofessionals to know how to instruct and handle different situations, classroom and special education teachers need to prepare, mentor, and supervise them. It becomes the practitioners' job to clarify and define the role(s) paraprofessionals play, establish the purposes for their instruction and support, and create opportunities for dialogue through which their insights are shared, questions and concerns are raised, and suggestions for daily implementation and evaluation of the IEP are discussed.

Creating parameters for what is expected leads to identifying who does what with the specific instructional program and tasks, when there is freedom to make choices, and the extent to which the schedule is fixed versus flexible. When paraprofessional responsibilities are explicit and support is provided, boundaries are established for what their roles are in delivering services and how expectations are defined for appropriate ways to support the student through delegated tasks (Gehrlach, 2004; Stetson et al., 2000). Establishing working relationships with reference to defined roles and responsibilities facilitates the classroom and special education teachers giving feedback to paraprofessionals regarding their performance in implementing the IEP and documenting student behavior and progress.

In planning for paraprofessionals as part of implementing the IEP and delivering services, consideration is given to these questions:

- How does the paraprofessional need to be prepared to understand what and how to teach and how to address behaviors to carry out his or her responsibilities with regard to the IEP?
- What are the roles and responsibilities of the paraprofessional with the student and in support of the classroom teacher and/or special educator?
- Who decides on a day-to-day basis what the paraprofessional does? What tasks are delegated to the paraprofessional? How are specific activities planned and communicated? Who creates lesson plans and gathers related materials?
- How clearly are implementation guidelines set with regard to planning instruction, intervening around behavior and performance challenges,

providing help to the student, and coexisting with professionals in the classroom and/or alternative settings?

- What aspects of the roles of the paraprofessional require supervision? How are his or her activities and interactions with the student monitored? Who serves as the direct supervisor of the paraprofessional for what aspects of the day? To whom does he or she report to give feedback and offer insights about student performance; ask questions about adjustments to instruction, materials, tasks, and activities; and evaluate the most appropriate environment for instruction?
- To what extent and how is the paraprofessional included in the collaborative efforts of the classroom teacher and special educators around supporting the progress of this student? To what extent and how does the paraprofessional participate in parent/caregiver conferences and IEP reevaluation meetings?

Cooperative Implementation

All implementers must work together, continuing to engage in communications to monitor delivery of the plan into action, check on how effectively ideas are working, respond to questions as they arise, share observations of the student, keep services coordinated, and foster their relationships. Synchronizing work with the student, cross-referencing teaching approaches with student performance, and evaluating service delivery strengthens the services provided to the student. As practitioners work together to implement, they:

- Share updates as student performance unfolds, keeping the flow of information relevant
- Problem-solve to support each other with implementation of interventions and modifications
- Address issues that arise relative to student performance, classroom chemistry, and/or curriculum
- Review and revise co-teaching options and involvement of paraprofessionals to enhance student learning and ensure professional support
- Collect data to document student progress to monitor program effectiveness

Step 3: Monitor Student Progress and Program Effectiveness

As professionals implement instruction, they must maintain ongoing communication about student progress. Documentation of student performance, participation, and progress is critical to making determinations about what is and is not working. When professionals design authentic tasks for assignments, they have opportunities to gain substantive samples of what the student is doing and how he or she is responding to instruction, materials, and/or settings. It is important to incorporate ways to monitor what is happening with the student during daily lessons to keep track of the student and get immediate feedback on the impact of instruction, interventions, and modifications. The team of program implementers is expected to collect evidence and respond to the following questions to address how the student is progressing in the area(s) of concern:

- What are the skills the student is expected to demonstrate? How are they documented over time?
- What types of ongoing tasks serve as authentic assessment tools to document student performance and evidence of possible growth? How do these measures reflect IEP goals and objectives?
- How effective are the instructional strategies, modifications, and interventions for enhancing participation and advancing student performance in the area(s) of concern?
- How are criteria from IEP objectives used to analyze student progress and challenges?
- How effective are instructional strategies and modifications for advancing student performance and enhancing participation in the area(s) of concern?
- How do assessment data link to revising the student's IEP?

Monitor Student Progress

Monitoring student progress is a commitment to collect evidence of student performance and behavior systematically. It is helpful for implementers to take the goals and objectives and list the pertinent skills to be tracked and criteria for judging student performance over time. Charts, lists on the face of file folders, and notebooks with organizing tabs offer systems for managing student responses to instruction, situations, and/or performance and participation under various conditions. When authentic tasks are used throughout lessons or units of study, examination of student use of skills in real contexts is readily available. The teacher may use the list of IEP objectives as a cover sheet to a file folder or notebook to help chart what documents provide verification of student performance. Or the teacher may engage the student in developing a portfolio of his or her work, giving guidelines for what to include. The portfolio provides an opportunity for the student to self-monitor, think about his or her performance, and develop a sense of making progress. The student and teacher can then share the portfolio with parents/caregivers to explain and substantiate student gains. However, when initially adopting an approach to ongoing monitoring of student progress, it is helpful to situate forms, questions, charts, and so on, to guide observations and/or serve as reminders to collect data.

Develop rubrics, checklists, portfolio baskets, and filing systems to keep evidence organized and information readily accessible, staying attuned to what is happening as a result of implementing the IEP. Ways to collect ongoing assessment data are described in the document. It is most helpful when assignments and activities directly address or embed the IEP goals and objectives so that student performance reflects the targets with authenticity. Gathering work samples or making anecdotal notes to capture student responses to situations and instruction are a part of implementing the educational plan. The documentation provides evidence to evaluate the extent to which the student is making progress—what the student is doing, what has or is changed, and what represents progress and participation (Alexandrin, 2003; Peck & Scarpati, 2005). Parents/caregivers are an important source in determining student progress and observing growing confidence. Remember to seek their input.

Different sources of assessment data are the activities in which the student is asked to respond. These assessments serve as data regarding student acquisition of IEP outcomes in relation to grade-level curriculum standards and corresponding benchmarks that are targeted through instruction. These data confirm progress or raise questions about the effectiveness of instructional practices used. IEP progress reports to parent(s)/caregiver(s) are informed by the documentation.

Monitor Program Effectiveness

The annual and/or triannual review requires the team to reconvene for the purpose of determining the effectiveness of IEP recommendations in terms of learning outcomes and access to general education and/or special education and related services for the student. The team engages in data-based decision making, reviewing evidence of how the student is functioning and progressing with regard to academic and social performance in the area(s) of concern, use of strategic thinking, and investment in relation to specific tasks, materials, and settings. The team examines progress according to IEP goals and objectives, referring to grade-level and/or modified general education curriculum standards and benchmarks to give implementers substantive information and points of reference for future planning.

Team members work together, collating the information to develop a holistic view for evaluating the overall effectiveness of the program. They examine the cohesiveness, benefits, and drawbacks of program elements. They take into account the extent to which different aspects impact and fit together for the student and substantiate what adjustments need to be made and whether more or less restrictive environments are appropriate. With what is gleaned, they make a commitment to update the IEP to be consistent with its current path and/or to address required changes that better meet student needs.

Maintaining documentation of performance and behavior is retaining evidence of what the student is doing for the purpose of evaluating the effectiveness of IEP recommendations, providing implementers substantive information for discussions. Regardless of the system the implementers set up, it is important to be attuned to the impact of the different aspects of the program and whether it supports student academic and social learning in the school environment.

Chapter Review: Focus and Decisions

Stage VI: Implement the Individualized Education Program and Monitor Progress

❑ Figure out how to apply the IEP systematically in and out of general education to address student needs:

- How does the IEP blueprint for instruction translate into daily activities for the student? What factors do the classroom teacher and special educator consider and incorporate when they plan units of study and daily lessons to address area(s) of concern (Interaction Formula)?

❑ Select appropriate instructional methods, materials, and settings designed to address IEP goals and objectives:

- In what ways do goals and objectives translate into explicit/direct instruction?
- How are objectives taught simultaneously?
- How, when, and to what extent is the general education curriculum used to infuse IEP-related instructional focuses, applying modifications and interventions to planned participation?
- What forms do specially designed instruction take to address student needs directly and/or supplement general education learning experiences?

❑ Co-plan to design the specific learning experiences in which objectives will be addressed to facilitate access to general education curriculum with or without modifications and/or specially designed instruction to make them meaningful:

- Agree on teaching approaches and authentic tasks/contexts in which those skills are infused
- Coordinate service delivery in ways that distribute responsibilities for planning specific tasks, adapting materials, providing instruction, offering support to student and teachers
- Describe how team teaching and/or cooperative learning is applicable to the situations in which the student is placed

❑ Decide on schedules to engage in co-planning and check-ins to ensure continued cohesiveness of student program.

❑ Translate IEP into practice. Establish meeting times for program implementers to prepare instructional plans identified in the IEP.

❑ Establish systems of communication and ongoing record keeping to ensure coordination of learning experiences and determine program effectiveness and student progress:

- How are elements of the IEP infused throughout the student's day in ways that allow for maximum access to the general education curriculum to make classroom learning experiences meaningful and productive?

- How are elements of the IEP infused throughout the student's day in ways to allow for coordination of specially designed instruction in and out of the classroom?
- How are actual instructional efforts coordinated and responsibilities distributed among implementers to ensure that student needs/the IEP are being addressed?
- What system(s) of record keeping support ongoing monitoring of student progress? How will program implementers share information regarding student participation and performance in instruction across settings?
- How will the student be involved and parents/caregivers informed of his or her progress in the area(s) of concern?

Stage VI: Apply and Learn

1. Interview a classroom teacher and/or special educator and ask what they do to prepare for implementing IEPs. Learn about the types of communication and collaboration used to support implementation. Find out how they collect ongoing data to document student progress and effectiveness of the plan. Review interview information to explain what the responses tell you about the usefulness of the IEP. Think about why the document does or does not serve professionals as a blueprint for instruction. Reflect on the kinds of communication established between the classroom teacher and special educator.

2. What steps will you take to prepare for implementing IEPs? What are your personal goals for cooperative teaming with colleagues? What needs to be accomplished? How will you go about planning and working together?

3. Explain co-teaming options in terms of roles, tasks, and responsibilities of the classroom teacher and special educator in relation to implementing the IEP. How will you co-plan or co-teach with a colleague? Try to identify one subject area to address from a collaborative approach. Describe how the two of you will establish an agreement, create a plan, and evaluate the effectiveness of your work together.

4. How will you work with a paraprofessional to support his or her role in implementing an IEP and monitoring student progress?

5. What types of documentation strategies make sense given the student situation and your roles and responsibilities as the implementer?

6. What types of ongoing communication with colleagues and parents/caregivers will you establish to ensure that the IEP is implemented effectively?

Establish a collaborative agreement:
☐ Set ground rules for working together
☐ Agree to set a common focus for each discussion with outcomes for time together
☐ Take notes during meetings to document ideas and solutions generated
☐ Establish consistent meeting and check-in times

Develop preliminary plans:
☐ Review the IEP, highlighting student needs and strengths
☐ Translate IEP goals and objectives/benchmarks into focuses for instruction
☐ Identify shared focuses for instruction, ones that overlap student instruction in and out of the general education curriculum
☐ Discuss general education curriculum to identify key skills/concepts and themes to determine compatibility with IEP focuses
☐ Determine what alternative instruction is necessary and what happens during allocated times
☐ Share ideas for approaches, materials, and instructional arrangements pertaining to student academic and/or social needs
☐ Organize ideas into units of study and lesson plans (intro, practice, independent, group activity, long-term assignment(s), etc.)
☐ Explore how learning across the curriculum, including the arts and physical education, may be achieved
☐ Give members assignments to collect materials and expand on preliminary teaching ideas

Create specific plans:
☐ Share ideas and materials pertaining to the focuses of instruction
☐ Sketch out the connections between targeted concepts and skills and instructional approaches, materials, tasks, and assignments
☐ Set expectations for behavior and performance
☐ Sequence the plan of ideas and materials and map out a schedule of instruction and assignments
☐ Assign roles for delivering instruction (e.g., develop materials, presentations, activities, readings, assignments, etc.)
☐ Identify assignments, tasks, and observation that will be used to document progress
☐ Determine where and when instruction will take place
☐ Identify the ways paraprofessional support will be used by defining expectations for implementation of plans, responses to student, documentation and feedback about his or her performance
☐ Set up formal and informal ways for implementers to share what is going on with the student and schedules

Develop co-teaching models and paraprofessional responsibilities:
☐ Select co-teaching styles suited for the different activities and learner needs
☐ Assign roles and responsibilities
☐ Set the schedule for *who* does *what when*

Deliver program and monitor student progress:

☐ Carry out agreed-on plans

☐ Make note of questions that arise as colleagues work separately and together

☐ Make note of student responsiveness, concerns, and performance during lessons

☐ Collect samples of student work

Evaluate program effectiveness:

☐ Hold conferences at different points during and after implementation

☐ Examine challenges and successes around content taught, approaches and settings used, student behavior/performance, and working together

☐ Process the approach to collaborations (comfort levels, quality of interactions, etc.)

☐ Jot down possible revisions for approaches to instruction and collaboration

☐ Report results to parent(s)/caregiver(s)

☐ Discuss the effectiveness of the IEP in guiding student instruction and suggest needed changes

☐ Contemplate possibilities of movement to least restrictive environment

Co-Planning in Detail	
Designing and coordinating learning experiences in and out of the General Education Curriculum	**Notes on ideas brainstormed; who does what by when?**
What to Teach/Skill clusters: *Plan how focuses for instruction address student needs and IEP proposals*	
Options in the general education curriculum: *How do student IEP skill priorities match up with upcoming unit or lesson objectives/ expectations?* ❑ Determine what general education units of study and/or lessons afford the student opportunities to develop skills targeted by instruction and how expected learning outcomes are relevant to IEP goals and objectives. ❑ Figure out whether the student has prerequisite skills to engage in instruction or whether the focus exceeds meaningful involvement. ❑ What types of supports will take into account student skill gaps to allow for participation in the general education curriculum? (e.g., charts for arithmetic facts, calculator, spelling notebook, handheld spell checker, computer-based prewriting webs, taped or alternate books, prompts on desk regarding behavior)? ❑ How might lesson or unit outcomes be adjusted to accommodate the student? ❑ What supplemental instruction is necessary to support the student in general education?	
Design alternative learning experiences: *What alternative instruction will target the skills identified on the IEP and support student progress in the area(s) of concern?* ❑ How is direct instruction organized in conjunction with general education? ❑ What other focuses are required? ❑ How are prior learning and personal experiences connected so the student benefits from the focus(es) of alternative lessons? ❑ How is the student taught to apply skill knowledge in context, using meaningful tasks, materials, and assignments?	
How to Teach/Formats for performance: *Plan what approaches to instruction afford the student opportunities to become competent in the area(s) of concern*	
Design options within the general education curriculum: *Based on student needs and responsiveness to different formats of performance/teaching approaches, how will he or she respond to proposed or existing. learning experiences in the general education classroom?*	

❑ Examine the specific formats for instruction; types of presentation approaches; practice opportunities; use and level(s) of materials, questions, and assignments; demands of independent tasks and long-term projects that address unit and lesson objectives.

❑ Figure out whether instructional experiences are suitable for the student to advance competence and/or benefit from involvement.

❑ How will the student be expected to gain from the designed learning experiences?

❑ What types of supports will be designed to promote student participation (e.g., advanced organizers, self-monitoring charts, preteaching experiences)?

❑ What will accommodate and support the student to gain from existing approaches (e.g., teacher illustrate concept, supplement talk with demonstration, think-aloud to model)?

❑ What alternative yet comparable materials provide the same information but are at levels appropriate for the student?

❑ What variations to assignments will give the student an opportunity to show what he or she is learning, how he or she is understanding (e.g., dictate vs. write vs. illustrate vs. talk)? Or how will criteria for grading be adjusted?

Design alternative learning experiences:
What alternative methodologies, materials, and assignments are needed to support student learning in the area(s) of concern that are not available through the general education curriculum?

❑ Develop alternative lessons to address skill needs directly, using teaching approaches that actively engage the student, explain and demonstrate them, offer various options for response and practice, give ample opportunities to rehearse in isolation and context, and ensure opportunities to show progress. How will alternative approaches, teaching strategies, tasks, materials, and assignments address the requirements/standards set by IEP objectives?

❑ How will approaches, teaching strategies, tasks, materials, and assignments promote student acquisition of the skills laid out in the IEP?

❑ How will tasks and assignments increase understanding of skills/concepts, allow for practice, and support mastery with reference to the requirements/standards set by the IEP?

❑ Teach the student how to engage in and respond to different formats for learning new skills/ concepts, practicing and demonstrating competence. How will these prepare the student to be more versatile and respond to different formats for performance?

❑ How will assignments be tailored to maximize student opportunity to show what he or she is learning?

❑ What informal measures will be used to evaluate student performance and participation?

Interaction Formula Co-Planning Toolbox

How to Approach/Strategic thinking (problem-solving approach): *Plan how organization and structures of instructional tasks and assignments promote strategic thinking relative to the area(s) of concern*	
Design options within the general education curriculum: *How is strategic thinking germane to the area(s) of concern addressed through teacher use of think-alouds, structure of instruction, and the design of assignments?*	
❑ Examine the opportunities in the general education curriculum in terms of how strategic thinking is infused in instruction and the structure of assignments to determine how the student is guided through the learning process.	
❑ What types of teacher cues (e.g., think-alouds, hints, questions, reminders, word/idea prompts) are used already?	
❑ What supplemental prompts (e.g., mnemonics, graphic organizers, identified steps, word banks, etc.) support the class through the thinking process and work completion?	
❑ What types of directions, tasks, or activities are used to facilitate strategic thinking?	
❑ How might strategic thinking be made more explicit and offer the student ways to process information, engage in tasks, or complete assignments systematically?	
❑ What types of modifications or alterations are needed to cue or guide the student to problem-solve and systematize approaches?	
Design alternative learning experiences: *How is strategic thinking and problem solving germane to the area(s) of concern addressed through direct instruction from the teacher, modeled through use of think-alouds,and guided through the structure of instruction and the design of assignments?*	
❑ Design direct instruction that teaches the student how to think, perform, and work strategically in the area(s) of concern.	
❑ Guide student use of strategic thinking in the context of activities in the area(s) of concern and help him or her develop self-monitoring techniques to ensure use.	
❑ What types of questions and structures help the student develop ways to prepare, engage in, complete, and self-evaluate through the respective process?	
❑ What cuing system or strategies will the student be expected to employ independently when attempting to problem-solve?	
❑ What types of lessons, guides, and lines of questioning support student acquisition of strategic thinking related to area(s) of concern (e.g., reading process—KWL, SQ3R, reciprocal questions; writing process—TOWER, COPS; participating—self-talk, FAST).	

Interaction Formula Co-Planning Toolbox

Under What Conditions/Context for participation: *Plan ways to optimal learning environments to promote comfort and productivity*	
Design options within the general education curriculum: *In what ways are existing environmental structures and arrangements conducive for student participation and performance in the setting?* ❑ Design structures to support student social interactions, attention to tasks, and self-management of tasks and work relative to the area(s) of concern. Consider how the existing instructional arrangements (flexible grouping strategies, amount of work, pace of tasks, large group, small group, cooperative tasks, teacher directed, peer directed, etc.) and physical setting (e.g., study spaces, desk clusters, use of bulletin boards, etc.) support or deter student involvement. ❑ What adjustments to the instructional arrangements or physical space will support student participation?	
Design alternative learning environments: *What considerations are to be taken to teach the student to interact flexibly in other learning and social contexts?* ❑ Create alternative learning arrangements in the setting to enhance student attention, engagement, involvement, and performance in instruction/activities related to the area(s) of concern. ❑ Introduce and teach ways to engage in different arrangements (e.g., how to be a member of a cooperative group, work independently).	
Why Teach/Investment: *Plan ways to capitalize on student interests and successes as part of topics and activities addressed in instruction*	
Design options within the general education curriculum: *How might student investment, confidence, and valuing the area(s) of concern be promoted within the general education curriculum and setting?* ❑ Examine opportunities afforded by the general education curriculum and instruction that engage the student, promote investment, and spark interest. ❑ In what way(s) do the adjustments made to instruction, tasks/activities, and setting enhance student success, interest, sense of purpose, and commitment to learning? ❑ Evaluate the extent to which content and skills are made relevant to his or her life and provide for success. ❑ What connections between accessing general education instruction, the area(s) of concern, and relevance to the student can be made to promote engagement in learning? ❑ Determine what adjustments may be introduced to enhance student investment in learning and working in the area(s) of concern.	

Interaction Formula Co-Planning Toolbox

❑ What types of attention, responses, incentives, and feedback need to be part of the instructional experiences to encourage building confidence, acknowledge efforts, and make learning relevant?	
Design alternative learning experiences: *What types of attention, responses, incentives, and feedback need to be part of the instructional experiences to encourage building confidence, acknowledge efforts, and make learning relevant?* ❑ Determine what the student needs and what can be done throughout instruction to enhance how he or she feels about performing and participating in the area(s) of concern and creates sense of purpose, sense of self, interests, and receptivity to expectations and feedback. ❑ What will help to build confidence, acknowledge efforts, and make learning relevant? ❑ What systems of attention, responses, incentives, and feedback guide student self-monitoring as vehicles to enhance investment?	

Chapter 8

Moving Forward

Geese, A Parable

Anonymous

When you see geese flying along in "V" formation, you might consider what science has discovered as to why they fly that way:

As each bird flaps its wings, it creates an up-lift for the bird immediately following. By flying in "V" formation, the whole flock adds at least 71 percent greater flying range than if each bird flew on its own.

People who share a common direction and sense of community can get where they are going more quickly and easily because they are traveling on the thrust of one another.

When a goose falls out of formation, it suddenly feels the drag and resistance of trying to go it alone, and quickly gets back into formation to take advantage of the lifting power of the bird in front.

If we have as much sense as a goose, we will stay in formation with those people who are headed the same way we are.

When the head goose gets tired, it rotates back in the wing and another goose flies point.

It is sensible to take turns doing demanding jobs, whether with people or with geese flying south.

Geese honk from behind to encourage those up front to keep up their speed.

What messages do we give when we honk from behind?

Finally . . . and this is important . . . when a goose gets sick or is wounded by gunshot, and falls out of formation, two other geese fall out with that goose and follow it down to lend help and protection. They stay with the fallen goose until it is able to fly or until it dies, and only then do they launch out on their own, or with another formation to catch up with their group.

If we have the sense of a goose, we will stand by each other like that.

Building Capacity

For there to be a constructive impact of the reauthorization of IDEA 2004 on life in school, the professionals involved need to be engaged in understanding the expectations the law sets and the promises it holds. Response to the reauthorization requires a schoolwide adoption of its goals, development of a system to organize the forms and functions of the special education process, approaches to interface the ways general and special education work together, and practices for identifying and meeting the needs of individual students. To advance the messages of IDEA 2004, it is important to build the capacity of schools by creating a culture of shared commitment and cooperation, designing an infrastructure, and supporting professional development to address the law (Hyatt, 2007).

Building capacity means the staff shares a common understanding of what special education legislation requires, determines what supports are needed and how they operate, articulates how to access resources, learns how to engage in cooperative efforts to provide coordinated services, and identifies strategies for how to work with students who struggle to acquire academic and social competence. Cultivating the school context for meaningful adoption of special education legislation requires creating a seamless system in which programs, services, and supports are aligned to provide assistance to educators, promote student growth and participation in general education, and/or offer alternative options to address individual student needs (Dearman & Alber, 2005; Sarason, 1982, 1990).

Framing the intended outcomes as a collaborative approach to IDEA paves the way to rethink the relationship of general and special education and to commit to mutually shared responsibilities. When professionals view the special education process as a part of the schoolwide problem-solving support system for teachers, students, and families, they pursue the sequence of interconnected *stages* linked to the specified *decisions*, which guide the *thinking and practices* for understanding learners and lead to individualized plans *as blueprints* for student outcomes (Gable, Mostert, & Tonelson, 2004; McIntosh, Chard, Boland, & Horner, 2006).

Ongoing dialogue related to the implications of IDEA and its reauthorization requires concerted efforts that involve the whole faculty in making commitments to its goals, definitions, procedures, access to the system, needed professional development, and involvement. It is through these discussions that the faculty can gain a collective understanding of how to interface systematically the perspectives, demands, and services of special education with the ongoing activity and programming of general education and the school. Giving faculty the opportunity to explore, choose, and mold the RSVP model means cultivating a school climate and culture to meet IDEA requirements. In doing so, the faculty create a system of meaningful supports from the prereferral stage, through cooperative and authentic assessment, through the development of IEPs, to the delivery of services in inclusive or alternative environments. When the faculty is involved in a process of refining, revising, or reconstructing, it is more likely that the groundwork, common directions, and investment for collaboration will be developed. It involves faculty in bringing multiple perspectives, sources of expertise, skepticism, and resources together to build infrastructure and to build collaborative relationships and professional confidence and competence.

Build Infrastructure

- Address the requirements of IDEA 2004 through the development of an infrastructure to support a seamless system of general and special education, one in which there is clarity around roles, procedures and access, purposes, resources, distribution of responsibility, and coordination of services and programs
- Evaluate how existing services, programs, and activities offer tiered supports with and for educators and students to augment, complement and/or supplement work in general education
- Confront the issues/potential barriers that undermine shared ownership and responsibility for the series of services that comprise prereferral, evaluation, and special education and those that interfere with instructionally relevant educational decision making, deter addressing individual needs, and impede professional effectiveness
- Examine the special education process as a part of the stages for gaining understanding of student needs and learning how to address them
- Construct a flowchart of how the existing support system for educators and students is linked, what the services are, how they are accessed, what purposes they serve (data generated, interventions provided, decisions involved), how they promote outcomes for students, and the types of documentation generated to indicate impact and provide evidence of work
- Determine what additional services would complement what exists
- Define roles and expectations of professionals with regard to engagement from prereferral to placement activity

Build Collaborative Relationships and Professional Confidence and Competence

- Develop collaborative relationships based on defining ways to work together, clarifying roles, recognizing the interrelationships among members' efforts, and making commitments to effective communication
- Establish ways to use general education curriculum and standards as points of reference for special education evaluation, services, and programming
- Develop a common language for looking at student needs, creating a shared path for the work to be done, and establishing clarity around practices and procedures that relate to enhancing student learning and behaving

- Create common ways to view student struggles and openness to examine the impact of instructional experiences and the environment and to shift away from a search for pathology to adopt proactive thinking and strategies
- Acknowledge the evolving nature of the process to grow an understanding of the challenges students face, recognize the impact of general education curriculum and settings, and figure out how to choose interventions systematically and monitor their effectiveness
- Equip general educators and special educators with the tools (assessment strategies, interventions, teaching approaches, resources, materials) and problem-solving competence to look at students, be attuned to what they are doing, evaluate how the environment and demands impact them positively and adversely to generate instructional and behavioral approaches and interventions and to treat plans as avenues for growth to be documented, reviewed, and revised

The geese parable challenges schools to establish common goals, continuously check for clarity, and sustain shared directions to achieve outcomes. In this way, faculty offer each other support. As structures are developed for achieving the goals, it is important to acknowledge and honor the perspectives, realities, styles, and creativity of others. Professionals need to figure out ways to work with each other and commit to looking out for each other, ensuring that voices and concerns are heard and addressed and hands are extended to offer help. Figuring out ways to look out for each other means investing the time, energy, and social connections involved in working with others. The Action Planning Toolbox at the end of the chapter guides professionals, beyond the *legalese* of IDEA 2004, to offering a practical framework for implementing a collaborative building-based special education process—one which enhances the thinking, decision making, and practices for constructive individualized education planning and guides the team in meeting student needs cooperatively and with fidelity.

Status In place (IP), Partially in Place, Not in Place	Tasks	Priority High, Medium, Low
	Building-Based Action Plan	
	FOUNDATION/VISIONS • Develop a clear understanding of the outcomes/purposes of special education evaluation, process, services, and service delivery options among school faculty • Set guidelines for procedures, paperwork, accountability, responsibility, and collaboration • Create a seamless system of supports, evaluating how existing services augment and complement each other and the purposes they serve • Identify a framework for looking at learner needs and challenges, one directly linked to educational demands	
	PREREFERRAL (Stage I) Outcomes: • Define what constitutes prereferral efforts (types of in-class assessments, modifications, tiered interventions, documentations) • Define the supports for prereferral efforts that address teacher and student needs making a distinction from types of help available during the special education process • Recognize the decisions involved in determining referral for special education evaluation and guide teachers and parents/caregivers in weighing options	
	Create guidelines for evaluating difficulties the student is experiencing	
	Identify ways to contact parents/caregivers	
	Define a system of prereferral support, looking at tiers of options for work with teachers and students	
	Articulate access to the prereferral support system (procedures, set of steps, membership)	
	Clarify expectations for the classroom teacher with regard to activity during the prereferral system	
	Clarify expectations for members of the prereferral support system	
	Outline agendas for related meetings that make productive and effective use of time	
	Indicate how prereferral efforts, strategies, and meetings are documented	

269

Action Planning Toolbox

Status	Tasks	Priority
	Referral (Stage I) Outcomes: • To design an approach or message that keeps students, parents/caregivers, and teachers involved in assessment and educational planning • To create a form that documents prereferral efforts: current understanding of the student in the area(s) of concern, summary of attempted modifications and interventions and the results; experiences and questions that lead to the decision to refer for special education evaluation, and expectations for participating in that process • To establish the outcomes of the special education process in light of concerns expressed on referral and the demands of the IEP	
	Purpose of form defined with regard to initiating a process, building on prereferral efforts and information, and responding to questions	
	Form designed to report relevant data, raise persistent questions, give voice to parent/caregiver and teacher concerns, and suggest which members participate on the evaluation team • Communicate expectations that prereferral efforts are made • Describe current understanding of student in the area(s) of concern • Indicate modifications attempted and results • Identify existing and/or persistent questions and concerns pertaining to the student • State hopes connected with submitting referral	
	Assessment Planning (Stage II) Outcomes: • To define a procedure for selecting team members to respond to referral for special education evaluation • To state the types of information that result from conducting special education assessments • To establish a procedure for choosing assessment tools in response to referral information • To get to know the student as a learner and understand the challenges he or she faces and how those challenges impact participation and progress in the identified area(s) of concern • To connect assessment to instructional planning without getting sidetracked by what is wrong with this student (why he or she is not learning, what needs to be fixed) • To examine what constitutes a practical/functional approach to the assessment process, staying focused on generating objective usable data that leads to instructional planning	
	Design a system for identifying professionals to be a part of the evaluation team	
	Create an explicit process for addressing referral information and questions that lead to selecting assessment strategies	
	Describe what constitutes an assessment plan designed to address questions, enhance understanding of the student, and guide assessment activity	

Action Planning Toolbox

Status	Tasks	Priority
	IEP Development (Stage III, IV, and V) Outcomes: • To use evaluation/assessment to build a comprehensive picture of the student, describing the student as a reader, writer, speaker, listener, mathematician, participant in the learning environment and/or member of the classroom community • To identify and understand the challenges student faces and how those challenges impact participation and progress in the identified area(s) of concern • To connect assessment to instructional planning without getting side-tracked by what is wrong with this student (why student is not learning, what needs to be fixed) • To construct an educational program according to student status (based on assessment data, profile, and present levels of performance) • To develop a program for the student (recorded on IEP) that defines curriculum, plans instruction, provides access to the general education curriculum, and articulates components of service delivery	
	Bring clarity to what constitutes an IEP as a working document	
	Identify agenda(s) for the IEP development meeting(s)	
	Establish expectations for team members to collate assessment information, setting criteria for what is helpful, informative, and guides instructional planning	
	Establish expectations for team members to design approaches to working with the student, setting criteria for what is helpful, informative, and guides teaching and interacting with the student	
	IMPLEMENTATION (Stage VI) Outcomes: • To design lessons, create modifications, access instructional materials and resources to address the IEP • To provide learning experiences and a coherent program to promote the student's participation and progress in the area(s) of concern • To monitor student progress to determine the effectiveness of instructional plans and modifications	
	Establish systems of communication among implementers proposed with avenues to set up ways to accommodate specific groups	
	Design systems of support for the student through which services are delivered (e.g., co-teaching, involvement of paraprofessional, grouping)	
	Translate goals and objectives to lesson objectives	
	Create systems for documentation established	

Action Planning Toolbox

Status	Tasks	Priority
	INTEGRATION Outcomes: • To connect the stages into a cohesive system • To evaluate the flow of procedures from one to another • To reexamine the values of tasks, activities in relation to IDEA, the special education process, and support for students and professionals	
	Create a flowchart	
	Examine how each stage addresses key decisions, builds on each previous one, offers supports to student and teacher, and generates documentation of efforts (developing meaningful paperwork)	

Source: Format adapted from Sugai, Horner, & Lewis-Palmer, 2001; Muscott & Mann, 2006.

References

Affleck, J. Q., Lowenbraun, S., & Archer, A. (1980). *Teaching the mildly handicapped in the regular classroom* (2nd ed.). Columbus, OH: Merrill.

Alexandrin, J.R. (2003). Using continuous classroom evaluations. *Teaching Exceptional Children, 36*(1), 52–57.

Ashlock, R. B. (1986). *Error patterns in computation: A semi-programmed approach* (4th ed.). Columbus, OH: Merrill.

Bahr, M., Walker, K., Hampton, E., Buddle, B., Freeman, T., Ruschman, N., Sears, J., McKinney, A., Miller, M., & Littlejohn, W. (2006). Creative problem solving for general education intervention teams: A two-year evaluation study. *Remedial and Special Education, 27*(1), 27–41.

Bahr, M. W., Whitten, E., Dieker, L., Kocarek, C. E., & Manson, D. (1999). A comparison of school-based intervention teams: Implications for educational and legal reform. *Exceptional Children, 66,* 67–83.

Banks, J. A. (2001). *Cultural diversity and education foundations, curriculum and teaching* (4th ed.). Boston: Allyn & Bacon.

Bateman, B. (1994). Who, how, and where: Special education's issues in perpetuity. *Journal of Special Education, 27*(27), 509–521.

Bateman, B. (1995). *Writing individualized education programs (IEPs) for success: Secondary education and beyond.* Learning Disabilities Association. Online 4/27/06: http://www.wrightslaw.com/advoc/articles/iep.success.bateman.htm

Bateman, B., & Herr, C. (2006a). *Better IEP meetings, everyone wins.* Verona, WI: Attainment Publications.

Bateman, B & Herr, C. (2006b). *Writing IEP goals and objectives.* Verona, WI: Attainment Publications.

Bateman, B. D. & Linden, M. A. (1998). *Better IEPs: How to develop legally correct and educationally useful programs* (3rd ed.). Longmont, CO: Sopris West.

Batsche, G., Elliott, J., Graden, J. L., Grimes, J., Kovaleski, J. F., Prasse, D., Reschly, D. J., Schrag, J., & Tilly, III, D. (2006). *IDEA 2004 and response to intervention: Policy considerations and implementation:* National Association of State Directors of Special Education.

Bauwens, J., & Hourcade, J. J. (1995). *Cooperative teaching: Rebuilding the school house for all students.* Austin, TX: Pro-Ed.

Bauwens, J., Hourcade, J. J., & Friend, M. (1989). Cooperative teaching: A model for general and special education integration. *Remedial & Special Education, 10*(2), 17–22.

Bauwens, J., & Korinek, L. (1993). IEPs for cooperative teaching: Developing legal and useful documents. *Intervention in School and Clinic, 28,* 303–306.

Beaver, J. (2001). *Developmental reading assessment.* Upper Saddle River, NJ: Pearson Learning Group.

Bergan, J. R., & Kratochwill, T. R. (1990). *Behavioral consultation and therapy.* New York: Plenum Press.

Black, S. (2007, January). A vigilant approach. *American School Board Journal,* pp.33–35.

Bradley, D. F., King-Sears, M. E., & Switlick, D. M. (1997). *Teaching students in inclusive settings: From theory to practice.* Needham Heights, MA: Allyn & Bacon.

Brimijoin, K., Marquissee, E., & Tomlinson, C. A. (2003). Using data to differentiate instruction. *Educational Leadership, 60*(5), 70–73.

Bryan, J. H., & Bryan, T. (1988). Where's the beef? A review of published research on the adaptive learning environments. *Learning Disability Focus, 4*(1), 9–14.

Buck, G. H., Polloway, E. A., Smith-Thomas, A., & Cook, K. W. (2003). Prereferral intervention processes: A survey of state practices. *Exceptional Children, 69*(3), 349–360.

Burns, E. (2001). *Developing and Implementing IDEA IEPs: An Individualized Education Program Handbook for Meeting Individuals with Disabilities Education Act (IDEA) Requirements.* Springfield, IL: Charles C. Thomas Publishers.

Cambourne, B. (1988). *The whole story: Natural learning and the acquisition of literacy in the classroom.* New York: Scholastic.

Chalfant, J. C., & Pysch, V. D. M. (1981, November). Teacher assistance teams: A model for within-building problem solving. *Counterpoint,* 16–21.

Chalfant, J. C., Pysch, V. D. M., & Moultrie, R. (1979). Teacher assistance teams: A model for within-building problem solving. *Learning Disabilities Quarterly, 2,* 85–96.

Chamberlain, S. P. (2006). Don Deshler: Perspectives on teaching students with learning disabilities. *Intervention in School and Clinic, 41*(5), 302–306.

Choate, J. S. (1992). Authentic assessment of special learner: Problems or promise. *Preventing School Failure, 37*(1), 6–10.

Clark, S. G. (1999). Assessing IEPs for IDEA compliance. *West's Education Law Report, 137,* 35–42.

Clark, S. G. (2000). The IEP process as a tool for collaboration. *Teaching Exceptional Children, 33*(2), 56–66.

Clay, M. M. (1991). *Becoming literate: The construction of inner control.* Auckland, NZ: Heinemann.

Cohen, C., Thomas, C. C., Sattler, R., & Voelker Morsink, C. (1997). Meeting the challenge of consultation and collaboration: Developing interactive teams. *Journal of Learning Disabilities, 30*(4), 427–432.

Coles, G. (1989). Excerpts from *The Learning Mystique:* A critical look at "learning disabilities." *Journal of Learning Disabilities, 22*(5), 267–273.

Coles, G. (2004). Danger in the classroom: 'Brain-glitch' research on learning to read. *Phi Delta Kappan, 85*(5), 344–351.

Conderman, G. J., & Nelson, N. (1999). A better IDEA for parents, students, and educators. *Kappa Delta Pi, 35*(4), 170–172.

Cook, B. G., & Schirmer, B. (2003). What is special about special education? Overview and analysis. *Journal of Special Education, 37*(3), 200–205.

Cook, L., & Friend, M. (1993). Educational leadership for teacher collaboration. In B. Billingsley, B. et al. (Ed.), *Program leadership for serving students with disabilities.* Richmond, VA: Chapter 14.

Cook, L., & Friend, M. (1995). Co-teaching guidelines for creating effective practices. *Focus for Exceptional Children, 28*(2), 1–12.

Corrigan, D., & Bishop, K. (1997). Creating family-centered integrated service systems and interprofessional educational programs to implement them. *Social Work in Education, 19*(3), 149–163.

Council for Exceptional Children. (1999). Bright futures for exceptional learners: An agenda to achieve quality conditions for teaching and learning. Reston, VA. Available from the Council for Exceptional Children, 1110 North Glebe Road, Suite 300, Arlington, VA 22201–5704 (800-CEC-SPED). http://www.cec.sped.org

Cramer, S. F. (1998). *Collaboration: A success strategy for special educators.* Boston: Allyn & Bacon.

Daly E. J., III., Witt, J., Martens, B. K., & Dool, E. (1997). A model for conducting a functional analysis of academic performance problems. *School Psychology Review, 26*(4), 554–574.

Dearman, C. C., & Alber, S. R. (2005). The changing face of education: Teachers cope with challenges through collaboration and reflective study. *The Reading Teacher, 58*(7). 634–640.

Dettmer, P. A., Dyck, N. T., & Thurston, L. P. (1996). *Consultation, collaboration, and teamwork for students with special needs* (2nd ed.). Boston: Allyn & Bacon.

Doyle, M., & Straus, D. (1976). *How to make meetings work.* New York: Berkley Publishing Group.

Drasgow, E., & Yell, M. L. (2002). School-wide behavior support: Legal implications and requirements. *Child & Family Behavior Therapy, 24*(1), 129–145.

Drasgow, E., Yell, M. L., & Bradley, R. (1999). The IDEA amendments of 1997: A school-wide model for conducting functional behavioral assessments and developing behavior intervention plans. *Education and Treatment of Children, 22*(3), 244–266.

Drasgow, E., Yell, M. L., & Robinson, T. R. (2001). Developing legally correct and educationally appropriate IEPs. *Remedial & Special Education, 22*(6), 359–375.

Dudley-Marling, C. (1985). Perceptions of the usefulness of the IEP by teachers of learning disabled and emotionally disturbed children. *Psychology in the Schools, 22*(1), 65–67.

Duncan, J., Griffiths, R., Ward, R., Hood, H., Hervey, S., & Bonallack, J. (1992). *Dancing with the pen: The learner as a writer.* New Zealand Ministry of Education. Learning Media Ltd.

Dykeman, B. F. (2007). Alternative strategies in assessing special education needs. *Education, 127*(2), 265–273.

Eber, L. (2003). *The art and science of wraparound: Completing the continuum of schoolwide behavioral support.* Bloomington: Forum on Education at Indiana University.

Edelen-Smith, P. (1995). Eight elements to guide goal determination for IEPs. *Intervention in School and Clinic, 30*(5), 297–301.

Edgemon, E., Jablonski, B. B., & Lloyd, J. W. (2006). Large scale assessments: A teacher's guide to making decisions about accommodations. *Teaching Exceptional Children, 38*(3), 6–11.

Education for All Handicapped Children Act of 1975, 20 U.S.C. & 1400 et seq.

Eidle, K.A., Boyd, T., Truscott, S. D., & Meyers, J. (1998). The role of prereferral intervention teams in early intervention of mental health problems. *School Psychology Review, 27*(2), 204–216.

Etscjeodt, S. (2006). Progress monitoring: Legal issues and recommendations for IEP teams. *Teaching Exceptional Children, 38*(3), 56–60.

Forest, M., & Pearpoint, J. (1992). Putting all kids on the MAP. *Educational Leadership, 50*(2), 26–31.

Fountas, I. C., & Pinnell, G. (1996). *Guided reading: Good first teaching for all children.* Portsmouth, NH: Heinemann.

Friend, M., & Cook, L. (1992). The new inclusion: How it really works. *Instructor 101*(7), 30–36.

Friend, M., & Cook, L. (2000). *Interactions: Collaboration skills for school professionals,* New York: Addison Wesley Longman.

Friend, M., Reising, M., & Cook, L. (1993). Co-teaching: An overview of the past, a glimpse at the present, and considerations for the future. *Preventing School Failure, 37*(3), 6–10.

Fuchs, D. (1987). *Preferral model: MAT.* Presentation at the Teacher Education Division Conference (CEC). Washington, DC.

Fuchs, D., & Fuchs, L. (1989). Exploring effective and efficient prereferral interventions: A component analysis of behavioral consultation. *School Psychology Review, 18,* 260–283.

Fuchs, D., Fuchs, L., & Speece, D. (2002 Winter). Treatment validity as a unifying construct for identifying learning disabilities. *Learning Disabilities Quarterly, 25,* 33–45.

Fuchs D., Mock, D., Morgan, P. L., & Young, C. L. (2003). Responsiveness-to-intervention: Definitions, evidence, and implications for the learning disabilities construct. *Learning Disabilities Quarterly, 18*(3), 157–171.

Fuchs, L. S. (2003). Assessing intervention responsiveness: Conceptual and technical issues. *Learning Disabilities Research & Practice, 18*(3), 172–176.

Fuchs, L. S., & Fuchs, D. (2006). A framework for building capacity for responsiveness to intervention. *School Psychology Review, 35*(4), 621–626.

Gable, R. A., Mostert, M. P., & Tonelson, S. W. (2004). Assessing professional collaboration in schools: Knowing what works. *Preventing School Failure, 48*(2), 4–8.

Gallagher, J., & Desimone, L. (1995). Lessons learned from implementation of the IEP: Applications to the IFSP. *Topics in Early Childhood Special Education, 15*(3), 353–358.

Garcia, T. (2007). Facilitating the reading process. *Teaching Exceptional Children, 39*(3), 12–17.

Gartin, B., Murdick, C., & Nikki, L. A. (2001). New IDEA mandate: The use of functional assessment of behavior and positive behavior supports. *Remedial and Special Education, 22*(6), 344–349.

Gartin, B., Murdick, C., & Nikki, L. A. (2005). IDEA 2004: The IEP. *Remedial and Special Education, 26*(6), 327–331.

Gehrlach, K. (2004). *Supervising paraeducators in educational settings: A team approach.* Austin, TX: Pro-Ed.

Gerber, M. (2005). Teachers are still the test: Limitations of response to instruction strategies for identifying children with learning disabilities. *Journal of Learning Disabilities, 38*(6), 516–524.

Gersten, R., & Dimino, J. (2001). The realities of translating research into classroom practice. *Learning Disabilities Research & Practice, 16*(2), 120–131.

Giangreco, M. F., Dennis, R. E., Edelman, S. W., & Cloninger, C. J. (1994). Dressing your IEPs for the general education climate. *Remedial and Special Education, 15,* 288–296.

Gleckel, E., & Koretz, E. (1993). Interaction model. Acton, MA: Educational Consulting Services.

Gleckel, E., & Koretz, E. (1996). Presentation of *The Interaction Model* at the Eleventh Annual Learning Disorders Conference, Harvard Graduate School of Education and the Research Institute for Learning and Development.

Gollnik, D. M., & Chinn, P. C. (2002). *Multicultural education in a pluralistic society* (6th ed.), Upper Saddle River, NJ: Merrill/Prentice Hall.

Goldstein, A. (1988). *The prepare curriculum*. Champaign, IL: Research Press.

Goodman, J., & Bond, L. (1993). The individual education program: A retrospective critique. *Journal of Special Education, 26*, 408–422.

Goodman, K. (1994). Reading, writing, and written texts: A transactional socio-psycholinguistic view. In R. B. Ruddell, M. R. Ruddell, & H. Singer (Eds.), *Theoretical models and processes of reading* (4th ed., pp. 1093–1130). Newark, DE: International Reading Association.

Goodman, Y., Watson, D., & Burke, C. (1987). *Reading miscue inventory: Alternative procedures*. Katonah, NY: Richard C. Owen.

Gottlieb, J., & Gottlieb, B. (1991). Parent and teacher referrals for a psycho-educational evaluation. *Journal of Special Education, 25*(2), 155–168.

Graden, J., Casey, A., & Bonstrom, O. (1986). Implementing a prereferral intervention system: Part I. – The model. *Exceptional Children, 51*(5), 377–384.

Graden, J., Casey, A., & Christenson, S. (1985). Implementing a prereferral intervention system: Part II—The data. *Exceptional Children, 52*(6), 384–487.

Gregory, G. (2003). *Differentiated instructional strategies in practice*. Thousand Oaks, CA: Corwin Press.

Gresham, F., & MacMillan, D. (1997). Teachers as tests: Differential validity of teacher judgements in identifying students at risk for learning difficulties. *School Psychology Review, 26*(1), 47–64.

Grimes, J., & Tilly, W. D. III. (1996). Policy and process: Means to lasting educational change. *School Psychology Review, 25*(4), 465–477.

Gronlund, N. (2004). *Writing instructional objectives for teaching and assessment*. Upper Saddle River, NJ: Merrill/Prentice Hall.

Harber, J. (1981). Assessing the quality of decision making in special education. *Journal of Special Education, 15*(1), 77–90.

Harp, B., & Brewer, J. (1996). *Reading and Writing: teaching for the connections*. Fort Worth, TX: Harcourt Brace.

Harrington, R., & Gibson, E. (1986). Preassessment procedures for learning disabled children: Are they effective? *Journal of Learning Disabilities, 19*(9), 538–541.

Henk, W., Marinak, B., Moore, J., & Mallette, M. (2003). The writing observation framework: A guide for refining and validating writing instruction. *The Reading Teacher, 57*(4), 322–333.

Henk, W., Moore, J., Marinak, B., & Tomasetti, B. (2000). A reading lesson observation framework for elementary teachers, principals, and literacy supervisors. *The Reading Teacher, 53*(5), 358–369.

Heward, W. (2003). Ten Faulty notions about teaching and learning that hinder the effectiveness of special education. *Journal of Special Education, 36*(4), 186–205.

Hitchcock, C., Meyer, A., Rose, D., & Jackson, R. (2002) *Access, Participation, and Progress in the General Curriculum: Technical Brief*. Peabody, MA: Center for Applied Special Technology, Inc. Retrieved from http://www.cast.org/ncac.

Horner, R. H. (1994). Functional assessment: Contributions and future directions. *Journal of Applied Behavioral Analysis, 27*, 401–404.

Horner, R. H., & Sugai, G. (2000). Schoolwide behavior support: An emerging initiative (special issue). *Journal of Positive Behavioral Interventions, 2*, 231–233.

Horner, R. H., & Sugai, G. (2001). "Data" need not be a four-letter word: Using data to improve school wide discipline. *Beyond Behavior, 11*(1), 20–22.

Hosp, J., & Reschly, D. (2003). Referral Rates for Intervention or assessment: A meta-analysis of racial differences. *Journal of Special Education, 37*(2), 67–81.

Huefner, D. S. (2000). The risks and opportunities of the IEP requirements under IDEA '97. *Journal of Special Education, 33*(4), 195–205.

Hyatt, K. (2007). The new IDEA: Changes, concerns, and questions. *Intervention in School and Clinic, 42*(3), 131–136.

Individuals with Disabilities Education Act. (2004). Washington, DC: U.S. Government Printing Office.

Individuals with Disabilities Education Act Amendments of 1997, 20 U.S.C. & et seq.

Individuals with Disabilities Education Act Regulations of 1999, 34 C.F.R. & 300 et seq.

Jardine, A. (1996). Key points of the authentic assessment portfolio. *Intervention in School and Clinic, 31*(4), 252–253.

Johns, B., Crowley, E. P., & Guetzloe, E. (2002). Planning the IEP for students with emotional and behavioral disorders. *Focus on Exceptional Children, 34*(9), 1–12.

Johnson, D. W., & Johnson, R. T. (1987). *Joining together.* Englewood Cliffs, NJ: Prentice Hall.

Johnson, D. W., & Johnson, R. T. (2000). *Joining together: Group theory and group skills.* Needham Heights, MA: Allyn & Bacon.

Junkala, J. (1972). Task analysis and instructional alternatives. *Academic Therapy, 8,* 33–40.

Kamens, M. W. (2004). Learning to write IEPs: A personalized, reflective approach for pre-service teachers. *Intervention in School and Clinic, 40*(2), 76–80.

Katsiyannis, A., Yell, M. L., & Bradley, R. (2001). Reflections on the 25th Anniversary of the Individuals with Disabilities Act. *Remedial & Special Education, 22*(6), 324–335.

Kauffman, J. M., & Hallahan, D. P. (2005). *Special education: What it is and why we need it.* Boston, MA: Allyn & Bacon.

King-Sears, M. (1997). Best academic practices for inclusive classrooms. *Focus on Exceptional Children, 29*(7), 1–23.

Knowlton, E. (2007). *Developing Effective Individualized Education Programs: A Case Based Tutorial, 2/e*—CD-ROM Only. Upper Saddle River, NJ: Merrill/Prentice Hall.

Koretz, E. (2003). *A study of the relationship between the literacy perspectives of primary grade teachers and their special education referral descriptions of struggling readers.* Unpublished doctoral dissertation, University of Massachusetts, Lowell.

Kroeger, S., Leibold, C., & Ryan, B. (1999). Creating a sense of ownership in the IEP process. *Teaching Exceptional Children, 32*(1), 4–9.

Lamorey, S. (2002). The effects of culture on special education services: Evil eyes, prayer meetings, and IEPs. *Teaching Exceptional Children, 34*(5), 67–71.

Lane, B. (1992). *Teaching & learning creative revision.* Portsmouth, NH: Heinemann.

Lane, K. L., Pierson, M. R., Robertson, E. J., & Little, A. (2004). Teachers' views of prereferral interventions: Perceptions of and recommendations for implementing support. *Education and Treatment of Children, 27*(4), 11.

Layton, C. A., & Lock, R. H. (2007). Use authentic assessment techniques to fulfill the promise of No Child Left Behind. *Intervention in School and Clinic, 42*(3), 169–173.

Lewis, T. J. (2001). Building infrastructure to enhance schoolwide systems of positive behavioral support: Essential features of technical assistance. *Beyond Behavior, 11*(1), 10–12.

Lewis, T. J., & Sugai, G. M. (1999). Effective behavior support: A systems approach to proactive school-wide management. *Focus on Exceptional Children, 31*(6), 1–33.

Lilly, M. S. (1987). Lack of focus in special education in literature in educational reform. *Exceptional Children, 53,* 325–326.

Lingnugaris-Kraft, B., Marchand-Martella, N., & Martella, R. C., (2001). Writing better goals and short-term objectives or benchmarks. *Teaching Exceptional Children, 34*(1), 52–58.

Lloyd, J. W., Crowley, E. P., Kohler, F. W., & Strain, P. S. (1988). Redefining the applied research agenda: Cooperative learning, prereferral, teacher consultation, and peer-mediated interventions. *Journal of Learning Disabilities, 21*, 43–52.

Logan, K., Hansen, C., Nieminen, P., & Wright, E. H. (2001). Student support teams: Helping students succeed in general education classrooms or working to place students in special education? *Education and Training in Mental Retardation and Developmental Disabilities, 36*(3), 280–292.

Lytle, R., & Bordin, J. (2001). Enhancing the IEP team: Strategies for parents and professionals. *Teaching Exceptional Children, 33*(5), 40–44.

MacMillan, D., Gresham, F., Bocian, K., & Siperstein, G. (1997). The role of assessment in qualifying students as eligible for special education: What is and what's supposed to be. *Focus on Exceptional Children, 30*(2), 1–8.

Mager, (2001). *Preparing: A critical tool in the development of effective instruction.* Belmont, CA: Fearon.

Mainzer, R., Deshler, D., & Coleman, M. R. (2003). To ensure the learning of every child with a disability. *Focus on Exceptional Children, 35*(5), 1–12.

Makuch, Gary. *Flowers are not in your IEP.* Reprinted with permission from the author.

Mamlin, N., & Harris, K. (1998). Elementary teachers' referral to special education in light of inclusion and prereferral: "Every child is here to learn but some of these children are in real trouble." *Journal of Educational Psychology, 90*(3), 385–386.

Mandlawitz, M. (2006). *What every teacher should know about IDEA 2004.* Laws & Regulations. (WETSKA Series). Boston, MA: Allyn & Bacon.

Marchand-Martella, N., & Martella, R. (2001). Maximizing student learning: The effects of a comprehensive school-based program for preventing problem behaviors. *Journal of Emotional and Behavioral Disorders, 10*(3), 136–148.

Marston, D. (2005). Tiers of intervention in responsiveness to intervention: Prevention outcomes and learning disabilities identification patterns. *Journal of Learning Disabilities, 38*(6), 539–544.

Marston, D., & Diment, K. (1992). Monitoring pupil progress in reading. *Preventing School Failure, 36*, 21–26.

Marston D., Muyskens, P., Lau, M., & Canter, A. (2003). Problem-solving model for decision making with high-incidence disabilities: The Minneapolis experience. *Learning Disabilities Research & Practice, 18*(3), 187–200.

Martin, J. E., VanDycke, J. U., & Christenson, W. R., 2006. Increasing student participation in IEP meetings: Establishing the self-directed IEP as evidenced-based practice. *Exceptional Children, 72*(3), 299–316.

Mastropieri, M. A., & Scruggs, T. E. (2000). *The inclusive classroom: Strategies for effective instruction.* Upper Saddle River, NJ: Merrill/Prentice Hall.

Mastriopieri M., & Scruggs T. (2005) Feasibility and consequences of response to intervention: Examination of the issues and scientific evidence as a model for identification of individuals with learning disabilities. *Journal of Learning Disabilities, 38*(6), 525–531.

McIntosh, K., Chard, D., Boland, J., & Horner, R. (2006). Demonstration of combined efforts in school-wide academic and behavioral systems and incidence of reading and behavior challenges in early elementary grads. *Journal of Positive Behavior Interventions, 8*(3), 146–154.

McLoughlin, J. A., & Lewis, R. B. (2001). *Assessing special students.* Upper Saddle River, NJ: Merrill/Prentice Hall.

Meisels, L. (1974). The student's social contract: Learning social competence in the classroom. *Teaching Exceptional Children, 7*, 34–35.

Menlove, R. R., Hudson, P. J., & Suter, D. (2001). A field of IEP dreams: Increasing general education teacher participation in the IEP Development process. *Teaching Exceptional Children, 33*(5), 28–33.

Merrell, K., & Shinn, M. (1990). Critical variables in the learning disabilities identification process. *School Psychology Review, 19*(1), 74–82.

Mount, B., & Zwernik, K. (1988). *It's never too early, it's never too late: A booklet about personal futures planning.* St. Paul, MN: Metropolitan Council.

Murphy, S. (1997). Literacy assessment and the politics of identity. *Reading & Writing Quarterly, 13*(3), 261–278.

Murray, D. M., (1998). "The maker's eye: Revising your own manuscripts." *The Writer*, Rpt. The McGraw-Hill Reader: Issues Across the Disciplines. Ed. Gilbert H. Muller. (8th ed.). Boston: McGraw-Hill, 2003, 56–60.

Muscott, H. & Mann, E. (2006). Universal Team Training Manual. New Hampshire: Center for Effective Behavioral Interventions and Supports (http://nhcebis.seresc.net)

Muscott, H., Mann, E., Benjamin, T., Gately, S., & Bell, K. (2004). Positive behavioral interventions and supports in New Hampshire: Preliminary results for a statewide system for implementing schoolwide discipline. *Education and Treatment of Children, 27*(4) 453–485.

National Council of Teachers of Mathematics (NCTM). (1989). *NCTM Standards.* http://www.nctm.org

National Joint Committee on Learning Disabilities, (2005). Responsiveness to interventions and learning disabilities. Retrieved from http://www.nrcld.org.

Nelson, P., & Smith, D. (1991). Prereferral intervention: A review of the research. *Education and Treatment of Children, 14*(3), 243–254.

NICHCY, (4th Edition, 1999). Questions Often Asked by Parents About Special Education Services. Accessed on http://www.nichcy.org/pubs/ideapubs/lg1txt.htm

Obiakor, F. E., (2007). Multicultural special education: Effective intervention for today's schools. *Intervention in School and Clinic, 42*(3), 148–155.

Ogle, D. (1986). KWL: A teaching model that develops active reading of expository text. The Reading Teacher, *39*, 564–570.

Paratore, J., & McCormack, R. (eds.) (1997). "Peer talk in the classroom: Learning from research," and "Designing for learning: Six elements in constructivist classrooms," G. W. Gagnon M. Collay; "The real thing: Doing Philosophy with Media," by C. Slade.

Peck, A., & Scarpati, S. (2005). Instruction and assessment. *Teaching Exceptional Children, 37*(4), 7–17.

Prasse, D. P. (2006). Legal supports for problem-solving systems. *Remedial & Special Education, 27*(1), 7–15.

Price, K., & Nelson, K. (2007). Planning effective instruction: Diversity responsive methods and management. Belmont: CA: Thomson Wadsworth.

Pugach, M., & Johnson, L. (1989). Prereferral interventions: progress, problems, and challenges. *Exceptional Children*, 217–226.

Pugach, M., & Johnson, L. (2002). *Collaborative practitioners, collaborative schools.* Denver, CO: Love Publishing.

Pugach, M., Johnson, L., & Hawkins, A. (2004). School-family collaboration: A partnership. *Focus on Exceptional Children, 36*(5), 1–12.

Reeve, P. T., & Hallahan, D. P. (1994). Practical questions about collaboration between general and special educators. *Focus on Exceptional Children, 26*(7), 1–12.

Reschly, D. J. (1996). Functional assessment and special education decision making. In W. Stainback & S. Stainback (Eds.), *Controversial issues confronting special education: Divergent perspectives*, 115–128. Needham Heights, MA: Allyn & Bacon.

Reschly, D. J. (1997). Utility of individual ability measures and public policy choices for the 21st century. *School Psychology Review, 26*(2), 234–242.

Reschly, D. (2005) Learning Disabilities identification: Primary intervention, secondary intervention, and then what? *Journal of Learning Disabilities, 38*(6) 510–515.

Reschly D., Hosp, J., & Schmied, C. (2003). *And miles to go: State SLD requirements and authoritative recommendations.* U.S. Department of Education, Office of Special Education Programs. Grant No: #324U0100004.

Rock, M. (2000). Parents as equal partners. *Teaching Exceptional Children, 32*(6), 30–37.

Salas, L. (2004). Individualized educational plan (IEP) meetings and Mexican American parents: Let's talk about it. *Journal of Latinos and Education, 3*(3), 181–192.

Salend, S. (2005). *Bright futures for exceptional learners: An action agenda to achieve quality conditions for teaching and learning.* Reprinted with permission from Council for Exceptional Children Today, online by the Commission on the Conditions for Special Education Teaching and Learning.

Samuels, C. A. (2005). States await special education testing rule. *Education Week, 25*(14), 16.

Sapon-Shevin, M. (1988, Summer). Working towards a merger: Seeing beyond distrust and fear. *Teacher Education and Special Education,* 103–110.

Sarason, S. (1982). *The culture of school and the problems of change.* San Francisco: Jossey Bass.

Sarason, S. (1990). *The predictable of failure of educational reform.* San Francisco: Jossey Bass.

Sarason, S. (1998). *The predictable failure of educational reform.* San Francisco: Jossey Bass.

Sarason, S., & Doris, J. (1979). *Educational handicap, public policy, and social history.* New York: Macmillan.

Schumm, J. A., Vaughn, S., & Leavell, A. G. (1994). Planning pyramid: A framework for planning for diverse student needs during content area instruction. *The Reading Teacher, 47*(8), 608–615.

Simmons, J. (2000). *You never asked me to read.* Needham, MA: Allyn & Bacon.

Simpson, R. L. (1996). *Working with parents and families of exceptional children and youth* (3rd ed.). Austin, TX: Pro-Ed.

Smith, S. W. (1990a). Comparison of individualized education programs (IEPs) of students with behavioral disorders and learning disabilities. *The Journal of Special Education, 24,* 85–110.

Smith, S. W. (1990b). Individualized education programs (IEPs) in special education—From intent to acquiescence. *Exceptional Children, 57,* 6–14.

Smith, S. W., & Brownell, M. T. (1995). Individualized education program: Considering the broad context of reform. *Focus on Exceptional Children, 28*(1), 1–11.

Smith, S. W., & Simpson, R. L. (1989). An analysis of individualized education programs (IEPs) for students with behavioral disorders. *Behavioral Disorders, 14,* 107–116.

Smith, T. (2005). IDEA 2004: Another round in the reauthorization process. *Remedial and Special Education, 26*(6), 314–319.

Soodak, L. (2000). Performance assessments and students with learning problems: Promising practice or reform rhetoric? *Reading and Writing Quarterly, 16*(16), 257–281.

Soodak, L., & Podell, D. M., (1994). Teachers' thinking about difficult to teach students. *Journal of Educational Research, 88*(1), 1–8.

Sopko, K., & Moherek M. (2003). The IEP: A synthesis of current literature since 1997 prepared for Project FORUM National Association of State Directors of Special Education (NASDSE). Accessed from: http://www.nasdse.org/publications/iep.pdf.

Stainback, W., & Stainback, S. (1984). A rationale for the merger of special and regular education. *Exceptional Children, 51*(2),102–111.

Stainback, W., & Stainback, S. (1985). *Inclusion: A guide for educators*. Baltimore, P.H. Brookes.

Stainback, W., & Stainback, S. (1992). *Controversial issues confronting special education: Divergent perspectives*. Needham Heights, MA: Allyn & Bacon.

Stetson, F., Jewett, R., & Mitchell, B. (2000). *What a great IDEA! Effective practices for children with disabilities*. IDEA Partnerships. Reston, VA: Council for Exceptional Children.

Strickland, B. B., & Turnbull, A. P. (1993). *Developing and implementing individualized education programs*. (3rd ed.) Upper Saddle River, NJ: Merrill/Prentice Hall.

Sugai, G., & Horner, R. (1994). Including students with severe behavior problems in general education settings: Assumptions, challenges, and solutions. In J. Marr, G. Sugai, & G. Tindal (Eds.), *The Oregon conference monograph, 6*, 102–20. Eugene, University of Oregon.

Sugai, G., & Horner, R. H. (1999). Discipline and behavioral support: Preferred processes and practices. *Effective School Practices, 17*(4), 10–22.

Sugai, G., Horner, R. H., & Lewis-Palmer, T. (2001). Effective behavior support team implementation checklist. Educational & Community Supports, University of Oregon, accessed from http://www.pbis.org

Sugai, G., Lewis-Palmer, T., & Hagan-Burke, S. (1999 – 2000). Overview of the functional behavioral assessment process. *Exceptionality, 8*, 149–160.

Switlick, D. M. (1997). Curriculum modifications and adaptations. In D.F. Bradley, M.E. King-Sears, & D. M. Switlick (Eds.), *Teaching students in inclusive settings, 225–239*. Needham Heights, MA: Allyn & Bacon.

Thompson, S. J., Thurlow, M. L., Quenemoen, R. F., Esler, A., & Whetstone, P. (2001). Addressing standards and assessments on state IEP forms. Synthesis Report 38. Minneapolis, MN: University of Minnesota, National Center on Educational Outcomes. Retrieved June 24, 2002 from http://www.education.umn.edu/NCEO/OnlinePubs/Synthesis38.html

Thurlow, M., & Ysseldyke, J. (1982). Instructional planning: Information collected by school psychologists vs. information considered useful by teachers. *Journal of School Psychology, 20*(3), 3–10

Tomlinson, C. (1999). *The differentiated classroom*. Alexandria, VA: Association for Supervision and Curriculum Development.

Tomlinson, C. A. (2002a). Invitations to learn. *Educational Leadership, 60*(1), 6–11.

Tomlinson, C. A. (2002b). Proficiency is not enough. *Education Week, 22*(10), 36–38.

Tomlinson, C. (2006). *An educator's guide to differentiating instruction*. Boston: Mifflin.

Torgesen, J. K. (2002). The prevention of reading difficulties. *Journal of School Psychology, 40*(1), 7–27

Tracy, A. E., & Maroney, D. (2000). Getting the most out of IEP meetings. *The Exceptional Parent, 30*(6) 70–71.

Tucker, B. F., Singleton, A. H., & Weaver, T. L. (2001). *Teaching mathematics to all children: Designing and adapting instruction to meet the needs of diverse learners*. Upper Saddle River, NJ: Merrill/Prentice Hall.

Tucker, D., & Bakken, J. (2000). How do your kids do at reading? And how do you assess them? *Teaching Exceptional Children, 32*(6), 14–19.

Turnbull, A. P., & Turnbull, H. R., III. (1997). *Families, professionals, and exceptionality: A special partnership*. Upper Saddle River, NJ: Merrill/Prentice Hall.

Turnbull, H. R. (2005). Individuals with Disabilities Education Act reauthorization: Accountability and personal responsibilities. *Remedial and Special Education, 26*(2), 321–326.

VanDeWeghe, R., (1992). What teachers learn from "kidwatching." *Educational Leadership,* *4,* 49–52.

Vaughn, S., Linan-Thompson, S., & Hickman-Davis, P. (2003). Response to instruction as a means of identifying students with reading/learning disabilities. *Exceptional Children, 69*(4), 391–409.

Vellutino, F. R., Scanlon, D. M., & Lyon, G. R. (2000). Differentiating between difficult to remediate and readily remediated poor readers: More evidence against the IQ achievement discrepancy definition of reading disability. *Journal of Learning Disabilities.* 33(3), 223–238

Walsh, J. (2001). Getting the "Big Picture" of IEP goals and state standards. *Teaching Exceptional Children,* 33 (5), 18–26.

Walther-Thomas, C., Korinek, L., & McLauglin, V. (1999). Collaboration to support students' success. *Focus on Exceptional Children, 32*(3), 1–18.

Walther-Thomas, C., Korinek, L., McLauglin, V., & Toler Williams, B. (2000). *Collaboration for inclusive education: Developing successful programs.* Boston: Allyn & Bacon.

Wang, M., Reynolds, M., & Walberg, H. J. (1986). Rethinking special education. *Educational Leadership.* 44(1), 26–31.

Weishaar, M. K. (1997). Legal principles important in the preparation of teachers: Making inclusion work. *The Clearing House, 70*(5), 261–264.

Weishaar, M. K., & Konya, M. (2001). The regular educator's role in the individual education plan process. *Clearing House, 75*(2), 96–99.

Wesson, C. L. (1992). Using curriculum-based measurement to create instructional groups. *Preventing School Failure, 36*(2), 17–22.

Wiederholt, J. L. (1988, Summer). *Restructuring special education services: The past, the present, the future.* Learning Disability Quarterly, *12*(3), 181–191.

Wiest, D. J., & Kreil, D. A. (1995). Transformational obstacles in special education. *Journal of Learning Disabilities, 28*(7), 399–408.

Wiggins, G. (1997). Practicing what we preach in designing authentic assessments. *Educational Leadership, 54,* 18–25.

Will, M. (1986). Let us pause and reflect, but not too long. *Exceptional Children, 51*(1), 11–16.

Wilson, P., Martens, P., & Arya, P. (2005). Accountability for reading and readers: What the numbers don't tell. *The Reading Teacher, 58*(7), 622–631.

Wood, W. M., Karvonen, M. D. W., Test, D., Browder, D., & Algozzine, B. (2004). Promoting student self-determination skills in IEP planning. *Teaching Exceptional Children, 36*(3), 8–16.

Wray, D., Medwell, J., Fox, R., & Poulson, L. (2000). The teaching practices of effective teachers of literacy. *Educational Review, 52*(1), 75–85.

Yell, M. L., Katsiyannis, A., Drasgow, E., & Herbst, M. F. (2003). Developing legally correct and educationally appropriate programs for students with autism spectrum disorders, *Focus on Autism & Other Developmental Disabilities, 18*(3), 182–191.

Yell, M. L., & Shriner, J. G. (1997). The IDEA amendments of 1997: Implications for special and general education teachers, administrators, and teacher trainers. *Focus on Exceptional Children, 30,* 1–19.

Ysseldyke, J. E. (2001). Reflections on a research career: Generalizations from 25 years of research on assessment and instructional decision making. *Exceptional Children, 67*(3), 295–309.

Ysseldyke, J. E. (2005). Assessment and decision making for students with learning disabilites: What if this is as good as it gets? *Learning Disability Quarterly, 28*(2), 125–128.

Ysseldyke, J. E., & Olsen, K. (1999). Putting alternate assessments into practice: What to measure and possible sources of data. *Exceptional Children, 65*(2), 175–185.

Ysseldyke, J. E., Thurlow, M., Graden, J., Wesson, C., Algozzine, B., & Deno, S. (1983). Generalizations from five years of research on assessment and decision making. *Exceptional Education Quarterly, 4*(1), 75–93.

Zigmond, N. (1997). Educating students with disabilities: The future of special education. In J. W. Lloyd, E. J. Kameenui, & D. Chard (Eds.), *Issues in educating students with disabilities,* 377–390. Hillsdale, NJ: Erlbaum.

Zigmond, N. (2001). Special education at a crossroads. *Preventing School Failure, 45*(2), 70–75.

Zigmond, N. (2003). Where should students with disabilities receive special education services? Is one place better than another? *Journal of Special Education, 37* (3),193–199.

Zigmond, N., Vallecorsa, A., & Silverman, R. (1983). *Assessment for instructional planning in special education.* Upper Saddle River, NJ: Prentice Hall.

Zickel, J. P., & Arnold, E. (2001). Putting the I in the IEP. *Educational Leadership, 59*(3), 71–73.

Zins, J., Curtis, M., Graden, J., & Ponti, C. (1988). *Helping students succeed in the regular classroom: A guide for developing intervention assistance programs.* San Francisco, CA: Jossey-Bass.

Name Index

Affleck, J. Q., 10
Alber, S. R., 247, 266
Alexandrin, J. R., 255
Algozzine, B., 4, 195
Archer, A., 10
Arnold, E., 194
Arya, P., 3

Badley, D. F., 45, 148
Bahr, M. W., 18, 30
Bakken, J., 108
Banks, J. A, 23
Bateman, B. D., 12, 57, 106, 155, 159,
    193–195, 245
Batsch, G., 4, 18
Bauwens, J., 57, 193, 195–196, 246, 251
Beaver, J., 86
Bell, K., 4
Benjamin, T., 4
Bergan, J. R., 18
Bishop, K., 18
Black, S., 17–18
Boland, J., 266
Bond, L., 13
Bonstrom, O., 17
Bordin, J., 246
Boyd, T., 17
Bradley, R., 12, 153, 193
Brewer, J., 43
Brimijoin, K., 217
Browder, D., 195
Brownell, M. T., 148
Bryan, J. H., 13
Bryan, T., 13
Buck, G. H., 17, 19
Burke, C., 86, 116, 134
Burns, E., 193

Cambourne, B., 65
Canter, A., 2

Casey, A., 17
Chalfant, J. C., 17–19
Chamberlain, S. P., 2
Chard, D., 266
Choate, J. S., 3, 47, 108
Christenson, S., 17
Christenson, W. R., 149
Clark, S. G., 18, 23, 43, 47, 56, 211, 246
Cloninger, C. J., 155
Cohen, C., 57
Coleman, M. R., 2
Coles, G., 47
Conderman, G. J., 57
Cook, B. G., 13
Cook, K. W., 17
Cook, L., 11, 30, 57–58, 153, 163, 251
Corrigan, D., 18
Cramer, S. F., 56, 147
Crowley, E. P., 18, 106, 193

Daly, E. J., III, 3, 45, 106–107
Dearman, C. C., 247, 266
Dennis, R. E., 155
Deno, S., 4
Deshler, D., 2
Desimone, L., 42
Dettmer, P. A., 147
Dieker, L., 30
Diment, K., 211
Dimino, J., 18
Dool, E., 3, 45, 106–107
Doyle, M., 58, 159
Drasgow, E., 12, 17, 147, 159, 193, 195, 203
Dudley-Marling, C., 193, 195, 245
Duncan, J., 90
Dyck, N. T., 147
Dykeman, B. F., 106–107

Eber, L., 153
Edelen-Smith, P., 193, 195–196

Edelman, S. W., 155
Edgemon, E., 158
Eidle, K. A., 17
Esler, A., 194
Etscjoedt, S., 45

Forest, M., 39, 148, 154, 159
Fountas, I. C., 47, 200
Fox, R., 43
Friend, M., 11, 30, 57–58, 153, 163, 251
Fuchs, D., 3–4, 9, 17, 152, 158
Fuchs, L. S., 3–4, 17–18, 152

Gable, R. A., 266
Gallagher, J., 42
Garcia, T., 116
Gartin, B., 2
Gately, S., 4
Gehrlach, K., 252
Gerber, M., 30
Gersten, R., 18
Giangreco, M. F., 155
Gibson, E., 18
Gleckel, E., 10
Goldstein, A., 190
Goodan, J., 13
Goodman, Y., 86, 116, 122, 134
Gottlieb, B., 42
Gottlieb, J., 42
Graden, J., 4, 17–18
Gregory, G., 216
Gresham, F., 42–43, 57
Griffiths, R., 90
Gronlund, N., 207
Guetzloe, E., 106, 193

Hagan-Burke, S., 107, 116
Hallahan, D. P., 11, 42, 147–148, 246
Harber, J., 10
Harp, B., 43
Harrington, R., 18
Harris, K., 30
Henk, W., 116
Herbst, M. F., 159
Herr, C., 193–194
Heward, W., 211
Hickman-Davis, P., 3
Hitchcock, C., 203
Horner, R. H., 2, 4, 18, 98, 107, 266, 272
Hosp, J., 3, 10
Hourcade, J. J., 251
Hudson, P. J., 148, 153

Huefner, D. S., 12, 42, 57, 193–94, 200, 246
Hyatt, K., 2, 207, 266

Jablonski, B. B., 158
Jackson, R., 203
Jewett, R., 158
Johns, B., 106, 193–94, 203
Johnson, D. W., 60, 160
Johnson, L., 11, 17–20, 58, 251
Johnson, R. T., 60, 160

Kamens, M. W., 195
Karvonen, M. D. W., 195
Katsiyannis, A., 153, 159, 193
Kauffman, J. M., 42
King-Sears, M. E., 45, 148, 155
Knowlton, E., 201, 207
Kocarek, C. E., 30
Kohler, F. W., 18
Koretz, E., 10
Korinek, L., 11, 57, 153, 193, 195–196, 246
Kratochwill, T. R., 18
Kreil, D. A., 13
Kroeger, S., 43, 159

Lamorey, S., 23
Lane, B., 90
Lane, K. L., 17
Lau, M., 2
Layton, C. A., 106
Leavell, A. G., 157
Lewis, R. B., 42–43, 49, 121
Lewis, T. J., 2, 17
Lewis-Palmer, T., 107, 116, 272
Liebold, C., 43
Lilly, M. S., 13
Linan-Thompson, S., 3
Linden, M. A., 57, 106, 155, 193, 195, 245
Lingnugaris-Kraft, B., 193, 195–196, 203
Little, A., 17
Lloyd, J. W., 18
Lock, R. H., 106
Lowenbraun, S., 10
Lyon, G. R., 3
Lytle, R., 246

McIntosh, K., 266
McLaughlin, V., 11, 153
McLoughlin, J. A., 42–43, 49, 121
MacMillan, D., 42–43, 57

Mainzer, R., 2, 13
Makuch, G., 245
Mallette, M., 116
Mamlin, N., 30
Mandlawitz, M., 159
Mann, E., 4, 272
Manson, D., 30
Marchand-Martella, N., 193
Marinak, B., 116
Maroney, D., 154
Marquissee, E., 217
Marston, D., 2, 4, 9, 18, 152, 158, 211
Martella, R .C., 193
Martens, B. K., 3, 45, 106–107
Martens, P., 3
Martin, J. E., 149
Mastriopieri, M., 18, 42
Medwell, J., 43
Meisels, L., 98
Menlove, R. R., 148, 153
Merrell, K., 13
Meyers, A., 203
Mitchell, B., 158
Mock, D., 3
Moore, J., 116
Morgan, P. L., 3
Mostert, M. P., 266
Moultrie, R., 17
Mount, B., 148
Murdick, C., 2
Murray, D. M., 90
Muscott, H., 4, 272
Muyskens, P., 2
Myers, J., 17

Nelson, K., 10, 203, 207
Nelson, N., 57
Nikki, L. A., 2

Obiakor, F. E., 3, 23
Ogle, D., 43
Olsen, K., 49

Pearpoint, J., 39, 148, 154, 159
Peck, A., 255
Pierson, M. R., 17
Pinnell, G., 47, 200
Podell, D. M., 42
Polloway, E. A., 17
Poulson, L., 43
Prasse, D. P., 4, 9
Price, K., 10, 203, 207
Psych, V. D. M., 17–18
Pugach, M., 11, 17–20, 58, 251

Quenemoen, R. F., 194

Reeve, P. T., 11, 147–148, 246
Reschly, D. J., 3, 10, 18, 42, 45,
    107, 152, 158
Reynolds, M., 13
Robertson, E. J., 17
Robinson, T. R., 12
Rock, M., 57
Rose, D., 203
Ryan, B., 43

Salas, L., 23
Salend, S., 207
Samuels, C. A., 2
Sapon-Shevin, M., 13
Sarason, S., 2, 4, 266
Sattler, R., 57
Scanlon, D. M., 3
Scarpati, S., 255
Schirmer, B., 13
Schmied, C., 4
Schumm, J. A., 157, 217
Scruggs, T., 18, 42
Shinn, M., 13
Shriner, J. G., 43, 201, 246
Silverman, R., 10
Simmons, J., 3, 43, 108
Simpson, R. L., 193–194
Singleton, A. H., 94
Smith, S. W., 148, 193–196
Smith, T., 2
Smith-Thomas, A., 17
Soodak, L., 42–43

Sopko, K., 193
Speece, D., 152
Stainback, S., 13, 42
Stainback, W., 13, 42
Stetson, F., 158, 252
Strain, P. S., 18
Straus, D., 58, 159
Strickland, B. B., 43, 201
Sugai, G. M., 2, 4, 17–18, 98, 107,
    116, 122, 272
Suter, D., 148, 153
Switlick, D. M., 45, 148, 155

Test, D., 195
Thomas, C. C., 57
Thompson, S. J., 194
Thurlow, M. L., 4, 13, 194
Thurston, L. P., 147
Toler Williams, B., 153
Tomasetti, B., 116
Tomlinson, C. A., 216–217
Tonelson, S. W., 266
Torgesen, J. K., 18
Tracy, A. E., 154
Tryscott, S. D., 17
Tucker, B. F., 94
Tucker, D., 108
Turnbull, A. P., 43, 57, 201
Turnbull, H. R., III, 57, 158

Vallecorsa, A., 10
VanDeWeghe, R., 49
VanDycke, J. U., 149
Vaughn, S., 3, 152, 157–158

Vellutino, F. R., 3
Voelker Morsink, C., 57

Walberg, H. J., 13
Walsh, J., 196
Walther-Thomas, C., 11,
    57, 153
Wang, M., 13
Watson, D., 86, 116, 134
Weaver, T. L., 94
Weishaar, M. K., 153–154,
    195, 249
Wesson, C., 4
Whetstone, P., 194
Whitten, E., 30
Wiederholt, J. L., 13
Wiest, D. J., 13
Wiggins, G., 107
Will, M., 13
Wilson, P., 3, 10, 106, 108
Witt, J., 3, 45, 106–107
Wood, W. M., 195–196
Wray, D., 43, 47

Yell, M. L., 12, 17, 43, 153, 159, 193,
    195–196, 201, 245–246
Young, C. L., 3
Ysseldyke, J. E., 3–4, 10, 13, 47, 49,
    108, 148, 200

Zickel, J. P., 194
Zigmond, N., 10, 42, 47–49, 94, 108,
    121, 194
Zwernik, K., 148

Subject Index

Achievement tests, 158
Action planning, 27, 246
Action Planning Toolbox, 269–272
Action-word word bank, 209
Antecedent-behavior-consequence, 79
Assessment data. *See* Collecting assessment data
Assessment planning, 6, 104
    assessment responsibilities, 56
    conducting assessments, 113–115
    How the team finds out, 46–50
    implementation of, 56, 106
    Interaction Formula, 44
    Know-Want-How Assessment Plan
      (example), 51–55
    Know-Want-How structure, 43–45
    logistic sequence of responsibilities, 110
    plan of action, 46
    preparing to conduct assessments, 109–113
    questions for evaluator, 114
    team collaborative perspective, 57–58
    to-do list for evaluators, 111
    what the team *Knows*, 43–44
    what the team *Wants* to learn, 45–46, 56
Assessment planning agenda, 58–60
Assessment session
    conducting session, 113–115
    explanation to student, 115
Assessment tools, 47–50
    authentic tools, 106, 115
    commercial instruments, 50
    informal interviews, 50
    mathematician tools, 130–131, 141–142
    observation, 49–50
    participant in classroom community tools,
      132–133, 143–145
    probe-level tasks, 49
    reader tools, 125–126, 134–136
    selection process for, 47–48
    survey-level tasks, 48–49
    writer tools, 127–129, 137–140

Authentic curriculum-based assessment, 3, 106

Behavior of the student as a participant/
    member, 79–85
Behavioral objectives, 155–156, 207–210
    action word word bank, 208
    behavior phrase bank, 210
    conditions behavior bank, 209
Brainstorming, 27–29, 45, 155
Building-based prereferral systems, 26

Charting data and analysis, 117–119
Checklists/rubrics, 21
Checklists to Guide Descriptions
    Toolbox, 118
    as mathematician, 181–183
    as participant in classroom community,
      184–190
    as reader, 167–174
    as writer, 175–180
Classroom teacher. *See* General education
    teacher
Clipboard cruising, 21
Collaboration, 28–30. *See also* Teams
    planning assessment as a team, 57–58
Collecting assessment data: mathematician,
    94–97
    analysis of data, 97
    assessment tools for, 130–131
    checklist to guide description, 181–183
    how to approach/strategic thinking, 95
    how to teach/formats for performance, 95
    probe-level tasks, 96–97
    rules of thumb, 94
    sample analysis chart, 141–142
    survey-level tasks, 94–96
    under what conditions/context for
      participation, 96
    what to teach/skill clusters, 96
    why teach/investment, 96

Collecting assessment data: participant in classroom community, 98–103
analysis of data, 102–103
assessment tools for, 132–133
checklist to guide description, 184–190
how to approach/strategic thinking, 99–100
how to teach/formats for performance, 98
probe-level tasks, 101–102
rules of thumb, 98
sample analysis chart, 143
survey-level tasks, 98–101
under what conditions/context for participation, 100
what to teach/skill clusters, 101
why teach/investment, 100–101
Collecting assessment data: reader, 86–89
analysis of data, 89
assessment tools for, 125–126
checklist to guide description, 167–174
how to approach/strategic thinking, 87
how to teach/formats for performance, 86
probe-level tasks, 88–89
rules of thumb, 86
sample analysis chart, 134–136
survey-level reading tasks, 86–88
under what conditions/context for participation, 88
what to teach/skill clusters, 88
why teach/investment, 88
Collecting assessment data: writer, 90–93
analysis of data, 93
assessment tools for, 127–129
checklist to guide description, 175–180
how to approach/strategic thinking, 91
how to teach/formats for performance, 90
probe-level tasks, 92–93
rules of thumb, 90
sample analysis chart, 137–140
survey-level tasks, 90–92
under what conditions/context for participation, 91
what to teach/skill clusters, 92
why teach/investment, 91

Commercial assessment instruments, 50
Communication skills/style, 28, 58
Comprehension/comprehension skills, 66–67, 169
Computational skills, 75–76, 181
Construction of assessment tools
mathematician, 130–131
participant in classroom, 132–133
reader, 125–126
writer, 127–129
Cooperative implementation, 253
Co-planning, 250
Co-teaching options/models, 251
Criterion-referenced tools, 50
Cultural reciprocity, 23
Curriculum-based measures, 50. See also Authentic curriculum-based assessment; General education curriculum modifications

Data-based decision making, 17
Data collection, 3, 5, 13, 18, 30. See also Collecting assessment data
charting and analysis, 116–118
clustering and integrating data, 120
cross-referencing data, 118–121, 144–145
developing forms for, 112
drawing statement of conclusions, 121–122
evaluator's copies, 113
interview data, 120
observation data, 120
preparation for, 109–113
task records, 112–113
tasks, tools, and activities, 107–109
Documentation of progress, 203, 211–215
Drafting strategies, 72

Environmental context/structures, 250
Evaluator's copies, 113
Evaluator's to-do-list, 111
Explicit/direct instruction, 215–216, 250

Facilitator, 59–61
Fluency/fluency skills, 65–66, 167
Focused observation, 214
Formats for performance, 46, 76–77, 151

Freewrite, 90
Frequency of behavior, 79

General education curriculum modifications, 217–220
adapt testing procedures/formats, 219
alter instructional materials/formats, 219
competence/mastery, 218
enhance investments, 220
practice, 218
providing enhancements, 219–220
specially designed instruction, 221
varying physical/instructional contests, 220
General education teacher
accessing support/pre-referral options, 26–27
conducting a conference, 25, 39–40
in-class adjustments, 22
initial concerns (case study), 19, 22
initial phone call to parents/caregivers, 24–25, 37–38
initiating special education process, 30–33
objective/informative descriptions, 20
ongoing communication, 25, 40
parents/caregivers and, 22–25
preliminary eligibility decisions, 152–153
preparing for conference, 25, 39–40
prereferral options, 26–30
prereferral period, 17–19
records of behaviors/performance, 21
referral document, 31–33
tasks as team member, 61
understanding student perspective, 21
Goals and goal statements, 203–204
behavior phrase, 205
examples of, 205–206
formulating goals, 204
how/way accomplished, 205
Grammar, 71, 176
Guideline Questions Toolboxes, 44, 46, 198
Guidelines for describing the student as a mathematician, 75–78
computation skills, 75–76

Guidelines for describing the student as a mathematician (*continued*)
conditions/context for participation, 77–78
how to approach/strategic thinking, 77
how to teach/formats for performance, 76–77
instruction/social aspects, 77–78
life skills, 76
number concepts, 75
overview, 75
problem solving, 76
student profile, 75
supporting detail, 75–78
what to teach/skill clusters, 75
why teach/investment, 78
Guidelines for describing the student as a participant in classroom community, 79–85
approach/strategic thinking, 82–83
awareness of others, 81
awareness of self, 80
communication, 80–82
conditions/context for participation, 83–84
describing behavior, 79
during learning experience, 83
how to teach/formats for performance, 82
interacts with peers/adults, 81
overview, 79–80
participant in learning, 79–81
postsituation, 83
preparation for an event, 83
qualities of situations, 83–84
reads, initiates, engages and responds, 81
student profile, 79
supporting detail, 80–85
what to teach/skill clusters, 80
why teach/investment, 84–86
work behaviors that support/detract from effectiveness, 82
Guidelines for describing the student as a reader, 65–69
fluency skills, 65–66
how to approach/strategic thinking, 67–68
how to teach/formats for performance, 67
instructional/social aspects, 68
language skills, 65
overview, 65

prereading, 67–69
qualities of materials, 67
retell/comprehension skills, 66–67
student profile, 65
supporting detail, 65–69
what to teach/skill cluster, 65–67
why teach/investment, 69
word recognition/word solving, 66
Guidelines for describing the student as a writer, 70–74
conditions/context for participation, 73
conventions of print/mechanics, 71
drafting, 72–73
evaluation of draft, 73
expression of ideas, 71
final copy, 73
grammar, 71
handwriting, 71
how to approach/strategic thinking, 72
how to teach/format for performance, 72
ideas, content, and organization, 70
instructional/social aspects, 73
overview, 70
prewriting, 72
qualities of assignment, 72
spelling, 71
student profile, 70
supporting detail, 70–73
what to teach/skill clusters, 70
why teach/investment, 74

Handwriting, 71, 176–177
How column, 46–50
How team finds out, 46–50, 104

Ideas, content, and organization, 70
IEP Implementer To-Do List Toolbox, 247, 258–259
Implementation of IEP, 246
collaboratively planning, 249–250
cooperative implementation, 253
co-planning activities, 250
co-teaching, 251
delivering the IEP, 250–253
instructional practices and, 248
paraprofessional's role, 251–253
preparing for, 247–249
program effectiveness, 255
student progress, 253–255
team members and, 247–248
In-class adjustments, 22

In-class behavior contract, 21
In-class solution options, 17
Individual assessment plans, 42
Individual education program meeting
agenda for IEP development, 160–162
composite picture of learner, 148–150
cooperatively pooling information, 148–150
design individualized curriculum, 154–155
determine eligibility, 157–158
develop context of IEP, 153–160
note taking, 159–160
overview of, 147–148
participate in performance assessments, 158
plan instruction, 155–157
preliminary eligibility decisions, 152–153
program components, 159, 162–164
summarize, draw conclusions, and hypothesize, 150–153
transition planning, 158–159
Individualized curriculum. *See also* General education curriculum modifications
documentation of progress, 211–214
goals and objectives, 203–211
record design of, 203–215
Individualized education plan (IEP), 1–3, 107, 115
academic/functional goal statements, 234
authoring the IEP, 194–196
as blueprint for student outcomes, 197
comprehensive picture of student, 196–197
criteria for progress/performance, 155
criteria for writing effective IEPS, 233–235
delivery of, 250–253
design of, 154–155
development of, 6, 153–154
direct instruction/alternative teaching, 234
documentation of progress, 211–215
example of, 226–232
functions of, 12–13
general education curriculum, 234–235

general-to-descriptive profile statements, 200
goals of, 154–155
implementation of, 6, 246
monitoring progress/effectiveness, 6, 234, 253–255
plan instruction, 155–157
present level of achievement and functional performance (PLOP), 196–197, 201–202, 233
profile/learning style/impact of disability, 196, 198–200, 233
RSVP and, 12–13
service delivery plan/program components, 221–223, 235
specific objectives/benchmarks, 155, 234
writing of, 6, 148, 154, 193–196, 215–221
Individuals with Disabilities Education Improvement Act (IDEA 2004), 1–2, 13, 152, 266
building capacity for, 266–267
challenges of, 2–3, 158
collaborative perspective and professionalism, 57, 267–269
determining eligibility requirements, 157–158
infrastructure for, 267
revisions to, 2
student challenges in general education context, 17
Informal assessments, 214
Informal interviews, 50
Informative referrals, 5, 30–33
Initial phone call to parents/caregivers, 24–25, 37–38
Interaction Formula, 10–11, 44, 46, 118, 149, 196, 198, 217, 221
Interaction Formula Assessment Analysis Toolbox, 118, 144–145
Interaction Formula Co-Planning Toolbox, 249, 260–264
Interview data, 120
Investment, 46, 152

Key decisions, 9–10
Know column, 44–46
Know-Want-How approach, 436
Know-Want-How Assessment Plan (example of), 51–55
Know-Want-How Assessment Plan Form Toolbox, 43

Language conventions, 71
Language cues, 66
Language skills, 65
Learning environment, 79
Learning experience, 83, 188
Learning outcomes, 250

Making action plans (MAPs), 159
Math concepts, 182
Monitoring and evaluation strategies, 211–215, 250, 253–255
Multidisciplinary evaluation teams, 11–12, 32

No Child Left Behind 2001 (NCLB), 2, 158
Note taking, 60–61, 159–160
Number concepts, 75

Objectives, 203, 207–212
Observation, 49–50, 214
Observation data, 120

Paraprofessional, 251–253
Parents/caregivers
    first conference with, 24–25, 39–40
    initial phone call to, 24–25, 37–38
    ongoing contact with, 25, 40
    prereferral period, 17–18, 22–25
    sharing information with, 23–24
    as team members, 61
Parents/Caregivers Contact Toolbox, 24–25, 37–40
Participation in conversation/discussions, 80–81
Peer/adult interactions, 81
Phonics, 88
Phonics rules, 66
Picture book, 171
Pictures aids, 66, 89
Plan instruction, 155–157
Postreading strategies, 68
Practice and evaluation activities, 250
Preliminary eligibility decisions, 152–153
Prereading strategies, 67
Prereferral data, 17
Prereferral options
    action plan, 27
    brainstorming ideas, 27
    collaborative emphasis for, 26–30

formal/informal options, 26–27
problem-solving agenda, 27–30
Prereferral period, 17–18, 22–25. See also General education teacher
    actions taken during, 17–18
    identifying concerns/initial actions, 19
    initiating special education process, 30–33
    parents/caregivers and, 17–18
Present level of academic achievement and functional performance (PLOP), 196–197, 201–202, 233
Prewriting strategies, 72
Probe-level tasks, 49, 107–109
    mathematics, 96–97
    reading, 88–89
    writing, 92–93
Problem-solving, 76, 183
    tiered problem solving, 8–9
Problem-solving agenda, 27–30
Profile/learning style/impact of disability, 196, 198–200
Profile narrative guidelines, 199
Profile statements, 200
Program components, 159
Prompts, 72

Qualitative criteria, 208
Quantitative criteria, 208

Reads aloud, 168
Recorder, 59, 61
Record-keeping, 112, 214
Referral document, 31–32
    case study example, 32–33
    guidelines for, 31–32
Referral process, 31
Responsive Stages, Voices, and Practices (RSVP), 1, 5
    assessment tools, 47
    graphic organizer, 14
    individualized education plans (IEP) and, 12–13
    interaction formula, 10–11
    introduction to, 4–12
    key decisions, 9–10
    multidisciplinary teams and, 11–12
    overview of stages, 5–7
    practices for, 10–11
    RSVP pyramid, 5
    stages and steps in, 7–8
    tiered problem solving, 8–9, 13

Responsive Stages, Voices, and
  Practices (RSVP) (*continued*)
  tools for organization, assessment,
    and planning, 10–11
Retelling, 66–67

Sample analyses charts
  mathematician, 141–142
  participant in classroom
    community, 143
  reader, 134–136
  writer, 137–140
Sample Analyses Charts
  Toolbox, 118
Schedule, 56
Self-awareness, 80, 184
Service delivery plan, 221–223
Silent reading, 171
Skill clusters, 46, 151, 202
Social situations, 81, 185
Special education process, 2–3
  challenge of, 2–3
  initiation of, 30–33
  as responsive process, 4
Spelling, 71, 177
Statements of conclusion, 121–122
Statewide assessments, 158
Strategic thinking, 46, 151
Student-centered focus, 3, 10
Student evaluations, 3, 6. *See also*
  Guidelines for describing
    the student
  access student perspective, 21

identifying expectations, 20
instructional/physical
  settings, 20
nonspecific terms in, 20
objective and informative
  descriptions, 20
observable vocabulary, 20
records of behaviors/
  performance, 21
Student performance
  charting and analyzing, 116–118
  cross-referencing data, 118–121
  drawing statements of conclu-
    sions, 121–122
  monitoring progress and effective-
    ness, 253–255
Student progress, 253–255
Survey-level tasks, 48–49, 107–108
  mathematics, 94–96
  participation, 98–103
  reading, 86–87
  writing, 90–92

Task records, 112–113
Teacher. *See* General education
  teacher
Teams
  assessment responsibilities, 56
  collaborative perspective of, 57–58
  communication style, 58
  evaluation/planning meeting,
    147–148
  group note taking, 61

How team finds out,
    46–50, 104
IEP writing, 193
implementation plan, 247–248
leadership, 32
multidisciplinary teams, 11–12
roles/tasks of team members,
    60–61
what the team *Knows*,
    43–44, 104
what team *Wants* to learn,
    45–46, 104
Tiered problem solving, 8–9, 13
Transition periods, 83, 158–159

What the team *Knows*, 43–44, 104
What the team *Wants* to learn,
    45–46, 104
Word recognition, 66, 167
Word solving, 66, 167
Work samples, 214
Written plan for instruction
  access to general education
    curriculum, 216–217
  example of, 226–232
  explicit/direct instruction,
    215–216
  mathematician areas, 240–241
  participant in classroom commu-
    nity, 242–243
  reader areas, 236–237
  special education services, 221
  writer areas, 238–239